The Rise and Fall of King Coal

THE RISE AND FALL OF
KING COAL

By Nick Pigott

First published in 2016
by Mortons Media Group

This edition published in 2022 by Gresley Books
an imprint of Mortons Books Ltd.
Media Centre
Morton Way
Horncastle LN9 6JR
www.mortonsbooks.co.uk

ISBN 978-1-911658-63-4

The right of Nick Pigott to be identified as the author of this work has been asserted in accordance with the
Copyright, Designs and Patents Act 1988.

Typeset by Jayne Clements (jayne@hinoki.co.uk), Hinoki Design and Typesetting.
Printed and bound by Gutenberg Press, Malta.

FRONT COVER: King Coal's golden crown is no more. The long reign of the deep mine in Britain came to
an end in 2015 after more than three centuries and now all the nation is left with are memories. This crown,
inlaid with a red diamond, adorned the upcast shaft at Nottinghamshire's Thoresby Colliery, one of the last
three deep mines to close in that final year.

Cover photo by Robin Stewart-Smith. Uncredited colour photographs are by the author.

Dedicated to my wife Suzanne, daughter Hannah and brother Geoff.

CONTENTS

THUMBS UP! When this picture was taken in 1979, the coal industry was in a powerful position as a major component of British society. PA

HEADS DOWN! By the end of 2015, the last handful of British deep miners had just lost their jobs and the nation that gave birth to the Industrial Revolution no longer possessed a single working deep colliery. PA

Introduction

A long and glorious reign

THE YEAR 2016 will be remembered as one of the most significant in the annals of industrial history, for it was the first for more than three centuries in which no deep-mined coal was produced in Great Britain.

That such a state of affairs could come to pass in the nation that gave birth to the Industrial Revolution is extraordinary and serves to underline the monumental social changes that have taken place in the UK in recent years.

For hundreds of years, 'King Coal' reigned supreme, reaching a pinnacle just before the First World War and remaining one of Britain's greatest industries until the mid-1980s. It is hard to imagine how the history of this island nation would have unfolded and how immensely different our lives would be now if it had not been for the 'black diamonds' lying beneath our feet.

Yet today there are millions of youngsters who've never

A stark reminder of past glories: Plinthed headstock pulley wheels in former mining communities, such as this one near Coalville, Leicestershire, are now often the only signs that a colliery ever stood in the vicinity.

even set eyes on a piece of coal in their lives and who wonder why they see so many "big wheels planted in the grass" when they travel through certain parts of the country.

Those wheels are, of course, the pulley sheaves that once sat proudly atop colliery winding towers, spinning day and night to send men deep into the bowels of the earth to win the fuel that powered the heavy industries of the 19th and 20th centuries. Today, either whole or cut in half, the sheaves sit in roadside memorial gardens in former mining communities … and are sadly often the only visible evidence that a pit ever stood on the site.

It is difficult to convey to anyone who never experienced it just how vast the British coal industry was at its peak. Just one large mine and its attendant housing, railway yards and spoil heaps could cover an area the size of a whole village, providing a living for as many as 3,000 men and their families. A mile or so down the road there would be another pit, then another, then another … and so it would go on right through the valley or coalfield – and those were just the surface structures, for coal mines were rather like icebergs; there was far more below the surface than was visible above, and their labyrinthine networks could spread as far as seven or eight miles from the colliery shafts.

An impression of the size of the industry as a whole can be gained from the fact that there were more than 900 such collieries in the coalfields of Britain when Queen Elizabeth II came to the throne and that at the height of the British Empire in the late-Victorian era there had been three times that many. Those were the days when the United Kingdom – possessing less than $\frac{1}{500}$th of the world's surface area – produced almost half the planet's mineral tonnage! Small wonder that the empire's industrial might is said to

Looking at the ancient wooden wagons, few people would guess that this evocative scene was captured as relatively recently as the mid-1980s. The location was Ashington Colliery, in Northumberland, and the National Coal Board's ex-British Rail diesel-hydraulic locomotive No.D9500 was passing its classmate D9521 as it arrived with loaded wagons from nearby Lynemouth Colliery on March 25, 1986. GORDON EDGAR

How the Ashington scene looks today: a slick new 'business park' with landscaped gardens and ornamental fountains.

have been built on a foundation of coal and steel.

At that time, it would have been utterly unthinkable for it all to have vanished little more than a century later, but the end of an era in Great Britain occurred on December 18, 2015 when the final shift ended at Kellingley Colliery in North Yorkshire.

The demise of that famous pit brought to a close an aspect of the industry so old that its genesis is impossible to accurately pinpoint but which is generally considered to date from the early-1700s … deep mining.

The small-scale extraction of shallow coal had been going on for many hundreds of years before that of course, as explained on the following pages, and some of the hand-dug bellpits had reached depths of 100ft or more in dry areas, but they didn't qualify as deep mines in the accepted sense that later saw men working at well over 20 times that depth.

The invention of water-pumping engines in the early 18th century made it possible to penetrate further into the earth's crust than had been possible with bellpits, but it wasn't until the first half of the 19th century that mines began to really grow in size. The final transition to the immense modern 'superpit' complexes of the later-20th century commenced just over a hundred years ago when it became a legal requirement to equip new mines with winding towers built of steel instead of timber.

Those towers, better known as headstocks or headgear, were the most visible surface aspects of any colliery — tall structures of steel or concrete often visible for miles around and forming a focal point for their community. Each tower was a symbol of industrial might, each mine a hive of activity, each community a source of pride.

Mining was one of the toughest jobs a man could do and the hardships and hazards were many, especially in the years prior to the creation of the National Coal Board (NCB) in 1947, yet most ex-miners say they wouldn't have

The decline of the UK's deep coal mines

Coal produced from deep mines (million tonnes)

1915 935,000 — Deep mines producing coal: **2,581**

Total mining workforce

1922 1,162,800

1947 707,700 — All mines nationalised

COAL NOT DOLE · NATIONAL UNION OF MINEWORKERS

1984 139,700 — Miners' strike: March 1984– March 1985

1926 General strike: May 4-13

1972 Miners' strike: Jan-Feb

1974 Miners' strike: Jan-Mar

1994 18,600 — All mines privatised

2015 2,168 — Deep mines producing coal: **9**

300 · 250 · 200 · 150 · 100 · 50 · 0

1915 · 2015

Source: UK Coal Authority, Department for Energy and Climate Change PA

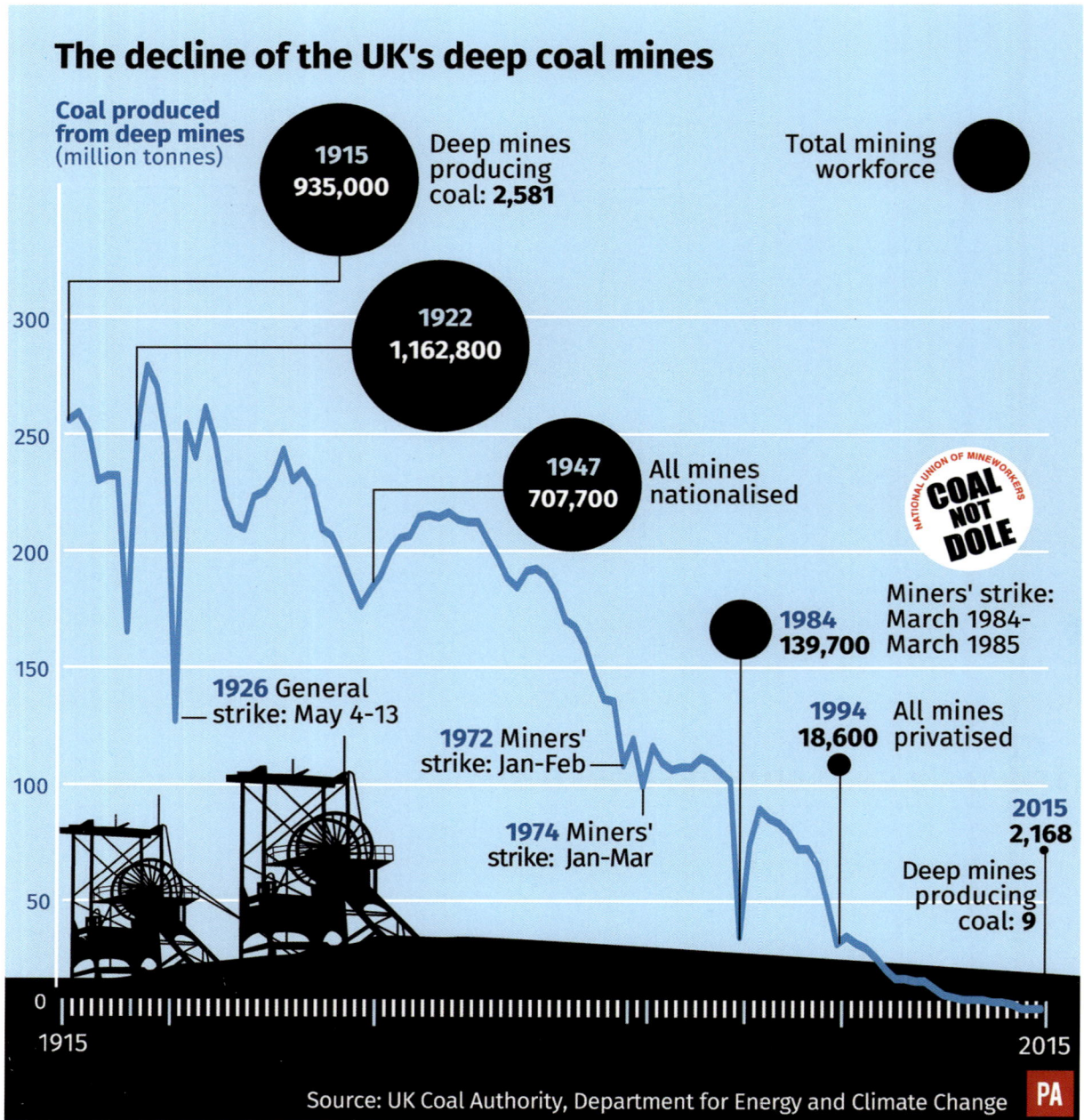

This graphic charts the decline of the UK coal industry between 1915 – when there were more than 2,500 collieries – and a century later, when there were no deep shaft mines at all. Significant landmarks in the history of the industry are shown, such as nationalisation, privatisation and the major industrial disputes.

wanted to do anything else. They had a love-hate relationship with their work, often claiming not to enjoy it ... yet they demonstrated fierce pride and loyalty to their pit and profession if ever they were threatened.

The passionate reactions of the Kellingley workers as they were interviewed by the media on their final day demonstrated heartbreak and anger in far greater measure than is usually the case in less-demanding industries ... and not simply because they were losing their jobs. In fact, so far did the emotions overflow as the men came to the surface for the last time that BBC Radio had to issue a public apology for expletives contained in a live news interview.

Most men have a soft spot for their former workplaces and are always saddened when they see how productive hives of industry have been flattened and replaced by housing estates, retail parks, warehouses or wasteland. This deep-seated fondness is borne out by the fact that a retired collier's home will usually have a brightly-polished safety lamp in pride of place on the lounge mantelpiece or sideboard.

In their working days, miners looked out for one another when underground – it was often the only way to survive

The close relationship between coal and power generation was established many decades ago and did much to prolong the longevity of the mining industry. With the cooling towers of Ferrybridge power station prominent in the background, Coal Products 0-6-0 saddle tank No.3 shunts in April 1976 at Glasshoughton, one of several Yorkshire locations containing both a colliery and a coking plant. BRIAN SHARPE

The UK's coal supply: how it's changed

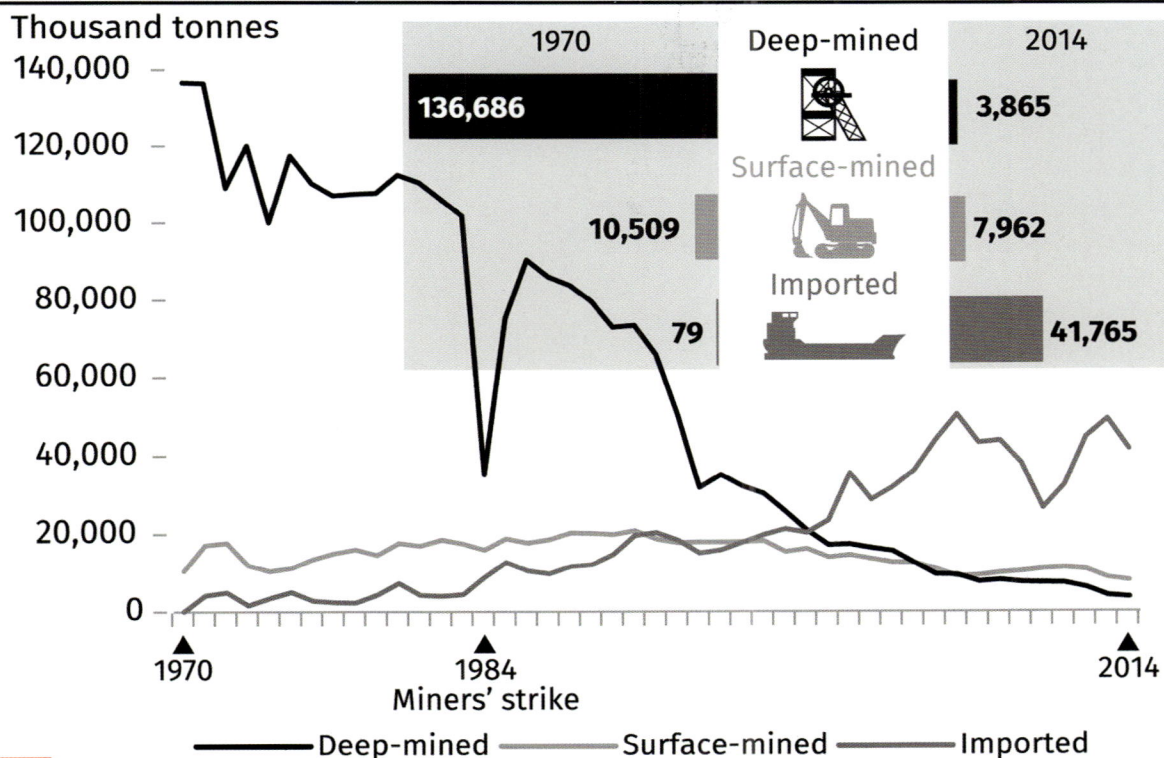

Thousand tonnes

	1970	Deep-mined	2014
	136,686		3,865
Surface-mined			
	10,509		7,962
Imported			
	79		41,765

1970 1984 Miners' strike 2014

——— Deep-mined ——— Surface-mined ——— Imported

PA Source: Department of Energy and Climate Change

This graphic shows how imported coal overtook the indigenous deep-mined product, the crucial point occurring at about the turn of the present century. The supply of surface-mined (opencast) coal remained fairly constant in comparison.

in such a potentially dangerous environment. As a result, strong bonds of friendship were formed between colleagues and their families and that led in turn to an unshakable sense of community that survives to this day.

Something that doesn't readily occur to members of the public is that coalface workers went every day where no human beings had ever been before! Notwithstanding the rapid shift towards sustainable energy in a bid to combat global warming, many people still harbour concerns that western governments have themselves taken a step into the unknown by depriving themselves of their deep-mining capabilities at a time when China, Russia, India and others continue on a major scale with such operations.

Old King Coal's death in Britain has been a protracted one, but the crown was finally knocked off by cheap imports and climate change fears. This was not an industry that died a natural death due to exhaustion of resources. On the contrary, enough coal remains under the British Isles to last hundreds of years and the nation has continued to consume millions of tonnes since 2015, mainly in steel manufacturing and electricity generation. The difference is that today's supplies are either dug from opencast mines (although that too is due to end in 2022) or purchased from abroad, much of it from countries with inferior working conditions and far poorer safety records than the UK.

The last few coal-fired power stations in Britain are due to be phased out by the end of 2024, leaving only a handful of steel and cement plants as large-scale consumers and only half a dozen or so drift mines , some with only a handful of workers each. Much controversy was, however, recently caused when the Government approved an all-new drift mine at Whitehaven, Cumbria, only to pause it ahead of the 2021 United Nations Climate Change Conference (COP26)…which Britain hosted in November 2021 (see pages 239 & 240).

At its peak in 1913, the United Kingdom was the world's largest producer of coal with 1.1m miners and an annual output of almost 300m tons. In 1947, the first year of nationalisation, 707,000 men were producing 187m tons and in 1980, the figure was still high at 128m tons and 150,000 men (the same number of miners as in the 1840s). By 1994, the year of privatisation, it had plummeted to 30m with a workforce of 18,000 and with the looming closure of the last opencast mines, both figures in the non-anthracite world are expected to stand at zero!

To rub salt into the wounds, foreign coal is now used instead and almost every closed colliery has been systematically wiped off the face of the earth by demolition men, leaving just a handful that have been converted to light industrial use or turned into museums.

The author 2,267ft (691m) below ground at Thoresby Colliery a few weeks before its closure in 2015. Thoresby was one of the most productive pits in Britain and, as our front cover image shows, was proud to proclaim itself the 'jewel in the crown' of the East Midlands coalfield. As was the case with many British mines in recent times, it closed despite possessing substantial reserves of coal.

The speed of the solar panel and wind turbine revolution really has been astonishing. At the start of the 21st century, Britain was reliant on coal for 40% of its energy; two decades later that figure has collapsed to just 2% and there have been several weeks since 2017 in which no coal whatsoever has been used to supply electricity to the National Grid.

Whatever the virtues of today's silent and virtually workforce-free sun and wind sites, there's no doubt that for hundreds of thousands of families who earned their living from coal, it's been a sad end for the industry that fired the Industrial Revolution, made almost every other type of works and factory possible and helped put the 'Great' into Britain.

The story of how this vast asset was gained and lost is a fascinating one and this book sets out to record its history for posterity and pay tribute to mining, mines and miners.

So large and varied is the subject that it's almost impossible to generalise when reporting on it, for there was at least one exception to virtually every rule and situation! It also has to be said that history books and reference sources contain often-conflicting information and varying statistics, particularly where 'first', 'last', 'largest' and so on are concerned. This book is therefore an attempt to iron out some of the imperfections and to present a general overview that will hopefully appeal to ex-mineworkers and their families as well as to those who simply have an admiration for the skills and advances associated with this most remarkable of industries.

Readers are asked to bear in mind that the terminology used in the pits has varied over the years, not only from area to area, but also from era to era. What was known commonly as a tub, for example, can be a tram, a dram, a hutch or a mine car, depending on which location and which timeframe is being referred to. Hundreds of years ago, a 'pit' was, strictly speaking, another word for a shaft, but in common usage it has come to be known as a general term for an entire colliery and is thus used as an alternative to mine or colliery in this publication.

By the same token, operating practices also differed; the way things were done at a certain location in Wales in the 19th century may not have been the way they were done in Yorkshire or Scotland in the 20th, and so on.

My own association with the industry began half a century ago and I was fortunate to be able to visit several collieries in their operational days, including Thoresby, Littleton, Bolsover, Rossington, Ashington, Maerdy, Snowdown, Asfordby, Eckington and Kellingley. My first trip was to Northumberland's Widdrington opencast mine in 1969 and my final underground visit in the UK took place at Thoresby in 2015. My occupation as editor of Britain's senior rail title, *The Railway Magazine*, for 21 years enabled me

to maintain close contacts with the colliery industry for the final two decades of its existence and I've also been privileged to visit working coalfaces abroad, notably in Poland and China.

I have attempted to steer a neutral line where politics and union affairs are concerned and to present both sides of an argument or simply state plain facts, but if it is felt I have inadvertently deviated from this line at any point, I apologise.

This book is a fully-updated and enlarged version of an edition printed in bookazine format in 2016 and as it was first published primarily to mark the end of the British deep-mining industry, I have opted to use the past tense in many chapters even though some of the practices and machines described continue to see use in other parts of the world.

Every precaution has been taken to ensure accuracy, but any errors are mine and mine alone. With a subject as vast and varied as coalmining, it's inevitable that readers will have comments and observations of their own, so if you feel you can add or amend anything, I would be delighted to hear from you at nickpigott@icloud.com

Last but not least, I am indebted to a number of former mineworkers and colliery managers for the granting of on-site and underground facilities. Among those whose help and advice I'm particularly grateful for are Roy Etherington, Barry Graham, Derek Main, Colin Stokes, John Watson, Gordon Banham, Kevin Sabin, Marek Growiek, David Amos, Bob Bradley, Jim Worgan, Robert Preston and the late Colin Mountford. An especially big thank you also to my wife Suzanne for bearing with me while I burned the 'midnight oil'... or should that be 'coal'?!

I hope this book serves as a record of a great and sadly-missed industry.
Nick Pigott,
Leicestershire, 2021.

CHAPTER 1

In the beginning

'Buried sunshine'

HOW COAL WAS FORMED

THREE HUNDRED million years ago, the area on which Britain now stands was a vast shallow tropical estuary into which great rivers flowed into the sea and deposited sand, mud and silt. The continents we know today had not yet formed and were constantly changing shape and position as violent upheavals took place in the earth's crust.

Every few million years, these changes would reduce the depth of water covering the land and create hot swampy conditions in which primitive ferns and trees could grow. Over thousands of years, these forests grew and died, forming a thick layer of decaying matter in the swamps and lagoons as they did so, until another change in the shape

of the land allowed the sea level to rise and water to flow over the area, depositing layer upon layer of mud and sand and burying the rotting vegetable matter.

As the water slowly subsided in these river deltas, as it did frequently during the earth's formative stages, the level of silt and clay gradually built up until there was sufficient depth for plants and trees to start growing again. Meanwhile, the previous layers of vegetable matter underneath were gradually being turned by pressure, heat and lack of oxygen into peat (a soft brown spongy substance) and the layers of sediment were slowly being solidified into rock under the tons of weight above them.

This cycle of growth, decay, flooding, sediment cover and

How coal seams were laid down: This bilingual diagram on display at Big Pit Colliery in Blaenafon, South Wales, shows how a prehistoric forest died and became covered by sea and mud, followed by a second forest once the water subsided, forming a second layer, which in turn became covered in mud, sand, silt and clay. Those substances eventually hardened into rocks and the process was repeated many times during the 62m-year Carboniferous Period.

Close-up of a coalface showing two coal seams interleaved with a layer of mudstone/shale above and a thin dirt band in between.

re-growth was repeated scores of times over the course of the prehistoric Carboniferous Period, which ran from approximately 360m years BC to 298m years BC – a time when the land that today forms the British Isles was located in a tropical region much nearer the equator (roughly where Florida is today). Each cycle formed a new layer of decomposed vegetation and a new layer of mud and sand. As each deposit was laid down, the ever-increasing heat and weight further compressed the older seams below, turning the peat into lignite and finally into coal.

To give an idea of the rate of compression, a 30ft depth of peat would take about 10,000 years to compress into 5ft of lignite (a form of soft brown coal), which in turn would compress over many more millennia into 3ft of hard, black bituminous coal.

This explains why coal is found in layers, for each seam represents one of the cycles mentioned above and the depth of each seam reveals roughly how long each cycle lasted. It also helps explain why coal burns, for the energy contained within it is latent energy from the sun that was absorbed by the trees and plants and trapped underground ever since. It is released when the coal is burned and gives rise to one of the affectionate nicknames coal has gained over the years – 'Buried Sunshine'.

Other names include 'Black Diamonds' and 'Black Gold' – although the latter is far more common as a description for crude oil.

The coal measures found in Britain were laid down during the Carboniferous Period and the stratified rocks normally comprise mudstone/shale, sandstone, siltstone, claystone and fireclay, as well as coal. It is a common error among members of the public to confuse coal seams with coal measures. The latter include the interleaved layers of rock and dirt and there can be as many as 100 seams within the measures, although many are only an inch or so thick and not worth mining. Anything above 2ft is commercially exploitable and in parts of Warwickshire and Staffordshire, the seams can be as thick as 30ft.

Every seam in Britain is identified by a name and those that ran for many miles, such as the Barnsley 'Top Hard', would be tapped by several different collieries. A fair proportion of the titles were based on local nicknames and if all the thin seams are taken into account, there were several hundred across the UK's coalfields as a whole.

Carboniferous means 'coal-bearing' and the 62m-year lifespan of that period coincided with primitive animal life on Earth. In fact, fossils of tiny invertebrates are sometimes found alongside fossilised leaves in the shale next to

- No 1 SHAFT -　　　NO 2 SHAFT

ENGINE HOUSE　　　　　ENGINE HOUSE

SURFACE PIT TOP LEVEL
74.80 mts ABOVE SEA LEVEL

BOTH SHAFTS 6.14 m DIA

SKIP FOR COAL
CAGE FOR MEN

BASE OF WATER BEARING MEASURES

260 m DEEP

COAL SEAM THICKNESS

Thickness	Seam	Depth
0.60 m	WALES SEAM	285 m
0.71 m	MAIN BRIGHT	344 m
0.62 m	ABDY	360 m
1.45 m	BRINSLEY	370 m
1.22 m	HIGH HAZLES	383 m
2.32 m	TOP HARD	444 m
	PIT BOTTOM	
0.86 m	DUNSIL	458 m
0.86 m	WATERLOO 1	480 m
0.97 m	WATERLOO 2	493 m
0.60 m	ELL	526 m
0.61 m	DEEP SOFT	588 m
0.30 m	DEEP HARD	604 m
2.10 m	PARKGATE	625 m
1.70 m	LOW MAIN	645 m
0.40 m	THREEQUARTERS	651 m
0.83 m	YARD	670 m
0.82 m	BLACKSHALE	686 m
0.82 m	ASHGATE	691 m

SUMP

BOREHOLE DRILLED DOWN
FROM SUMP LEVEL
BOTTOM OF HOLE 747 mts DEEP

TOP HARD SEAM
55 DISTRICTS PANELS WORKED
3 MILES TO 51s & 3 1/2 TO 24s NW
FROM PIT BOTTOM

ROPE MANRIDER 1 IN 6 DRIFT
CONVEYOR MANRIDER 1 IN 5 DRIFT
CABLE BELT FOR COAL 1 IN 4 DRIFT

1 IN 6 DRIFT

PARKGATE SEAM
19 PANELS WORKED
4 1/4 MILES TO 47s

1 IN 6 DRIFT

LOW MAIN SEAM
36 PANELS WORKED
5 MILES TO 121s

BLACKSHALE / ASHGATE SEAM
4 PANELS WORKED
4 MILES TO B S 4s
FROM PIT BOTTOM

SHAFTS SUNK 1927 - 1928

TOP HARD 1928 - 1968

LOW MAIN 1946 - 1993

PARKGATE 1964 - 1986

BLACKSHALE / ASHGATE 1993 - 1997

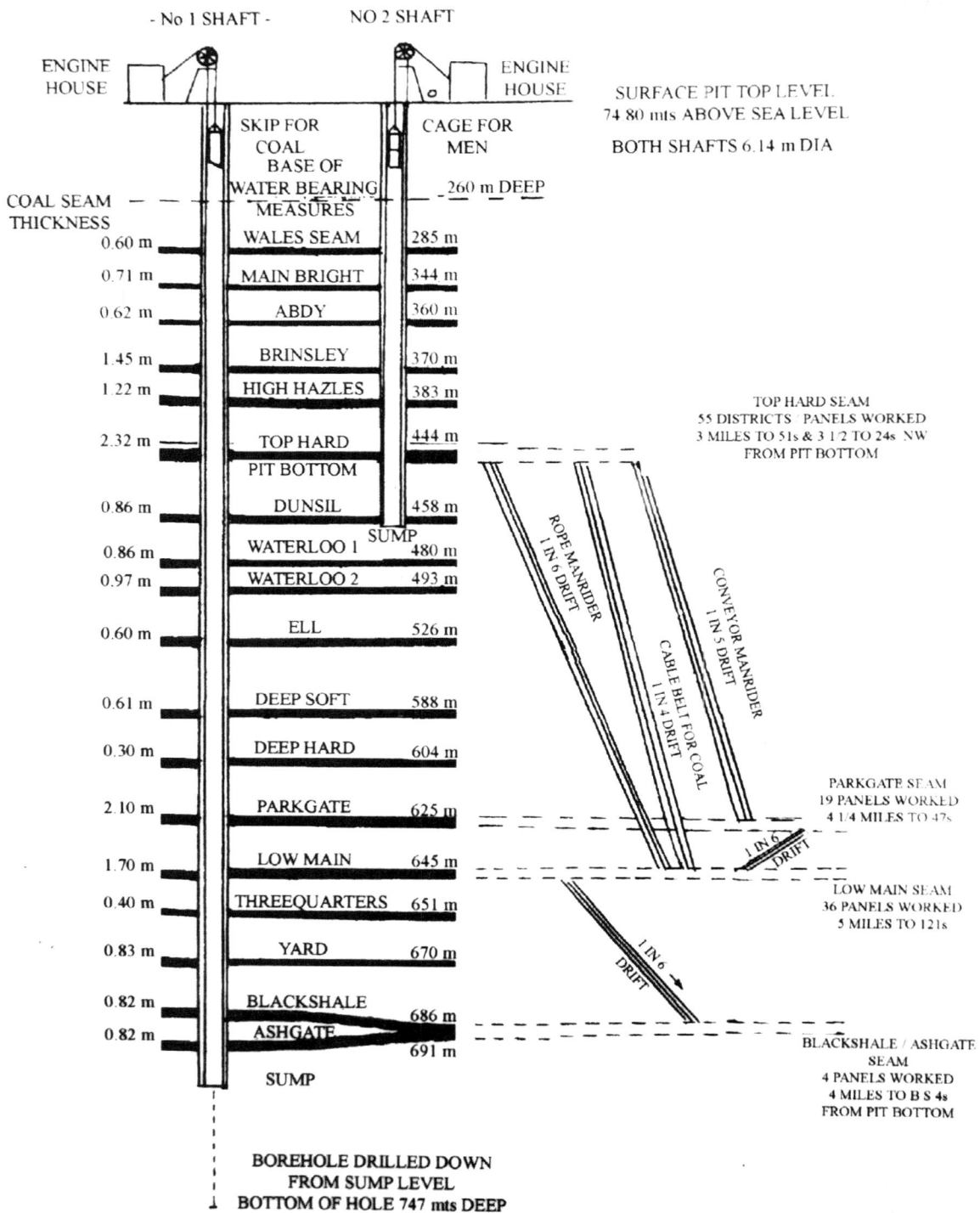

- BILSTHORPE COLLIERY -
- SHAFT SECTION -
NOT TO SCALE

Eighteen seams: A cross-section of the two vertical shafts and five subterranean drifts at Bilsthorpe Colliery, Nottinghamshire, showing the names, depths and thicknesses of the seams they passed through. At this particular mine, No.2 shaft was used for man-riding and provided access to the Top Hard, with drifts at gradients of between 1-in-6 and 1-in-4 descending from there to access lower seams. Illustration by Robert Bradley.

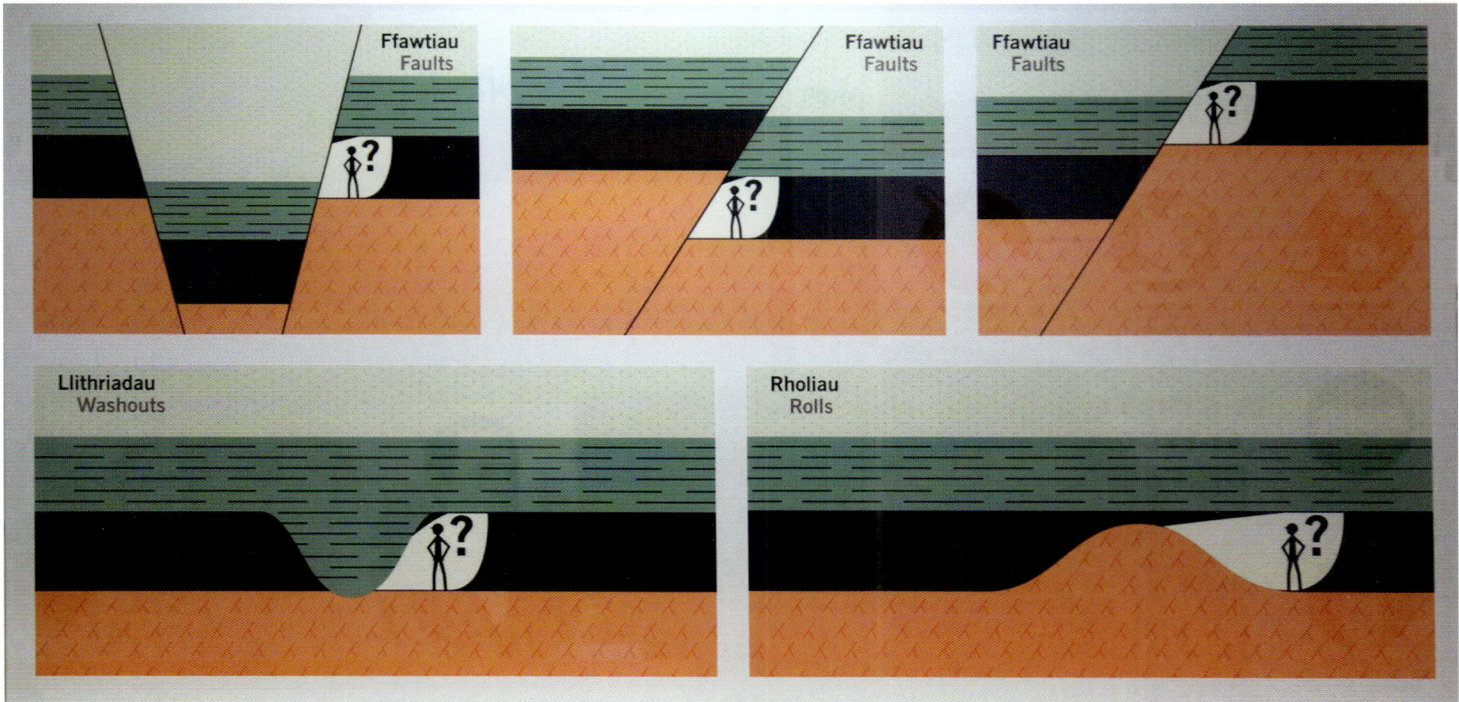

There were several ways in which the results of geological phenomena baffled early miners and five of them are illustrated at Big Pit Colliery. In each case, the green and orange levels represent rocks with the black coal seam falling or rising in relation to them, depending on the type of fault. A washout usually occurred when a subterranean river removed a portion of coal that had been lying in its path, while a roll would be caused by the forcing-up of rock by the natural movement of the earth.

the coal and in one East Midlands colliery an entire band of fossilised shellfish was revealed. Larger fossils such as those of dinosaurs are restricted to 'younger' depths nearer the surface, but calamites (basically fossilised tree trunks still standing vertically) are occasionally discovered in carboniferous measures.

Coal is usually found lying in 'basins', a reference to the swamps in which it was formed, and there are five primary basins beneath the mainland of Britain containing a total of about 50 accessible coalfields if the small ones are included.

When the measures were first laid down, they were reasonably level, but towards the end of the Carboniferous Period, colossal earth movements began to develop, forcing the land containing the seams into undulating folds known as anticlines and synclines (the hills and valleys we know today). Over millions of years, seams that had ended up on top of the raised anticlines became worn away through the erosive action of frost, ice, wind, rain and rivers, which explains why there is no coal on top of the Pennines, for example.

Other seams fell victim to massive faults and fractures in the earth that broke their continuity, so they appeared to stop abruptly but in fact continued at different heights or depths. Subterranean washouts of seams in certain locations posed similar problems for miners, as did prehistoric volcanic activity, for larva that forced its way through the

ground solidified to form igneous rocks, some of which were able to mimic sedimentary rocks by turning horizontal and running parallel to coal seams.

The thickest seams lie at about 10,000ft (too deep to be economically mined by conventional means), but most of the workable ones in Britain are found between 200 and 2,000ft. Measures overlaid by more recently-formed sedimentary rocks, such as those laid down in the Jurassic and Triassic periods, are known as concealed coalfields, while those that appear close to the surface are referred to as 'exposed' even though they may be covered by layers of soil and sub-soil. They are usually only literally exposed at the edges of the basins or in places such as cliffs where natural erosion has taken place.

Coal comes in many ranks, the most abundant of which is bituminous, so called because it contains a hydrocarbon substance called bitumen. The bituminous family contains many varieties but can broadly be separated into two basic usage types: thermal and metallurgical, the latter also known as coking coal. The distinction relates to the different types of plant and organic vegetative matter from which they were originally formed and the metallurgical varieties normally have a higher carbon content and lower levels of ash, moisture, sulphur and phosphorus.

They are generally used for the production of coke in the steel-making industry while the thermal types, which are unsuited to the production of commercially-viable coke, are usually supplied to the domestic, power-generating, heating and steam-producing industries.

Thermal and coking coals can both be further sub-divided into hard, medium and soft varieties, the harder types tending to occur in coalfields such as Yorkshire and the Midlands, while South Wales is noted for softer forms.

Bituminous, sometimes known as 'black coal' to distinguish it from brown coal (lignite) is by far the commonest rank found in Britain. It splits readily along its cleats and can be cleaved by hand-held picks fairly easily, but has a relatively high gaseous content.

Also found in South Wales and in a few areas of northern Britain are deposits of anthracite, which is the highest-ranking grade in terms of carbon content, but also the rarest, accounting for only 1% of global coal reserves.

Ranks of coal

COAL HAS been described by a scientist in America's University of Pennsylvania as "the most complex solid ever analysed". The number of varieties and permutations is almost limitless and the situation is further complicated by considerable overlaps between the various types. It does, however, conform to an official ranking system in terms of maturity, carbon content, volatility and so on and these, along with some of their individual properties, are as follows:

ANTHRACITE: A hard, shiny coal with few impurities formed by exposure of bituminous coal to volcanic activity or other naturally-occurring heat and pressure at great depth. It has an extremely high fixed carbon content of between 85 and 97% and the highest calorific value of all true coals. Its sulphur levels are low, its volatile matter averages only around 5% and its inherent moisture content can be as low as 2%. Sometimes known as stone coal, it ignites with difficulty but burns with great heat, low ash and virtually no smoke, making it exempt from restrictions on other forms of coal-burning. It is the most mature type of coal and is good for steel-making, gas generation and central heating. It is also the rarest type globally, with South Wales containing some of the world's finest quality deposits.

SEMI-ANTHRACITE: This slightly higher volatility variety burns more readily than pure anthracite and has a carbon content of 83-93%. The volatile matter averages 8-15% and it gives off less smoke than bituminous types when burning.

SEMI-BITUMINOUS (STEAM COAL): Lying between the anthracites and the main bituminous varieties are the Steam Coals, which are particularly prevalent in the South Wales coalfield and are excellent for raising steam in boilers. They contain low ash and reasonably low volatile matter and those with the lowest moisture and hydrogen content are classed as 'dry' coals, meaning they exude virtually no moisture product of decomposition when heated.

BITUMINOUS: This is the most abundant rank and has more than 70 principal varieties. It is sometimes known as household coal and is good for domestic, industrial, power station and (confusingly) steam-raising uses, but it can be smoky due to a relatively high content of gaseous constituents and a volatile matter of 15-25%. Its fixed carbon can be anything between 47 and 86% depending on which coalfield and seam it is extracted from. Almost all are made up of layers, but whereas some are 'soft' and friable and crush easily on impact, the 'hard' varieties found in coalfields such as South Yorkshire are far more durable. Appearance-wise, some are bright and shiny, others dull and sooty. N.B.: 'Thermal' coal and 'metallurgical' (coking) coal both belong to the overall family of bituminous/semi-bituminous types, but the coking varieties used in steel-making almost invariably have a higher carbon content and lower amounts of ash, sulphur and phosphorus.

SUB-BITUMINOUS: A cross between bituminous and lignite and occasionally known as black lignite. Typically containing 35-45% fixed carbon, it has a higher volatility and slightly lower heating value than bituminous and is primarily used as a fuel for electricity generation in steam-turbine power stations.

CANNEL: A form of bituminous coal sometimes classified as oil shale. It has a fixed carbon content similar to sub-bituminous plus high hydrogen and low ash content. It burns with a long bright flame like a candle (hence its similar name) and is occasionally known by the nickname 'parrot coal' by virtue of its tendency to make a crackling or 'chattering' noise when burning. Dull and fairly hard in consistency, it has no layers and can be hand-carved and polished into small sculptures. (Note, however, that many coal ornaments sold in souvenir shops today are produced in moulds from coal dust & resin.)

LIGNITE: The lowest rank due to its relatively low heat

The energy stored in coal is released by burning it and the main constituents are basically carbon, hydrogen, oxygen, nitrogen, moisture, ash and hydrocarbons in widely-varying proportions. When heated, it first gives off water vapour and then its volatile matter, which tends to be sulphurous and can cause 'black smoke' pollution if insufficient heat or air is present in the fire.

Once the volatiles have been driven off, the flames subside to leave fixed carbon, which is so-called to differentiate it from any carbon present in the volatile matter. After complete combustion, the inherent ash content is left on the grate, sometimes badly clinkered if the coal contained too many impurities or the fire had been poorly managed by an unskilled boiler stoker or locomotive fireman.

The main ranks of coal and their individual properties are given in the panel below.

To the untrained eye, most coal looks the same but there are numerous types, three of which are shown in this Scottish Mining Museum display. The most common is bituminous (right), which in the case of this particular exhibit is bright, glossy and layered. The parrot, or cannel, on the left is dull and hard, not unlike shale at first glance, while the anthracite at the top is shiny and hard with a semi-metallic sheen and few signs of layers.

value and greater moisture content. It is much younger than fully-formed coal and the process of conversion from peat (see below) is incomplete. It is reasonably soft and certain varieties of it are sometimes known as 'brown coal'. It contains 25 to 35% carbon, a high volatile matter of around 40% and the highest ash content.

In addition to the above are peat, graphite and coke. **Peat** is a soft combustible substance consisting of partly-decayed plant and mineral matter occurring near the surface. In some cases, the geological conversion of peat into lignite is how the process of coalification began, leading over millions of years to bituminous and higher ranks. Capable of being burned in power stations, despite giving off less heat than lignite, peat has a high moisture and medium carbon content and occurs in large outcrops in countries such as Ireland (where it also known as turf), Finland, Germany, Poland and Indonesia.

At the top end of the ranking scale is **graphite,** which is 99% fixed carbon and therefore almost impossible to ignite. It is not mined for the same purposes as coal.

Man-made **coke** is a lightweight, hard, grey, porous and virtually smokeless substance left after the volatile matter has been extracted from coal by baking or 'cooking' in the absence of air using a specialised oven. It has a high carbon content, low volatility, few impurities and is most commonly used as a fuel and for the smelting of iron ore (see Chapter 16). Forms of coke have sometimes also been created deep underground by a natural geological process in which intrusions of volcanic magma act as a natural 'oven'.

CHAPTER 2

The coalfields

Where coal is found

BRITAIN IS often described as an 'island of coal', but only certain regions are classed as coalfields. The largest ones are basically to be found in South Wales, the East and West Midlands, West and South Yorkshire, Lancashire, the North East and central Scotland.

The reason for the specific and highly localised nature of the boundaries shown on the map on the facing page is that the fields represent only the relatively exposed and accessible parts of the coal measures. In many locations, deposits of coal extend far further afield but are concealed beneath millions of tons of younger rocks. This explains, for example, why Lincolnshire is not considered a coalfield, even though deposits are known to exist at great depth beneath it all the way from the Nottinghamshire border to the North Sea coast.

The land that now constitutes the British mainland was once largely covered in coal measures (apart from areas such as central Wales and the Scottish Highlands, which in prehistoric times had been covered by solid terrain rather than by swamps), but, as explained in the previous chapter, earth upheavals and subsequent erosion mean that only certain areas are formally classified as coalfields.

The region considered for many years to be the principal mining district, even though it wasn't the largest, is **South Wales**. This field extends almost 90 miles east to west across the bulk of the famous 'mountains and valleys' region of Glamorgan and Monmouthshire and although less than 20 miles across at its widest point, it covers some 1,000 square miles and contained more than 600 collieries in its heyday.

In the peak year of 1913, almost 20% of South Wales coal was being exported through Barry or Cardiff docks and the two together accounted for the largest coal-exporting port complex in the world at the time. Back in 1851, only 951 people lived in the Rhondda valley; by 1924, there were 167,000!

The last deep mine in the Valleys was Tower Colliery, which closed for the second and final time in 2008.

The field was basically formed of three types of coal — bituminous in the south, low-volatile steam coal in the north and anthracite in the west. Beyond the latter is the **Pembrokeshire** field, a smaller and less productive continuation of the main South Wales field and separated from it by Carmarthen Bay. Sometimes known as the Daucleddau, its seams are mostly thin and plagued by fault lines and the best anthracite could be found only at considerable depth. Its last mine closed at the end of the 1940s.

Moving east, we come to the coalfields aligning the River Severn. On the eastern side of the river can be found the various contiguous seams generally known as the **Somerset & Gloucestershire** and **Bristol** coalfields. These are believed to be an extension of the South Wales coalfield but their seams are generally thinner. The main section is about 20 miles long and runs roughly through the gap between Bristol and Bath, extending from Yate in the north to Radstock and Vobster in the south. Coal is first recorded as being mined there in 1223 and the last colliery, Kilmersdon, closed in 1973.

Although part of Gloucestershire, the **Forest of Dean** is considered a coalfield in its own right. It lies on the western bank of the River Severn roughly between Cinderford and Coleford and, although only 34 square miles in area, it is one of the oldest in Britain, having been worked since at least Roman times. It is also one of the best known by virtue of the Forest Free Miners (see Appendix E).

FIFE COALFIELD

CLACKMANNAN
COALFIELD

LANARKSHIRE
(OR CENTRAL)
COALFIELD

● Glasgow

● Edinburgh

LOTHIAN
COALFIELD

DOUGLAS
VALLEY
COALFIELD

Ayr ●

AYRSHIRE
COALFIELD

MACHRIHANISH
COALFIELD

CANONBIE
COALFIELD

DURHAM &
NORTHUMBERLAND
(THE GREAT
NORTHERN
COALFIELD)

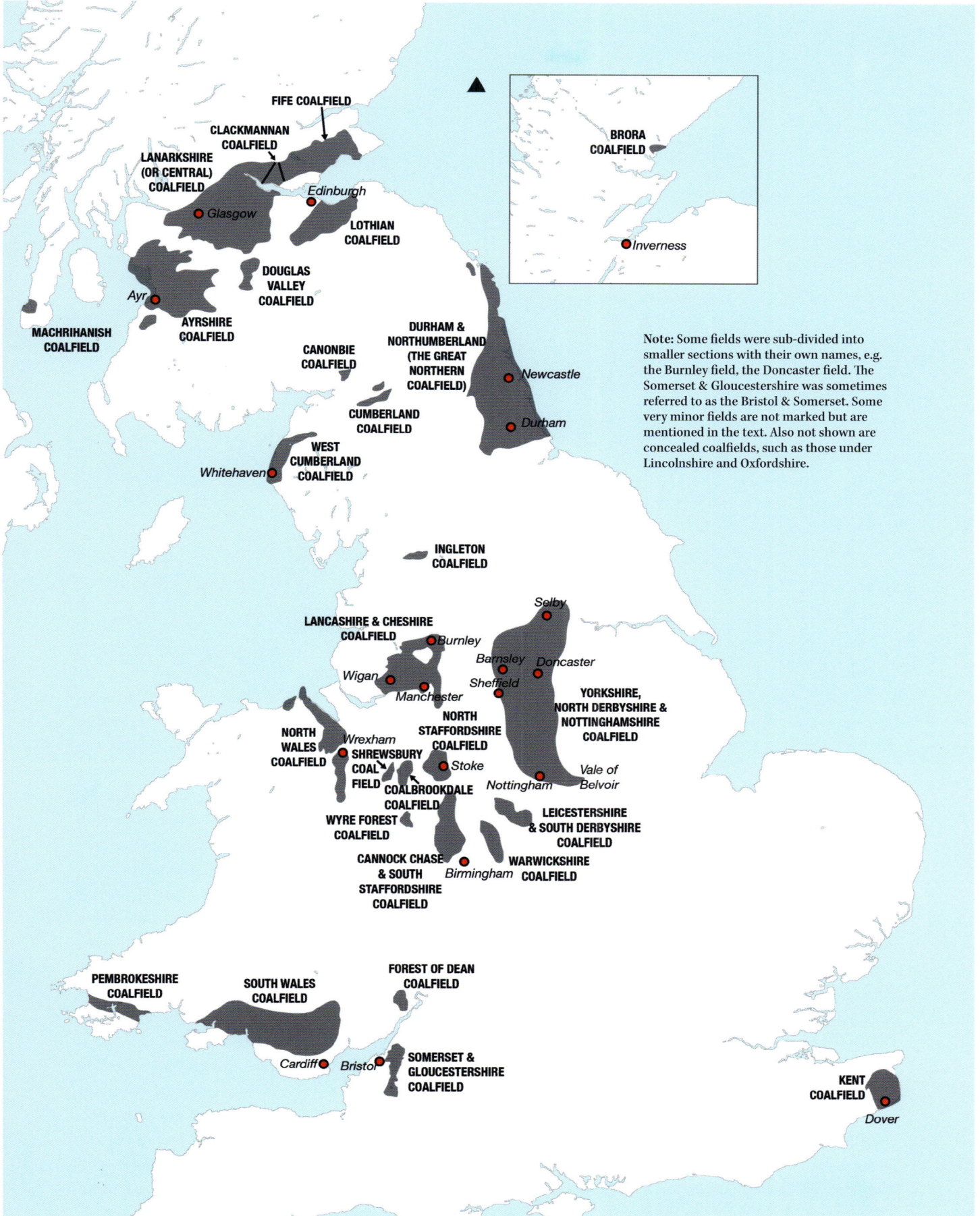

● Newcastle

CUMBERLAND
COALFIELD

● Durham

WEST
CUMBERLAND
COALFIELD

Whitehaven ●

BRORA
COALFIELD

● Inverness

Note: Some fields were sub-divided into
smaller sections with their own names, e.g.
the Burnley field, the Doncaster field. The
Somerset & Gloucestershire was sometimes
referred to as the Bristol & Somerset. Some
very minor fields are not marked but are
mentioned in the text. Also not shown are
concealed coalfields, such as those under
Lincolnshire and Oxfordshire.

INGLETON
COALFIELD

● Selby

LANCASHIRE & CHESHIRE
COALFIELD

● Burnley

Barnsley ● ● Doncaster

Wigan ●

● Manchester

Sheffield ●

YORKSHIRE,
NORTH DERBYSHIRE &
NOTTINGHAMSHIRE
COALFIELD

NORTH
WALES
COALFIELD

Wrexham ●

SHREWSBURY
COAL
FIELD

● Stoke

NORTH
STAFFORDSHIRE
COALFIELD

COALBROOKDALE
COALFIELD

WYRE FOREST
COALFIELD

Nottingham ●

Vale of
Belvoir

LEICESTERSHIRE
& SOUTH DERBYSHIRE
COALFIELD

CANNOCK CHASE
& SOUTH
STAFFORDSHIRE
COALFIELD

● Birmingham

WARWICKSHIRE
COALFIELD

PEMBROKESHIRE
COALFIELD

SOUTH WALES
COALFIELD

FOREST OF DEAN
COALFIELD

Cardiff ● ● Bristol

SOMERSET &
GLOUCESTERSHIRE
COALFIELD

KENT
COALFIELD

● Dover

Typical of the South Wales coalfield was the small town of Mountain Ash, whose colliery nestled in the narrow Cynon Valley. This view shows NCB loco No.7139 shunting the pit's busy yard in 1972. ROGER SIVITER/COLOUR-RAIL

The **North Wales** coalfield is 45 miles long from north to south but less than 10 miles wide. Its exposed area stretches from the Irish Sea coast down to Oswestry, in Shropshire, but to the east the deposits extend beneath a covering of newer strata and are continuous underground with the Lancashire and Staffordshire measures. It is sometimes considered as two coalfields – the **Flintshire** and the **Denbighshire**.

Although its seams are heavily faulted, North Wales contained one of the largest and most prolific collieries in Wales – Llay Main, near Wrexham, which as early as 1929 broke into the 'millionaires club' with an output of 1,057,592 tons. The region also possessed one of the principality's last operational collieries, Point of Ayr, which didn't close until 1996. There is also a tiny and little-known isolated coalfield on the island of Anglesey, but mining there ceased in the 1880s.

In addition to the extremity of the North Wales field near Oswestry, the county of Shropshire has three coalfields of its own – the **Shrewsbury**, **Coalbrookdale** and **Wyre Forest**. Of these, Coalbrookdale (also known as the Shropshire field) is the largest and is considered one of the cradles of

the Industrial Revolution thanks to the iron ore smelting developments of Abraham Darby. Although the Wyre Forest field has been a memory since its last mine, Highley, closed in 1969, it retains a link with coal to this day as steam locomotives of the Severn Valley Railway run through Highley en route from Bridgnorth to Kidderminster.

The **South Staffordshire**, or Dudley coalfield as it is sometimes known, covered an area of about 80 square miles extending from Wolverhampton down into north Worcestershire. It was renowned for its 'Ten Yard Coal', a seam approaching 30ft in thickness that was actually a dozen thin seams overlying each other with no intermediate layers of dirt or rock. This lay less than 400ft below the surface in some places and no other part of Britain had so much coal available at such a shallow depth. A number of South Staffordshire's mines flooded due to lack of maintenance during the 1921 miners' strike and never reopened, but Baggeridge – the last colliery in the 'Black Country' – survived until 1968.

Immediately north of this field is the **Cannock,** or Cannock Case, coalfield, which for administrative purposes is sometimes considered part of the South Staffordshire but

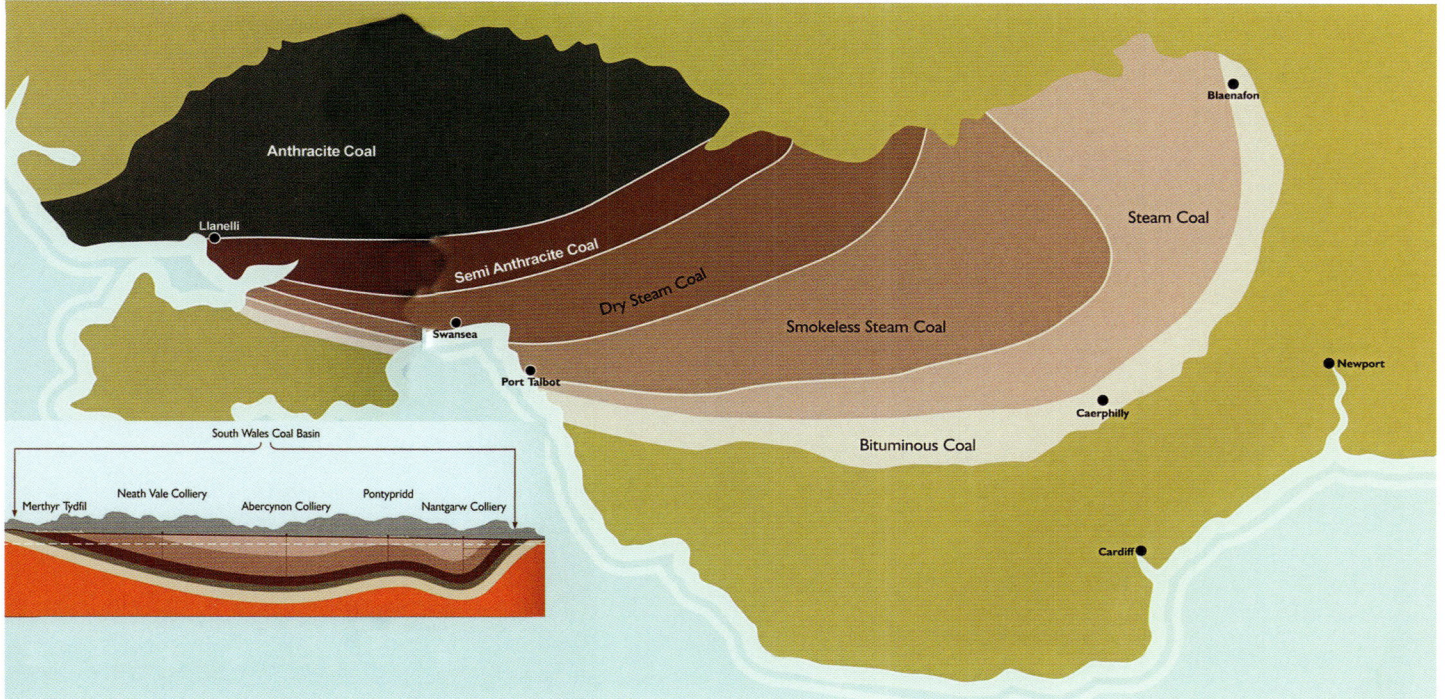

The South Wales coalfield is a complex one containing several classes of coal – bituminous in the south, grades of steam coal in the centre and north, and anthracite in the west. The inset shows a cross-section running from north (left) to south.

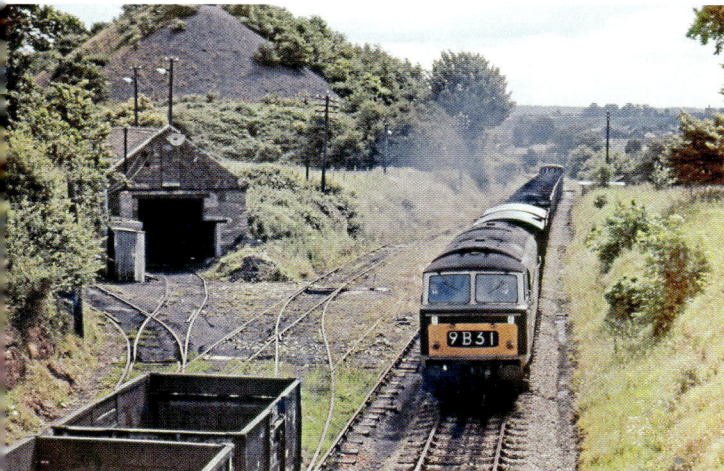

One of the smaller British coalfields lies in Somerset but its mines are long-closed. In July 1965, BR diesel-hydraulic No.D7046 passes the spoil heap and engine shed of Old Mills Colliery as it gets away from Midsomer Norton with loaded coal wagons from Radstock to Bristol. RAIL PHOTOPRINTS

which is physically separated from it by a major geological division known as the Bentley Fault. Cannock Chase contained Littleton Colliery, which continued in production until 1993, and Lea Hall, which in 1960 had been one of the NCB's all-new showcase superpits.

The largest of the West Midlands' coalfields is the **North Staffordshire**, most of which is taken up by the Potteries field, whose 100 square miles in the Stoke-on-Trent and Newcastle-under-Lyme districts contained some of

Britain's largest and most modern superpits. There are more than 30 workable seams in this field, making a total thickness of almost 150ft, more than anywhere else in Britain, but some are so faulted as to be almost vertical (so-called 'rearer' workings). The Cheadle field was one of three smaller outliers adjacent to the main Potteries area.

Some of the thickest seams in Britain, ranging from 7ft to 23ft, are in the **Warwickshire** (or North Warwickshire) coalfield. Lying in the Coventry/Warwick/Nuneaton district, it's an indication of how prodigious it was that Daw Mill Colliery, eight miles north-west of Coventry, was expected to be the last operational mine left in Britain until a major underground fire caused its shock closure in 2013.

The **Leicestershire** and **South Derbyshire** coalfields lie close to an ancient geological area known as Charnwood Forest and stretch 17 miles from just east of Burton-upon-Trent to just west of Leicester. They are sometimes thought of as one field, but lie on different sides of a major geological dividing point known as the Ashby Anticline.

Each part contains a sizeable mining town — Coalville in Leicestershire and Swadlincote in Derbyshire — and each possessed about a dozen collieries in NCB days. Records of workings go back to medieval times and evidence of old pillar & stall workings were recently uncovered in opencast operations.

In the late-1980s, Asfordby Colliery became the last deep coal mine built in Britain when it was sunk near

A cross-section of northern England showing how the Pennine hills divide the coal measures on either side. Note the extensive amount of faulting, especially in Lancashire.

Melton Mowbray to exploit a hitherto unexploited part of Leicestershire, the **Vale of Belvoir** coalfield. Unfortunately, geological and political problems combined to condemn the project to a short life and it closed in 1997.

One of the best-known mining areas is the **Lancashire** coalfield, a symbol of England's industrial might in the early 20th century when there were more than 300 collieries there employing 94,000 workers and lifting almost 25m tons of coal a year. It is divided into three smaller fields – **Burnley**, **South Lancashire** and **East Manchester** – and parts of the area are sometimes further sub-divided, with **Wigan**, **Oldham** and **St Helens** all having been credited at various times with fields named after them.

The southern part of the East Manchester is known as the **Cheshire** field and although the whole area is usually referred to as the Lancashire & Cheshire coalfield, the latter section forms only a narrow strip to the east of Stockport.

The majority of the Burnley section was physically cut off from the main area and, being in hilly terrain, featured more drift mines than was the case in the rest of the county

At its peak, the Lancashire field as a whole was a large one with numerous easily accessible seams, but they were mostly thin, with the majority being only 2 to 3ft in height. Several of the workings also had a reputation for wetness and it is said that mines in the Wigan field used to pump four tons of water for every ton of coal. East Manchester was the most productive part and contained some large collieries, such as Moseley Common, Astley Green and Agecroft. Lancashire's products were mainly bituminous and it was known for high-quality coking and gas-making coals.

Separated from Lancashire by the Pennine mountains

is Yorkshire, which forms the northern section of Britain's largest coalfield.

This is known as the **Yorkshire, North Derbyshire & Nottinghamshire** coalfield, but for administrative purposes is usually divided into its respective counties and treated as three separate sections.

Sometimes known as the Midland coalfield, it stretches 60 miles from the Leeds and Huddersfield area down to Nottingham, taking in Barnsley, Rotherham, Doncaster and Mansfield, and is larger and deeper than the South Wales field, from which it took over the mantle of Britain's premier mining region in the latter part of the 20th century.

In fact, so large is the area that the four aforementioned towns are sometimes thought of as sub-division coalfields in their own right.

Until the Industrial Revolution and the huge demands the iron and steel-making factories of Sheffield and Rotherham began placing on the mining industry, workings were confined to the 'exposed' western part of the coalfield but, from the 1920s onwards, new sources of coal had to be found and the mining companies thus began migrating eastwards to tap into the deeper concealed parts of the measures.

The eastern boundary of the accessible part of the field stretched for 75 miles in an almost straight line from the southern part of the Vale of York to the northern part of the Vale of Belvoir and the most easterly collieries were strung out along that imaginary line. Beyond it, the seams descended too far beneath newer rocks to be commercially viable and as an indication of how low and how far they extend, test-boring in 1927 found coal 4,000ft beneath Lincoln Cathedral!

Another test bore even further east – at Woodhall in

The extent of the East Midlands coalfield in Nottinghamshire and North Derbyshire can be seen in this NCB map. Almost 100 collieries are visible – and this excerpt doesn't even show those at Manton (near Worksop) or Ollerton, Bevercotes and Bilsthorpe, which lay east of Thoresby.

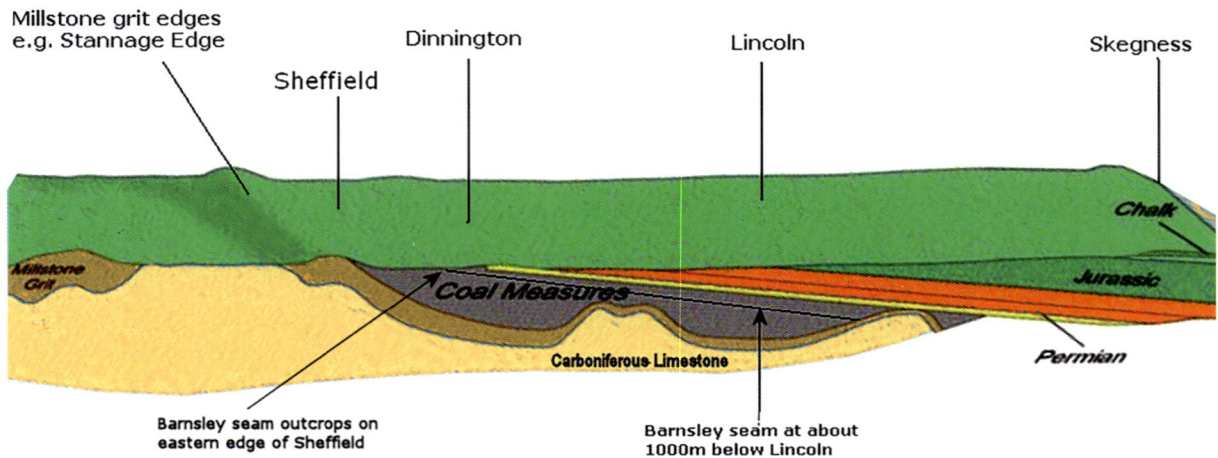

Millstone grit edges e.g. Stannage Edge

Sheffield

Dinnington

Lincoln

Skegness

Coal Measures

Carboniferous Limestone

Chalk

Jurassic

Permian

Barnsley seam outcrops on eastern edge of Sheffield

Barnsley seam at about 1000m below Lincoln

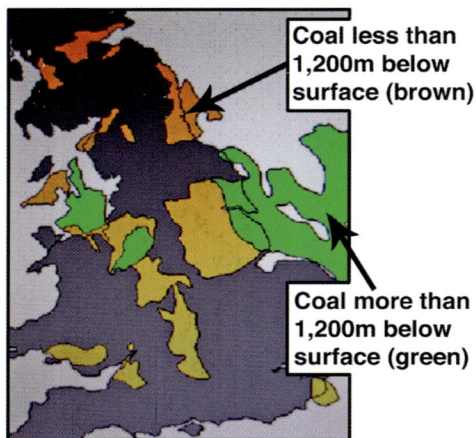

Coal less than 1,200m below surface (brown)

Coal more than 1,200m below surface (green)

WOODHALL SPA

Coalfields fall into two main categories – exposed and concealed. The latter usually lie below more recently-laid rock strata and the diagram above left shows how the Midland coalfield extends at great depth all the way under Lincolnshire and far out into the North Sea, while the top diagram above shows how the Permian and Jurassic strata begin to descend rapidly under Lincolnshire, forcing down the coal seams (whose deep eastern under-sea sections aren't shown on this cross-section). In Victorian times, boreholes were dug in Lincolnshire to ascertain depths and this Woodhall Spa road sign contains an incongruous headstock image as a reminder of those days.

1811 — couldn't quite reach the coal but did discover brine water, which gave the village a major new lease of life as an internationally-famed health spa. Coal board engineers had more luck many years later when they tapped into a southern appendix of the Nottinghamshire field under Belvoir vale and found enough coal between Melton Mowbray and Grantham to justify three new mines — Saltby, Hose and Asfordby. Only the latter was actually built.

Just west of the aforementioned imaginary line in north Nottinghamshire is an area known as 'the Dukeries' because of the number of stately homes in and around that part of Sherwood Forest. In the 1920s, a series of large collieries were built in the district and during the 1950s and 60s, the NCB concentrated a number of superpits there and in Yorkshire to serve new power stations in the Trent and Aire valleys.

The mines built at the northern end of the Yorkshire field were those of the all-new **Selby** coalfield — notable for its use of small and relatively unobtrusive pithead shafts

linked underground to a single large coal processing and loading point at Gascoigne Wood. The complex was developed between 1972 and 1984 and at the time it was the most modern in Europe. In order to ensure maximum coal extraction, one of Britain's fastest and most important railways, the East Coast Main Line, had to be diverted (see Chapter 19).

There is a small isolated field in north-west Yorkshire, at **Ingleton**, and other limited deposits in the Askrigg, Lune Valley and North York Moors districts. The Westmorland villages of Stainmoor and Shap once contained very minor deposits too, but those small outcrops mainly supplied local needs only, as did the **Cumberland** coalfield in the Alston and Midgeholme area.

Of far more importance was the **West Cumberland** field, which hugs the Irish Sea coast in the Workington and Whitehaven district. It occupies a narrow strip of land but extends westwards, necessitating under-sea mining from

With the West Cumberland coalfield partly extending under the sea, Haig Colliery was perched on a clifftop near Whitehaven and in this 1972 scene, its yard is being shunted by Barclay saddle tank *King*. Haig survived demolition after its 1986 closure but was shut down as a museum at the end of 2015. Ironically, Whitehaven is again in the news in the early-2020s over plans for a new deep mine near the town. GORDON EDGAR

as early as the 18th century. At one point, Whitehaven was one of the most important coal-shipping ports in the country, sending huge tonnages over to Ireland, which had no large coal reserves of its own, mainly only peat and lignite.

By far the oldest and most traditional source of coal in England are the **Durham** and **Northumberland** fields. This is often thought of as two separate entities but geologically it is only one, known collectively as the Great Northern (or Great North) Coalfield. It embraces an area of about 800 square miles and runs for 50 miles from Amble in the north to Hartlepool in the south, stretching inland for about 30 miles towards Middleton-in-Teesdale.

It was from this field that 'sea coal' was shipped to London from medieval times, that name deriving partly from the fact that it was transported by sea and partly because the first supplies were washed up on the Durham beaches. As the easily-won supplies at the western end of the field became exhausted, the collieries migrated eastwards much earlier than they did in Yorkshire and Nottinghamshire with Wearmouth Colliery in Sunderland being sunk to a depth of 1,725ft in 1825-35, making it the deepest coal mine in the world, a record it held for many years. The magnitude of such an engineering feat at that time can be gauged by the fact that Britain's first proper public railway, the Stockton & Darlington, didn't open until 1825 and Stephenson's *Rocket* wasn't built until 1829.

In 1911, the Great Northern Coalfield produced a staggering 56m tons. It all came to an end in 2005 with the closure of Ellington Colliery following an underground flood.

North of Amble, there is only one tiny field—the

The Kingdom of Fife possessed substantial coal deposits and boasted some 30 pits in NCB days, several of which were served by the Wemyss Private Railway, whose Barclay 0-6-0T No.20 is storming out of Methil West yard in 1967. W J V ANDERSON/RAIL ARCHIVE STEPHENSON

Scremerston (or Tweed), near Berwick — until one reaches the central lowlands of Scotland, when they reappear with a vengeance. This area of Scotland, like Durham and South Wales, was peppered with collieries at one time, but there are two significant features that characterise Scottish coalfields.

Firstly, some of the deposits had their properties altered millions of years ago by the action of volcanic larva thrusting up through the seams, and secondly, not all the seams lie in the coal measures … just under half are found embedded in carboniferous limestone.

Coal that came into contact with igneous molten larva was converted by the forces of nature into coke or anthracite, the latter being more valuable than ordinary bituminous coal.

There are four main regions of Scotland in which coal was mined — Ayrshire, Lanarkshire, Lothian and Fife — but the disjointed nature of the occurrences has resulted in several separate coalfields, some sub-divided.

The **Lanarkshire** (or Central) field is the largest, extending from Glasgow and Lanark up towards Stirlingshire and at its peak it produced 17m tons of coal, about 60% of Scotland's output. In addition, it produced fireclay and ironstone for the nation's industries and blast furnaces.

The next largest is the **Ayrshire** coalfield, which stretches all the way from Glengarnock in the north to Dalmellington in the south, with small outlying fields at **Sanquhar** and **Dailly**. Although deep mining in Ayrshire ceased in 1989, large-scale opencast operations have continued well into the 21st century in the New Cumnock and Auchinleck areas. The south-eastern tip of this coalfield is sometimes considered a separate area known as the **Dumfriesshire** field.

The large **Fife** coalfield runs for about 30 miles along the north bank of the Firth of Forth (which is itself a concealed coalfield). For centuries, outcropping coal was collected on the seashores of the area and some of the colliery coalfaces extended under the sea.

The coal measures extend beneath the Firth of Forth to become the **Lothian** coalfield on the south bank, a few miles east of Edinburgh, and it is in this field that the popular Scottish Museum of Mining can today be found in the former Lady Victoria Colliery at Newtongrange.

A small coalfield, just six miles by four and known as the **Clackmannan**, lies to the west of the Kingdom of Fife and the very last operational colliery in Scotland, Longannet, was situated about four miles south-east of Clackmannan. It closed in 2002.

Other minor fields 'north of the border' are **Canonbie**, **Douglas Valley**, **Machrihanish** (on Mull of Kintyre) and **Brora**, the last of which is interesting in that it is the most northerly coalfield in the whole of the British Isles. Situated in Sutherland, some 50 miles north of Inverness, its coal is of Jurassic origin formed only 160m years ago and consequently not of the highest quality. It was mainly used locally to supply a brickworks, distillery and woollen mill.

Brora Colliery was nevertheless considered important enough to be modernised with pithead baths in the late-1930s and it survived as a private mine licensed by the NCB, not closing completely until the early-1970s.

This just leaves one established British coalfield to be dealt with – the one that surprises most people when they are told about it for the first time. It is the **Kent** coalfield, an industrial anachronism in the 'Garden of England'.

It wasn't even discovered until the late-Victorian era and then only as the result of an assumption by mining engineers that the large coalfield of northern France and Belgium might continue under the English Channel. In 1890, boreholes were sunk near Dover's Shakespeare Cliff by a company involved in an ill-fated Channel Tunnel rail scheme and the hunch was indeed confirmed.

Nine mines were built to tap into the field's 14 seams, but the first of those, Dover Colliery (sometimes known as Shakespeare Colliery), was not a success and was closed after just a few years in 1915, as were those at Guilford and Cobham. Stonehall (also known as Lydden) and Wingham were abandoned without ever producing coal but the other four – Snowdown, Betteshanger, Tilmanstone and Chislet – were far more successful and long-lived. The latter was a large mine modernised by the NCB in the early-1960s and notable for featuring an underground overhead electric railway system.

All four NCB pits in Kent were built on a large scale with headgears and winding engines of massive construction to deal with the extreme shaft depths of more than 3,000ft, but only continuous pumping enabled them to cope with the salty water found in the strata. Kentish coal mining came to an end with the closure of Betteshanger in August 1989 and it was thus the shortest-lived of Britain's significant coalfields.

In addition to those detailed above, there is a concealed coalfield beneath parts of Oxfordshire and Berkshire that

The most northerly coalfield in Britain was the small Brora field, which lay in the county of Sutherland, almost 40 miles north of Inverness as the crow flies. Unlike the great majority of British coal, which was laid down in the Carboniferous Period, Brora deposits belonged to the more recent Jurassic Period. The colliery closed in 1969 but the measures continued to be worked from nearby drifts until the mid-70s.

The Coal Mine on the Beach

Dover Colliery, Shakespeare Cliff.

The English coalfield most isolated from the rest was located in Kent and in NCB days it possessed four major collieries – Chislet, Tilmanstone, Snowdown and Betteshanger. Few people are aware that there had at one time been other mines in the 'Garden of England', the biggest of which was Dover Colliery, known as 'the Coal Mine on the Beach'. Its remarkable position at the foot of Shakespeare Cliff can be appreciated in this early 20th century postcard photograph.

has never been commercially exploited, plus a little-known field near Bovey Tracey, in Devon, but the latter contains lignite, rather than fully-formed coal, and is therefore the only deposit found in England that does not date back to the Carboniferous Period.

Coalfields on the island of Ireland are mainly of the concealed type, although mining in a relatively minor way has taken place over the years in the Munster, Leinster, Connaught and Tyrone areas (the latter in Northern Ireland) and there are also extensive peat deposits.

In the world as a whole, coalfields are located in more than 70 countries on every continent (including Antarctica) with the largest by far being in Russia, China, the United States and Australia and it is estimated that there are still more than 850billion tonnes of accessible coal reserves worldwide.

CHAPTER 3

Early years to 1800

Setting the stage for a revolution

C OAL HAS been known to man since the dawn of civilisation and there is carbon-dated evidence of it being used for cremation pyres in what is now Wales about 3,000 years before the birth of Christ. Bronze Age axe-heads have been found embedded in coal and excavations of Roman sites in Britain have found traces of coal ash, indicating that it was used in a modest way during the military occupation of 43 to 410AD.

The Romans are known to have smelted iron using local coal and ore at their fort in Caerleon, near modern-day Newport, and they had discovered outcrops in the Somerset coalfield too, for there is evidence of coal being used in the city of Bath to fuel hot springs and feed a sacred flame in the Temple of Minerva.

More than 400 years after the Romans left Britain, the chronicles of Peterborough Abbey reveal that 12 loads of 'fossil coal' were purchased in the year 852, but the Domesday Book of 1086 makes no mention of the mineral, even

This is how a typical English rural coal mine would have appeared in the late-1700s. Winding of men and coal at this Shropshire pithead was done by the horse 'gin' in the centre of the picture and the coal was taken away on the narrow gauge track on the left and by packhorse. ('Gin' was a short form of the word engine.)

An indication of how crowded the coalfields were in the early years of mining can be gained from this engraving from the late-1700s. There are three mines within very close proximity, each with its own timber headgear, the latter by then already beginning to resemble the huge structures they would develop into over the next century and a half.

though lead and iron mines are recorded, and it is not until the 13th century that documents show 'sea coal' being sent to London by sailing vessels from the north-east of England.

In those days, coal was not mined in the modern sense but retrieved; either by collecting it from shores and beaches where it naturally washed up with every tide or by burrowing into riverbanks and other shallow locations.

Records of the 12th century show that wood, charcoal and peat were the fuels universally employed in the British Isles at that time. In the homes of the common people, a peat or wood fire would lie in a hole in the floor, exhausting through a hole in the roof and to prevent the wooden houses from burning down at night when the inhabitants were asleep, a law was introduced whereby a bell would be rung at dusk telling everyone to cover their fire (*couvre feu*), from where the word curfew originates.

By the 12th century, many urban dwellers had switched to burning sea coal from the North Eastern and Scottish coastal areas and towns were beginning to suffer so much from the effects of smoky environments that Queen Eleanor felt forced to cut short a stay in Nottingham, complaining of foul-smelling fumes. The problem was that most of the primitive little houses in the cities didn't have proper chimneys, resulting in pungent smoke swirling around the narrow cramped streets. Attempts were made to ban use of the fuel in London, but with little effect.

It might appear from this that Britain was already a coal-fired society in the 13th to 16th centuries, but nothing could be further from the truth. Coal accounted for only a minuscule fraction of the fuel burnt in the country at that time. The vast majority was wood, much of which was also being used to produce charcoal to supply Britain's fledgling workshops.

However, the amount of charcoal needed to smelt just one ton of iron for weapons or cannon required a whole acre of woodland to be destroyed, which is why suitable types of timber were becoming scarce. Exacerbating the situation in the 1500s to 1700s was the sheer volume of wood required to build the great Navy ships of the time (a single large warship required the timber of 4,000 oak trees), and laws were therefore passed protecting woods and forests from unauthorised felling.

Therein lies one of the main reasons for the future success of coal, for the effect was to make wood and charcoal prohibitively expensive ... so much so that in the 1590s, the price of firewood rocketed by 800%, causing the English Parliament to ban the use of charcoal for all but the most important uses and encourage the population to burn coal instead. Up until that point it had still been relatively small fry – a mere 210,000 tons produced annually in the entire country ... less than the output of a single medium-sized colliery in the 20th century.

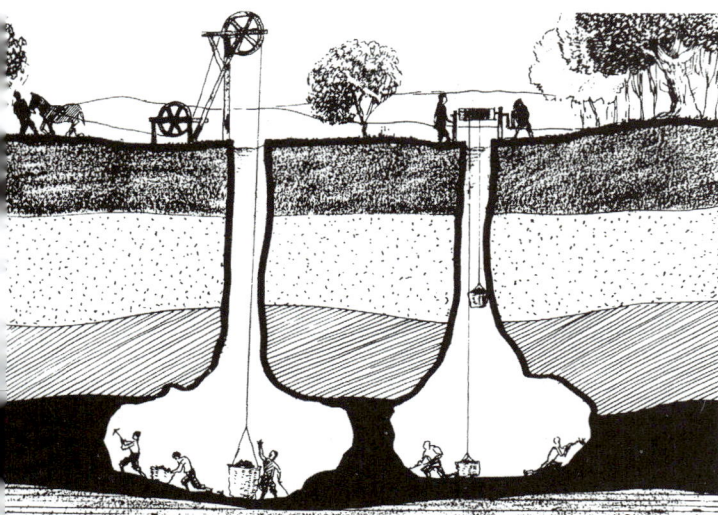

Above: An illustration of an 18th century scene showing the transition between the hand-operated windlass type of bellpit and the horse-powered pulley wheels that were to form the basis of the large steam and electricity-driven headstocks of the future. Note the closeness of the two pits in the above image, only a small pillar of coal supporting the roof.

Right: Shallower or freshly-dug bellpits could be accessed via ladders, as depicted in this model at the Scottish Mining Museum.

In the early-1600s it was reported in the vernacular of the time that "sea-cole and pitt-cole is become the general fewell of this Britaine island, used in the houses of the nobilitie, clergy and gentrie in London and in all other cityes and shires of the Kingdome as well as for dressing of meate, washing and brewing".

The resultant demand for sea coal and outcropped coal, especially from the capital, saw the fleet of 'collier' sailing ships plying between there and the Great Northern coalfield increase more than tenfold to 900 by 1660, there being no quick or cheap means of moving large quantities of coal over land for such a distance until the great canal-building era arrived in the 18th century. In fact, it was revealed in 1675 that it was cheaper to move coal 300 miles by sea than it was to move it 20 miles by horse.

Once the search for coal became more widespread, the sea coal retrievers, outcroppers and shallow 'pitt-cole' diggers began to be joined by burrowers (the forerunners of modern drift miners) who would dig what is known as an 'adit' into a hillside and literally follow a seam horizontally or at a slight incline for as far as they dared before flooding, foul air or the risk of a collapsed roof forced them to abandon the orifice and start another close by.

In less hilly areas, a deeper form of pit-digging was becoming more widespread. This was the vertical bellpit, so called because of their shape in profile (see illustrations),

bellpits were initially shallow enough for the coal to be carried out via ladders but as they grew deeper, hand-operated wooden windlasses were erected around the openings in order to winch baskets up and down on ropes.

Once a collier sensed that removing any more coal would cause the soil and rock above him to collapse, the pit would be abandoned and a fresh one would be dug alongside. Although it might seem from a modern viewpoint that it would make sense to support the roof to prevent it collapsing, archaeological evidence indicates that the hewers of the day clearly considered it quicker and easier to simply start a new one.

Vertical pits were more productive than the previous methods as they could tap more than one seam if they went deep enough and in certain coalfield areas of the 17th and 18th centuries, the countryside was peppered with such holes, above which stood gins or windlasses. We know this because they appear as illustrations in the diary of Reinhold Angerstein, a Swedish industrial spy who was sent by his government to travel surreptitiously through England monitoring the extent of industrial progress in 1753-55.

After being abandoned, the holes became serious hazards once their entrances had become partly obscured by long grass and bushes. There are many records of local people and livestock being injured or killed as a result of falling into old pits. Gradually, they were filled in but, with no record of

generated. This was the genesis of arguably the most important aspect of the entire mining industry – the principle of upcast and downcast air flow – and it has dictated how mines and shafts have been constructed ever since (see Chapter 14).

The ventilated pits enabled the early colliers to venture further into the ground and although they learned to hold up roofs with props of timber, numerous collapses – and no doubt injuries and deaths – made them realise it was much safer to leave blocks of coal in situ as support pillars. These allowed them to make incursions into the seam on all four sides of each block as well as advance further into the terrain in relative safety. The size and shape of the pillars (also known as 'stoops') was a matter of skill and careful judgment and depended on the depth of the working and the nature and hardness of the roof.

As more and more sections of coal were removed from between the supports, the subterranean scenes began to resemble honeycombs of rooms and pillars, hence the term 'room & pillar mining' (more commonly known as pillar & stall, and also as bord & pillar or stoop & room).

Most stalls were too small for two men to work in, lest they accidentally struck each other with their picks, but some colliers chose to work with a mate, who would fill the tub with the loose coal he had hewed. As they advanced, the distances back to the shaft entrances grew longer, so women and children were engaged to assist the menfolk by carrying or dragging the full baskets, or 'corves', along

Before the advent of proper collieries, Britain's coalfields were peppered with a plethora of shallow pits, as depicted in this scene near Wednesbury, West Midlands, in April 1754. It was sketched by Reinhold Angerstein, a Swedish industrial spy who made a two-year journey through Britain at that period to gather information on the fledgling Industrial Revolution for his government.

where they all were, it took centuries for these man-made 'rabbit warrens' to be made safe. An idea of the size of the task can be gained from the fact that in 1947 the newly-formed NCB identified no fewer than 442 abandoned mine workings in the Sheffield area alone!

Roof support did eventually come after it was noted that in bellpits that had been 'holed through' under the ground to adjacent ones, the air was fresher and that a breeze was

Once bellpits had been succeeded by subterranean passageways, the only way pioneer miners could keep their tunnels clear was to waft out the gas with large cloths and remove water by means of bucket chains.

With mines growing larger in the late-1700s, pockets of methane lurking in roof cavities began to be encountered on a regular basis. That led to the need for 'firemen', whose hazardous job it was to crawl into tunnels with a naked flame on the end of a long pole and explode the gas!

the dark passageways and hooking them on to the windlass rope.

The disadvantage with the pillar & stall system, of course, was that it was dreadfully inefficient, for only about half the coal was mined, the rest being left untouched in the ground, yet despite this it is still deployed in numerous parts of the world today – and was in daily operation at Derbyshire's Eckington Colliery drift mine until its closure in January 2019.

Britain's first waggonway had been built as early as 1604 to convey coal from Strelley pits to Wollaton, just west of Nottingham. Similar horse and gravity-powered forerunners of railways quickly appeared in the North-East, using wooden-bodied chaldron waggons. By the late-1700s, coal was starting to become a significant player in the commercial fabric of the nation and the era of deeper mining was beginning to dawn, with some larger pits already being dug down to 300ft or more.

The ever-increasing lengths of the subterranean passageways brought a second headache – methane gas. Known colloquially as 'firedamp', it was prevalent in most mining districts and in the early days the only way the pioneer colliers had been able to cope was to waft it out with a large cloth or use a hand-operated bellows to generate a flow of

Not until Thomas Newcomen invented an atmospheric water-pumping engine in 1712 could mines be kept sufficiently dry to enable regular production. Rapid advances in the technology of stationary steam engines between then and the early 1800s produced more efficient and powerful machines and enabled the sinking of shafts below the water-bearing measures. This fine model is housed at the Scottish Mining Museum and a full-size working replica of the 1712 engine can be seen at the Black Country Living Museum in Dudley.

air. Both methods proved hopelessly inadequate, so until the invention of safety lamps in the early years of the 19th century there was nothing for it but to employ a 'fireman'.

A fireman's job was to wrap himself in thick water-soaked garments, crawl forward and ignite the pockets of gas with a naked flame on the end of a long stick … or with a candle pulled along with a string while he crouched down as best he could. Because of their monk-like hoods and short life expectancy, such men were known by their fellow mineworkers as 'the Penitents'.

Such remarkable bravery cleared the danger, but only for a few hours at a time. To ventilate mines on a longer-lasting basis, fire baskets (later replaced by furnaces), were placed at the bottom of upcast shafts so that the air currents

caused by the flames would draw ventilation through the mine workings, but there was always a risk that the air would become charged with methane while travelling through the passageways and explode when it reached the furnace. This remained a problem until the furnaces were eventually replaced by fans.

So far, most pits and tunnels had been created relatively close to the surface, staying above the natural water table. There were drift mines that had been dug into the sides of notoriously wet hills and they usually ascended slightly so that a) the water would drain away into the valleys of its own accord and b) it would ease the task of hauling the loaded coal from the face to the exit of the mine. In locations where it was not always possible for the main

Most room & pillar mining was conducted before the advent of photography and, even afterwards, cameras were only allowed down mines under strict safety precautions. It was not until the introduction of opencast mining in the 1940s that unexpected surprises such as this began to come to light. This example was unearthed at Blindwells, in East Lothian, Scotland, and the large amount of coal left to support the roof shows just how inefficient some of those early mines were.

haulage road to ascend, a smaller adit would be driven to the outside of the hill or valley to act as a drain. Vertical shaft pits, however, had to rely on a horse gin or water-wheel-driven bucket-and-chain system, often using the same shaft as the coal (which hampered production).

As early as 1700, the percolation of water into the galleries of many mines was proving a big problem, for the depth a collier could work at was limited by the level of flood water.

Although several experiments had been made with rudimentary waterwheel and wind-powered pumps in the 1600s, it wasn't until 1712 that Thomas Newcomen produced the first efficient atmospheric engine to drain mines of water. The colliery at which the pioneering machine was installed

is believed to have been at Coneygree, near Dudley Castle in the West Midlands. It worked not as a steam-driven engine but by using the pressure of the atmosphere to push a piston against a partial vacuum created in the cylinder by condensing the steam. Its efficiency was less than 1%, but it could lift ten gallons of water 153ft with each stroke of its beam – about 5,000 gallons an hour.

Over the next half-century, Newcomen-style machines of improving types, and more efficient James Watt-designed steam engines, spread rapidly across the nation's coalfields, reducing fuel costs and making the early collieries more profitable for their owners.

The advent of the Newcomen pumping engine just over 300 years ago is thus generally considered to represent the

37

birth of deep mining, although 'deep' is a relative term, for those crude early developments merely paved the way for the ultra deep-mining era of the 19th and 20th centuries that were to revolutionise the entire world. Until then, it had been assumed by engineers that mining at depths greater than 350ft or so would always be unattainable due to water ingress.

In 1763, Walker Colliery, near Newcastle, took delivery of the largest engine in the world at the time – a Newcomen product with a 74in cylinder that had been cast by the Coalbrookdale Company of Shropshire and could pump water from a then-unprecedented depth of 530ft. A further major milestone was reached 17 years later at another Northumberland colliery, Willington, when a Watt-designed engine was used for coal-winding (as opposed to mine-draining).

Also appearing in mid-18th century chronicles was the first written mention of what would much later become the main alternative to room & pillar mining – the longwall technique. This required rows of wooden props to hold up the roof while colliers standing alongside each other hewed coal from the face at a fairly uniform rate in order to remove a panel of coal in a single operation. In doing so, they created what was literally a 'long wall'.

This had the advantage that it recovered virtually 100% of the coal compared with 50-60% in room & pillar, but it was far more hazardous as it left a huge expanse of roof strata exposed above the coalface and relied on the strength and stability of the props and the skill of the colliers in positioning and inserting them correctly.

As the face advanced, thick stone walls (known as packs) were erected to help support the roof alongside the roadways and also the roof above the extracted part behind the colliers – an area known as the 'goaf' or 'gob'. In many mines, the roof was allowed to cave into this waste area as long as there were no buildings or roads on the surface above it. In most cases, coal removal that would undermine important structures such as churches, farmhouses or stately homes was generally avoided.

The strenuous efforts being made by engineers to tackle the problems of ventilation and flooding were paying dividends, but there was a third major obstacle that would need to be overcome before mining could really take off as a major industry – transport.

The Britain of that era had few major roads and turnpike tolls were charged to use them. Elsewhere, the population had to put up with unmetalled tracks which turned to mud in winter and were unsuitable for heavy loads. The only way to shift coal long distances was by coastal vessels – but the second half of the 18th century marked a great canal-building era in the country, most with the carriage of coal as their prime objective. Well over 100 inland waterways were built in a relatively short space of time to enable the advantages of widely available coal to be felt in all parts of the country rather than just London, the North and the coastal towns.

One canal, built by the Duke of Bridgewater to link his Worsley Colliery with the centre of Manchester, reduced the cost of that pit's coal by no less than a half, showing what enormous potential there was in reforming inland transport.

Railways as we know them would not arrive until the first half of the 19th century, although preliminary work had started on a horse-drawn rail system at Middleton, Leeds, as early as the 1750s and within the internal layouts of numerous collieries themselves, waggonways with wooden rails were in fairly widespread use.

The year 1767 saw the first use of cast iron for rails, at Coalbrookdale, and 16 years later came the first *bona fide* waggonway to be laid underground in a British mine – at Sheffield Park Colliery, in Yorkshire. This was a development of the primitive 'hund' system that had been used in central European mines since the late Middle Ages, a hund being a small, wheeled tub.

Until the beginning of the 19th century in Britain, coal had remained a largely local industry, operated by reasonably wealthy families and restricted by lack of proper transport to areas where naturally-occurring outcrops and shallow seams could be accessed. But the canals started to change that – and the social fabric of the country began to change with it, writer Arthur Young noting in 1791 that "all the activity in the kingdom is fast concentrating where there are coalpits."

While an unsuspecting population waited for the steam railway age to burst upon it and change the nature of the nation forever, coal shipments from the Great North coalfield continued to grow and exceeded a million tons for the first time in the late-1700s. The South Wales field was also a big player, sending out a quarter of a million tons a year through Swansea dock alone. The annual amount of coal produced in Britain as a whole in the 1780s was a shade over 10m tons.

What is sometimes known as the 'First Industrial Revolution' had started circa 1760, fired largely by the availability of cheap and plentiful coal, and thanks to pumping engines, mines were becoming deeper and deeper. Percy Main Colliery, near Newcastle, had attained a depth of 960ft in 1799 – making it the deepest in the country until overtaken by Wearmouth 30 years later.

The stage was set for the coming of the railways and the phenomenal growth in the coalmining industry that would see Great Britain become the 'workshop of the world'.

CHAPTER 4

1800-1946

Britain ... workshop of the world

IT IS no exaggeration to say that the Industrial Revolution could not have occurred if it had not been for coal. If there had been no deposits in the British Isles, the great social phenomenon Britain gave to the rest of the world would have taken place in another country and probably much later.

The revolution might not even have started at all if the kingdom had not suffered serious deforestation in the 16th century, triggering laws forcing Britons to start burning coal instead of wood and charcoal.

By the turn of the 19th century, all the building blocks were in place for arguably the biggest social upheaval in the annals of human history.

Most historians put the genesis of the Industrial Revolution at 1760, some as early as 1700. Those, however, are the dates at which early mechanisation began to make its presence felt in the relatively modest workshops of the day, most of which were locally based and self-contained. It has to be remembered that Britain at the beginning of the 1800s was still primarily an agricultural society. There was a relatively small population, no railways, few proper roads ... hardly any means by which labour forces and heavy products could be moved around the country except on water or drawn by horses.

The Industrial Revolution scenes beloved of history and geography teachers — of countless smokestacks belching out smoke, grimy goods trains and row upon row of terraced houses — still largely belonged to the future.

Even Richard Trevithick's idea of turning the concept of the colliery water-pumping engine into one that could use wheels to propel itself along a track was still four years away in 1800 and not even those with the most vivid of imaginations could have foreseen what a vast difference

that invention would have made by the time babies born that year reached their 100th birthdays.

Ironstone had been found in close proximity to coal in several locations, so much so that 90% of British iron was being smelted in South Wales by the time Trevithick's first locomotive took to the rails near Merthyr Tydfil in 1804. Other inventors soon began to improve on the design and by 1812, the Middleton Colliery in Leeds was operating the first commercial steam trains. Up in the North-East, Wylam Colliery was experimenting with the rudimentary locomotives *Puffing Billy* and *Wylam Dilly*.

The big breakthrough on the world stage came in 1825 with the opening of the Stockton & Darlington Railway — generally accepted to be the world's first 'main line' route. It was an extremely successful venture, carrying 52,000 tons of coal by its third year and running more than 30 trains a day by the time the world's first inter-city passenger railway opened between Manchester and Liverpool five years later.

Potential income from coal was one of the prime factors

The workshop of the Welsh Mining Museum at Big Pit in Blaenafon.

This fine classical painting by Victorian artist John Carmichael depicts Murton Colliery, County Durham, in 1843 and shows that tall head-stock-mounted pulley wheels were in use by then (although an old-style horse gin can be seen in front of the largest building). The long-backed hat and waterproof over-garment worn by the man in the foreground indicates that he is a shaft-sinker.

The opening of a new colliery was a grand occasion, often accompanied by a banquet for coal owners, local dignitaries and possibly even miners and their families. Such a gala is depicted in the grounds of Gyfeillion Colliery (later renamed Great Western Colliery) in August 1851. The Hetty shaft winding house of this mine has been preserved.

that fuelled the 'railway mania' in the 1840s, for the great coalfields of Britain were crying out for rapid connection with the major markets of London and the South-East, and vice versa. The railways are dealt with in more detail in Chapter 19.

By the 1850s there were 2,397 collieries in Britain, but many of those were still small, primitive and grouped very close together, as evidenced by the fact that there were 516 mines in Staffordshire and Worcestershire — more than twice as many as in Durham and Northumberland — yet the amount of coal they produced annually was well under half the 15m tons mined by the 225 collieries in the latter two counties.

Even Yorkshire possessed only 270 pits at that time, but the spread of railways had seen the search for coal reach frantic proportions with 50 shafts being sunk close to Barnsley in quick succession and new seams being found at ever-greater depths. As with the railways, many fortunes

An 1814 view of Middleton Colliery, near Leeds, which two years earlier had started using steam locomotives. The painting, by contemporary artist George Walker, is entitled The Collier but it appears to depict him in his 'Sunday best'.

An early-1820s sketch of Hetton Colliery and two of its George Stephenson-built locos.

were made during the coal equivalent of the 'gold rush' and towns in the region began to boom as Britons turned their hands to manufacturing virtually everything under the sun.

Indeed, it's no exaggeration to say that without the coal industry, very few other industries would have been possible. Coal was quite simply the catalyst that changed the world.

So great was its rate of extraction that 'experts' were predicting as early as the 1860s that supplies would soon be exhausted … yet more and more new seams were located and sleepy rural villages were transformed almost overnight from agricultural to industrial ways of life.

In fact, so many new coalfaces were opened up that the forests couldn't keep pace with the demand for pit props (shades of the deforestation crisis of the 16th century) and timber had to be imported from Russia and Finland. The result was that by the end of the 19th century, the relatively small island of Britain possessed an estimated 3,000 coal mines.

Between 1862 and 1880, some of the independent producers began to amalgamate and by 1864 the Powell Duffryn combine, with 59 pits and 30,000 employees, had become the world's largest coal producer, followed by Lewis Merthyr and the Ocean Coal Company.

The lives of the moguls who ran such enterprises were a million miles from those of the men who toiled hundreds of feet beneath their feet. Although it had been made illegal for women and children to work underground since 1842, the hardships faced underground had changed little and despite the passing of numerous parliamentary Acts designed to improve their lot, the 20th century dawned with thousands of men still having to risk death or injury from roof collapses, dust-clogged lungs and naked flames in gas-laden atmospheres.

In those days, many colliers worked in pairs and it was the job of the senior man and his mate not only to cut

the coal but to advance the face and erect the props as they went. They also had to bore holes, break up the waste stone and, in many mines, pack it tightly in the void (the 'goaf') to support the roof as the face advanced. On top of all that, the early colliers had to buy their own tools (usually by deduction from wages) and had to lock them up at the end of every shift to prevent them being stolen by unscrupulous colleagues.

Although the men were not always favourably inclined towards their work, they had huge pride and self-respect in their ability to perform such a tough task year after year.

At most collieries they were on piece-work and toiled under the control of charter masters, or so-called 'butties', who paid them only for the amount of coal they produced from their 'stint' each day and often manipulated pay and working conditions to maximise their own profits. The mining companies themselves could be unscrupulous in that respect and this led in 1877 to colliers at each pit earning the legal right to appoint an honest and impartial 'checkweigher' to ensure the weight of each tub matched what was recorded by the company.

Given such circumstances, it was unsurprising that unrest was rife. There had been numerous local strikes, lockouts and other instances of dissent in the coalfields in the 19th and early 20th centuries but the first national strike of British miners occurred in 1912 and secured a minimum wage to ensure that colliers who worked in difficult seams weren't disadvantaged.

Whether by coincidence or design, the very next year, 1913, turned out to be the all-time peak year for production in the UK with 288m tons won from the 3,000 or so mines great and small, and more than a million people employed in the industry — about one in ten of the entire working-age male population of the country at the time. When it's considered that workable coalfields covered only

An indication of the colossal scale of Great Britain's coal-exporting industry in its heyday can be gained from this aerial view of Cardiff's Queen Alexandra Dock. The photograph is undated but was taken during the era of private colliery ownership, so before 1947. There are well over 1,000 wagons waiting to be unloaded and similar scenes would be enacted at other docksides across the UK. Hard though it is to believe, the annual British output of 287m tons in 1913 would, if placed into wagons, have formed a train long enough to stretch almost four times around the world!

a relatively small proportion of the British Isles, the statistic takes on an even greater resonance.

The nation's railway system was at its zenith too, with well over 20,000 locomotives burning coal every day, and the British Navy ruled the waves with the Admiralty preferring South Welsh steam coal because its near-smokeless qualities meant warships wouldn't give their position away to an enemy too easily. (On the other hand, warship captains were often grateful for a spare batch of bituminous coal in the boiler room, for it enabled them to order the creation of a thick black smokescreen to hide their vessels from enemy guns.)

Exports were booming at that time too — in 1913/14 the pits of South Yorkshire alone sent seven million tons of coal through Hull docks, much of it to Russia, which at that time had not begun to seriously exploit its own vast coal reserves.

The British mining industry had only recently been overtaken by the US as the largest of its kind in the world, so

the future of the pits, like the future of the British Empire, looked rosy in 1913. But a rude awakening lay ahead … just a few months later the First World War broke out, destroying Great Britain's export trade almost overnight (it never fully recovered) and causing huge manpower losses.

Many miners, like other workers, enlisted for military or naval duty in huge numbers.

For the young unmarried ones, it was an adventure, a chance to travel to foreign places they could never have afforded to visit otherwise. Miners made particularly good soldiers, fearless, determined and unafraid of the unknown, as British military leader Sir Douglas Haig recognised when he said: "There are no more gallant or enduring men on the battlefields of France than the miners of Britain." *The Times* newspaper weighed in by thundering: "The pit has no mercy for the weedy or the timid."

The war itself produced a massive demand for coal to keep the nation's steelworks supplied for the manufacture

Stripped to the waist because of the heat and wearing only soft flat caps, two hewers work on their 'stint' in the pre-mechanisation era. Their allocated tub on the right is full and almost ready to be taken to the pitbank for weighing and unloading.

of tanks, cannon and other munitions (naval orders alone increased ten-fold) but the rush to sign up for the forces left the mines in disarray, so in 1916 the Government decided to put the industry under state control to ensure continued supplies during the hostilities.

An unusual aspect connected with the conflict concerned a group of German and other European workers who had been sinking the shafts of a new colliery at Harworth, north of Retford. The assets of the mine's Anglo-German development company were impounded by the Government at the outbreak of fighting in 1914 and the men were interned for the duration of the hostilities, although some are believed to have fled back to Germany in the nick of time. The Harworth work was put on hold for four years and not completed until the return of peace, the original partly-built shafts being abandoned in case the Germans had spiked them with explosives.

Putting Britain's collieries into public hands during the war had given many miners a hope that the industry would

be nationalised after the Armistice, but in 1919 the pits were handed back to their private owners, contributing indirectly to another bitter strike in 1921. A triple alliance between miners, railwaymen and transport workers fell apart and the three-month dispute left the miners on poorer terms.

There were other negative developments; not only had the war destroyed Britain's coal export trade, but the Royal and Merchant navies began converting ships from coal to diesel fuel and the newly-formed Southern Railway pressed ahead with widespread electrification of London commuter routes. In a development far more damaging to the economy, however, nations that had previously been paying for imported coal from Britain began building up their own coalmining industries.

In 1926 came the General Strike, bringing the nation to a virtual standstill and affecting industries in every walk of life, but after nine days it was called off and the miners were left to continue their dispute alone for six months

The headstocks at Harworth Colliery in the early-1920s shortly after construction. The sinking of the shafts there had been delayed as German and Austrian specialists working on them had either fled or been arrested upon the outbreak of the First World War. This picture makes an interesting comparison with the 21st century view in Chapter 7 as it can be seen that the winding house was without its eastern section at both the very start and the very end of its life. INDUSTRIAL RAILWAY SOCIETY

until hunger forced them back to work.

The situation was exacerbated by the mass unemployment that resulted from the global recession of the late-1920s and the 'hungry 30s', so that by 1932, employment in mining had fallen by more than a third from its pre-strike peak of 1.2m. Colliers would be seen sitting by the side of the road eating bread and dripping and their kids would be playing in the street with no shoes on their feet because the families couldn't afford to clothe them properly.

The effects of the 1930 Coal Mines Act resulted in railway grouping-style amalgamations for some colliery companies, such as Powell Duffryn Ltd (formed from 14 firms with 43 mines), Amalgamated Denaby Collieries Ltd (a merger of four colliery firms) and the Lambton, Hetton & Joicey Collieries Co, formed by a merger of local operations in the North-East. Unlike the railway company groupings, the amalgamations were voluntary.

The industry was in the doldrums relative to how it had been 20 years earlier and few pits were making a profit due to cut-throat competition between the various coal owners. The writing had started to appear on the wall a few years earlier for some of the older mines in the west and central parts of England and Scotland as it was clear their reserves were finite, so boreholes were sunk further east in an attempt to maintain production.

Small mines that had received little or no investment had become uncompetitive and mining in the small Cheshire field ceased altogether as early as 1935 due to thin and worked-out seams. The drift to the east was also felt hard in Barnsley, whose traditional position at the centre of the

South Yorkshire coal industry was coming under threat from the Doncaster and Rotherham areas, where more modern pits were being sunk in virgin territory.

Some of the new shafts in Yorkshire and the East Midlands could be half a mile or more deep and thus extremely hot with low air pressure and many miners who had transferred from the shallower, cooler mines of South Wales, West Derbyshire and the North-West couldn't handle the harsh conditions and left the industry.

In South Wales, the number of miners slumped to 136,000 and annual production in that part of the UK dropped to 35m tons. It took the Second World War to change everything completely. Jobless miners flocked to enlist in the armed forces and, ironically, the industry moved from having tens of thousands of unwanted men to a serious labour shortage.

As there was a renewed demand for coal to help the country re-arm in the face of the Nazi threat, the Government made mining a reserved occupation to prevent any more men from joining up and then, in 1942, it took control of the entire industry, just as it had in the First World War. A new Coal Act decreed that all reserves belonged to the nation for the duration of the hostilities, although the mining industry itself remained in private hands. The only exceptions were the small coal deposits belonging to Forest Free Miners in Gloucestershire and extremely thin seams found at locations where adjacent minerals were more plentiful and more important than coal.

Those government moves still didn't provide enough miners to meet demand, which led to the introduction of the Bevin Boy system (see panel).

Small old-fashioned pits began to feel the pinch between the wars as the industry struggled for survival during the years of economic depression. Bannockburn Colliery – seen here in scale model form at the Scottish Mining Museum – was one that managed to keep trading through the Second World War but was condemned along with many others during the first few years of nationalisation.

Many worked-out pits had closed in the 1930s but a number of uneconomic ones were kept open after 1939 to contribute to the war effort, often being run by managers from more-productive neighbouring mines.

Because there had been a feeling in the industry for many years that nationalisation was inevitable, most of the coal-owning companies had been reluctant to invest in new equipment, with the result that many small mines were still working on the traditional pick-and-shovel method and the British mining industry had become uncompetitive compared with its German and American counterparts, especially where underground haulage was concerned.

By the end of the Second World War, most people in Britain, regardless of their political persuasion, accepted that the coal industry was worn-out, demoralised and in need of expensive modernisation. There was also a strong feeling among victorious soldiers returning from the front that they didn't simply want to revert to a pre-war state of affairs. The Labour Party included full nationalisation of the industry among many radical changes in its manifesto for the 1945 general election and won by a landslide.

The stage was set for the NCB.

Bevin Boys: Fighting Hitler at the coalface

At the height of the Second World War, the British Government realised that so many men were enlisting to fight in the armed forces that there would soon be a shortage of coal for the war effort if the mines weren't adequately manned.

The Minister of Labour in the Coalition Government, Ernest Bevin, therefore decided that every 10th conscript aged 18 would be sent to the collieries, whether he liked it or not.

The 'Bevin Boy' system was introduced in December 1943 and between then and the end of the war in 1945, 21,800 youths were recruited and trained in the scheme, 7,000 of whom actually worked underground at the coalface.

The selection process was conducted fairly on a ballot basis and Mr Bevin went on record as saying: "None of you would funk a fight with the enemy and I do not believe that it would be said of any of you boys that you failed to respond to the call for coal upon which victory so much depends."

However, considering they'd had no choice in the matter and had been prepared to fight on the battlefields, they were treated very shabbily after the war and not allowed to march in the annual Remembrance Day parades at the Cenotaph in London—a situation not rectified until as late as 1995. Probably because the scheme was extended into the 1950s as an alternative to National Service, many also had to put up with abuse from ill-informed members of the public as a result of a mistaken but widespread impression that they were somehow 'shirkers' or conscientious objectors.

Among famous Bevin Boys were England footballer Nat Lofthouse and comedians Eric Morecambe and Brian Rix.

CHAPTER 5

Hardships and harshness

Not worth a light!

O NE OF the most shameful episodes in the history of coal mining concerns the subterranean employment of women and very young children in the 18th and early 19th centuries.

Unfortunately, it has to be said that many of the private coal owners at the time were shameless when it came to the exploitation of their workers. Until prevented from doing so by law in 1842, they allowed women and children to work alongside men; they took a penny-pinching view to unsafe working practices such as naked flames and insufficient roof props ... and they encouraged climates of fear in which colliers dared not speak out for fear they would lose their livelihood.

Children as young as five toiled in the pits and most were naked or near-naked due to the intense subterranean heat — as were the adults; a situation that naturally led to debauchery underground.

Many pregnant women suffered miscarriages by having to hew or haul coal 14 hours a day, six days a week for virtually the full nine months of their expectancy, but health

Strain and misery etched on their faces, two shoeless boys struggle to bring a heavily-loaded tub out of a mine. Note how the rope of the first lad passes around his neck and between his legs. COURTESY COAL AUTHORITY

Male and female hewers working naked in a hot mine in the 1830s.

deeper shafts and longer tunnels began to be developed, it became necessary for the helpers (who were rather ironically known as 'hurriers') to drag their heavy loads of coal while crawling on all fours like animals along low, dark passageways.

For such work, a woman would usually be harnessed to a cart by a chain or rope that passed between her legs, even if she was pregnant. Some of the bigger children might also be engaged in such tasks, but mostly they were employed as 'trappers'. For this, kids as young as five would be dragged from their beds at 4 o'clock in the morning and made to sit for up to 12 hours or more in a cramped recess about the size of a domestic fireplace, doing nothing but pulling on strings to open ventilation doors whenever anyone approached.

Air in those pre-electric fan days moved through mines very slowly due to the use of furnaces to induce a flow, so there was little chance of draughts blowing out naked flames, yet most trappers were not even allowed a candle and had to sit in pitch blackness for the whole day, hence the phrase 'not worth a light'.

In the early-1840s, Lord Shaftesbury went underground in South Wales and spoke to trapper boys. What he heard and saw shocked him so much that he resolved to return to London and press for reform. Politicians subsequently learnt that children were taken down the mines by their parents, not so much because they were too young to be left on their own, but because they were needed for work in the family team. In the 1830s it is estimated that there were more than 5,000 children under the age of 10 working underground in such conditions and when 26 children (11 of them girls) were drowned in an underground flood at Silkstone, Yorkshire, in 1838, a Parliamentary commission

and safety was of no consequence to the bosses, whose only consideration was profit. Life was cheap in those days and the workers were simply too impoverished to object.

This state of affairs had its origins in the primitive bell-pits of earlier times when a self-employed collier hewing coal at his own risk and own expense would more often than not have his wife and kids carry the coal baskets up a ladder to the surface. While such work was being undertaken in the relatively shallow, light and airy environs of a bellpit, the problem wasn't too serious, but when

Children whose job it was to move tubs were known as 'hurriers' or 'putters'. Whether due to artistic licence or not is unknown, but this drawing seems to depict youngsters little more than three or four years of age pushing a loaded tub underground while another, not much older, pulls open a heavy wooden ventilation door. Although the artist has depicted a candle on the front of the tub, the poor 'trappers' normally had to sit in the dark for their entire shift, hence the phrase 'not worth a light'.

An early Victorian view showing the perilous ascent women and young girls had to make in the shafts before the law change of 1842. Not only did they have to climb rickety ladders laden with heavy sacks but they had to run the risk of being injured or even knocked off by coal falling from those above them.

was set up to look into working conditions.

The reports of the inspectors make for sober reading. One sub-commissioner wrote: "It is a most painful thing to contemplate the dungeon-like life these little creatures are doomed to spend, a life for the most part in solitude, damp and darkness."

After seeing women struggling to drag iron-keeled boxes holding a quarter of a ton of coal, sub-commissioner Robert Franks commented: "It is almost incredible that human beings can submit to such employment, harnessed like horses, over soft slushy floors … more difficult than dragging the same weights through sewers in consequence of the inclination, which is frequently as steep as 1-in-3 to 1-in-6."

Another inspector reported: "The heat in the mine is so great that the men work totally naked in some cases, surrounded by females of all ages, from girls of six to women of 20, with many of the females also naked to the waist. So covered in coaldust and sweat were the boys and girls that their sex was only recognisable by their breasts. I had some difficulty on occasions pointing out which were girls and which were boys and that caused a great deal of laughter and joking."

In another report it was stated: "The colliers are naked apart from a pair of clogs or hobnail boots and a thin pair of drawers, but sometimes the heat is so oppressive that even the drawers have to be discarded."

And one clearly shocked sub-commissioner wrote: "One of the most disgusting things I have ever seen was of young females, dressed like boys in trousers, crawling on all fours, with belts round their waists and chains passing between their legs, in pits near Holmfirth and New Mill. Two of the girls had worn large holes in their trousers and any sight more revolting can scarcely be imagined than those girls at work — no brothel can beat it."

The language in the pits was said to be bawdy in the extreme, with the women often being more foul-mouthed than the men. Noted one inspector: "It is impossible for a woman to be decorous or genteel in such conditions," while a Justice of the Peace from Yorkshire who visited a local pit as part of the inquiry said: "It is little wonder that passions are naturally excited."

After hearing that numerous illegitimate babies were being conceived in the coal mines of Britain and that children aged seven or eight were having to work 14-hour shifts starting as early as 4am, Parliament passed the Mines & Collieries Act of 1842 prohibiting boys under the age of 10, and all women and children, from working underground.

Unfortunately, the new law was not backed up immediately by the appointment of a sufficiently large team of

Pit brow lasses (or 'pit brow wenches' as the original postcard caption described them). The seven young ladies in this hand-tinted photo worked in the Wigan coalfield.

inspectors, which enabled some of the more unscrupulous mine owners to continue employing willing females for a few years longer. Sadly, there was no shortage of girls prepared to turn a blind eye to the law in order to earn a few shillings at a time when money in other occupations was hard to come by.

Generally speaking, though, most colliery companies abided by the law, and the result was a massive increase in the number of pit ponies deployed underground (see Appendix D).

Boys over 10 continued to work legally, mainly in seams that were too thin for a grown man to crawl into, but attendance at school was made compulsory by Parliament in the 1860s.

Women were allowed to continue working on the surface, often as 'pit brow lasses' picking stones from the coal in the washery screens, and it wasn't until as recently as the 1970s that the last ones retired. Somewhat ironically, equal rights legislation in recent years enabled women to return to subterranean work if they wished, although very few took up the option.

Hardships continued to be part of the job for the men and youths left behind after the females had gone and the following quotation from an unknown 19th century collier encapsulates much of the problem they faced on a daily basis:

"The Devil made coal, made it black like himself and hid it in the deepest recesses of the earth so that he might drive men mad in the finding of it."

As if a job that involved lying in two or three inches of foul black water in seams as low as 18in was not difficult enough, there were myriad additional impositions on the old-time colliers until the advent of the NCB brought standardisation of working conditions across the country.

Hard though it may be to believe today, many colliery companies forced their miners to pay a weekly sum for the hire of lamps and that continued to be the case at some 'unenlightened' mines until as late as the 1930s. The policy was imposed even though the men couldn't see to do their jobs without a lamp, so they had no choice but to hire them and, at threepence or sixpence a week, they effectively paid for the original purchase price many times over. If a miner broke his pick or shovel while at work, the cost of the replacement was normally deducted from his wages.

Eyes and ears suffered terribly in the days before goggles and ear-defenders were issued. Sharp slivers of coal flew every time a pick slammed into a seam or a large lump, dust and grit swirled into eyes, nostrils and mouths, and if a lamp or candle went out in a part of the mine in which a man was alone, there would be no point at which his

So heavy were some of the loads the women had to carry that many became permanently stooped in later life. This sad image is on display in the South Wales Miners' Museum.

eyes would ever grow accustomed to the pitch darkness until he could reach an illuminated part of the mine. That could prove disorientating and frightening to anyone but a hardened collier.

Small wonder that some miners in the early years used to keep a handful of fish scales in their pockets, those of certain deep-sea breeds having a remarkable ability to glow in the dark, although the luminosity they gave out was really too weak to be of any practical use.

Eardrums took a hammering once mechanisation began to be introduced, for although the machines sped up the process, they made a deafening racket in the confined space below ground. They also made the operation more hazardous, not only because the noise disguised tell-tale creaking sounds in the roof but because the increased rate of extraction left dangerously large stretches of roof unpropped for longer … exacerbated by the machines' vibrations shaking everything loose. (This was in the days before powerful hydraulic advancing roof supports had been invented.)

The inhalation of coal and stone dust thrown up by the early machines was one of the biggest and potentially most dangerous problems the men had to contend with because it could lead eventually to lethal lung diseases. There were no face masks, so most old miners chewed tobacco while at work, the reason being that it enabled them to keep their mouth closed and breathe through their nose, the latter's natural defences being better equipped to filter out the dust. "The baccy rotted our teeth but saved our lives," said one old-timer.

Another hardship the men had to put up with occurred in the years when colliers were paid wages or bonuses on piecework according to the number of tubs they filled during the course of a shift. In a tightly-run mine, the tubs returned from the shaft on a regular basis and there was no problem, but in badly-managed pits there were long delays and shortages of trams, leaving colliers at the coalface angry, frustrated and even sometimes idle. Consequently, it was perhaps only human nature for fights to break out for the right to claim a tub and take it back to their stall.

Where a deputy (foreman) was on duty, this would not be a problem as he would decide who got the next tram – although the officials had their personal favourites

So hot were many deep mines that some workers had to drink up to eight pints a day simply to replace what they lost in sweat. Bottles were normally carried on the belt and varied in size according to personal choice, but filling them before going on shift was essential.

among the men and that often resulted in unfair treatment. Some deputies were even more despised than the mine owners and some were downright cruel and deceitful.

Bert Coombes, a miner from South Wales at around the time of the First World War, told of a deputy who ordered a team of repairers to clear a bad roof fall that was preventing loaded tubs from being sent out of the mine. The repairers told him the hole in the roof was still dangerous and that they would need to shore it up with timber supports before they could start to clear the obstruction. The official, however, threatened them with the sack if they didn't get the rocks removed straightaway.

Fearful for their jobs, they reluctantly agreed. The result ... another roof fall and the crushing to death of an experienced repairer.

After the body had been removed, the foreman, thinking he was alone, was seen placing timber in among the rocks before the investigators arrived in order to make it look as though he had agreed to the repairers' original request. That would have been in a bid not only to save his own skin but to salve his guilty conscience ... for if a death could be

shown to be accidental, a widow would receive compensation but if there was even a hint of negligence, the insurers would not pay a penny.

There was no pension scheme in those days either, so most older men — many with dust-clogged lungs — had to keep on working, desperately hoping the deputies or under-managers wouldn't notice they were coughing frequently and could no longer keep up the pace. Without wages in the pre-welfare state, they often had to rely on 'parish relief' — a poor reward for a lifetime of hard and dangerous toil.

Many of the discomforts encountered before nationalisation are not immediately apparent to a non-miner. Take the problem of rats and mice, for example. The vermin were inadvertently taken underground in sacks of grain and bedding straw intended for the horses and ponies but then began breeding in the mines, thriving on scraps of food accidentally dropped by the men.

Consequently, miners had to ensure their packed lunches were kept out of the way, either by keeping them in tightly-sealed metal tins or by suspending them in mid-air from lengths of string. "If you left your sandwiches in your jacket

As if toiling in a mine all day wasn't hard enough, colliers didn't even have the occasional luxury of oversleeping! Like railwaymen, they had to work frequent night shifts but on a cold winter's night or after an evening 'on the ale', waking up on time could be a problem. Companies thus employed retired men as 'knockers-up', their job being to tap (or hammer!) on the doors and windows of miners' homes until they got a reply.

Lads left home white at the beginning of their shifts and came back black! This picture is undated but it is believed to date from late-Victorian times, so this pair probably worked in the screens or a similarly dusty part of the surface mine.

pocket by mistake, you'd often find they'd gone with just the shape of them left in the paper," recalled Staffordshire miner George Shufflebotham, adding that some mines even suffered flying insect infestations in the shape of thousands of crickets! (In the 2010s it was revealed that this latter phenomenon is still prevalent in Czechia's last deep mine in Karvina.)

Another problem in some of Britain's older mines were cockroaches and it is ironically said with black humour that the only good thing about the year-long 1984/85 strike was that it rid the mines of vermin!

A pitman's packed lunch was known pretty universally throughout the industry as 'snap' and usually comprised something simple such as jam sandwiches (cheese being liable to melt in the heat). It was usually contained in a special snap tin designed to prevent the contents being pinched by mice or even the ponies themselves. Few miners ate much in the old hand-worked mines, though, because the crouching position in which many had to work all day could cause heartburn. Even at home, some miners in the years before full mechanisation would occasionally feel

the need to crouch or sit on a low seat in order to eat a meal comfortably.

With temperatures that could rise in some deep mines to an almost unbearable 90 or 100°F (32-37°C), one thing the colliers did take plenty of when going underground was water, usually carried in a sturdy flask known as a 'Dudley'. Some men preferred cold tea.

Clothing was another aspect of discomfort in the days before pithead baths, when miners had to change and wash at home. That is unless it was a searingly hot mine in which men had to strip to their underpants to work. The normal physical exertions would result in shirts and trousers being so soaked in sweat and dirt that they'd almost stand up on their own when they were taken off. Yet, in those early days, water was precious and sometimes only available from a well or standpipe at the end of the street, so as it needed to be conserved for drinking purposes, the clothes would not be washed, merely dried in front of the fire every night. Putting such trousers on the next morning and trying to walk or cycle to work in them was not a comfortable experience.

Before the nationwide issuing of standardised (latterly

Despite the dangers and hardships they faced every day, miners never lost their strong sense of humour and camaraderie. Cheerful faces at Eckington Colliery in 2016 as coalface workers settle down for a few minutes break at 'snap' time. NICK PIGOTT

orange-coloured) NCB overalls, men wore a miscellaneous variety of clothes for pit work, moleskin trousers with an old jacket and waistcoat being pretty common.

On days when it rained, the coal dust that lay thick on the ground of every colliery would turn into a mass of cloying grey paste and on such occasions, sacks and cloths would have to be put down in residences to protect the furniture or floor coverings whenever work clothes were taken off.

Many colliers had to work night shifts, but on a cold, dark winter's night or after an evening 'on the ale', oversleeping was a problem, so in the days before alarm clocks and telephones, the coal companies—like the railway companies—employed retired men as 'knockers-up', their job being to tap (or rap!) on the doors and windows of miners' houses in the dead of night until they got a reply. Some carried a long pole to enable them to reach the bedroom windows.

As with any industry, there were good bosses and bad, but in the era of privately-owned mines, a depressingly high proportion of coal owners drove their men hard for little pay and minimal rights.

Benevolent owners, on the other hand, cared for the wellbeing of their workforces and provided schools, chapels, free coal, electricity and water in addition to good quality housing, sports pitches, bowling greens and, in the case of Kiveton Park Colliery, near Sheffield, even a hospital.

Some of the pits were under the control of sizable combines such as Powell Duffryn, while others were owned by families—often the same family whose ancestors had first sunk the mine several generations earlier.

Miners employed by religiously-aware Quaker families were paid regular wages and were provided with schools, shops, chapels and comfortable houses. The Tredegar Company was also a socially aware employer and built houses and hospitals at the turn of the 20th century.

Elsewhere, housing shortages and, in later years, pit closures presented the additional hardship of travelling to other collieries in order to remain in a job. For miners who couldn't afford cars at the time (and that was the majority), it would entail a trek of anything up to five miles each way on foot and in all weathers. In South Wales, the journey would involve much uphill slogging over the mountains separating one valley from the next, or a train journey of 20 miles or so, the extra distance being caused by the need to go down to the end of a vale, change trains and then travel up another.

Despite the drawbacks, most boys born in mining villages 50 to 150 years ago automatically went down the pit as soon as they were old enough. There was virtually nothing else for them to do. Skills and camaraderie were handed down from generation to generation, creating fierce loyalty to the profession.

The nature of life in 19th and early 20th century collieries could be unregulated and rather haphazard, yet there was nevertheless a sort of pecking order and succession policy; most young boys would start as trappers (before 1842) and then graduate from the age of about 12-14 to become a pony driver, leading the animal as it pulled a rake of tubs through the underground passages.

After a couple of years doing that, a lad would become a putter, manhandling the tubs, both empty and loaded, and trying to ensure that the hewers they either idolised or feared never had to wait long for a tram to be delivered to their part of the face. While working as a putter, he would be given the opportunity to cut coal whenever possible and, at the age of about 21, he would finally attain the noble (and yes, even coveted) position of hewer.

In what little free time they had, miners played hard and, in common with their 19th century contemporaries, the railway-building navvies, they had a fearsome reputation for heavy drinking and rebel-rousing... yet many were also God-fearing and would attend church with their families on Sundays.

Unlike the navvies, who were forced by the nature of their work to be nomadic, colliers became rooted in close-knit communities that were to last for generations until pit closures and increasing car ownership from the 1960s onwards obliged or enabled them to work miles away and thus meet potential partners from other areas.

Even in the early 21st century, there were miners who had gone into the industry straight from school and never worked at anything else, but there had been many others of course, especially in the 1930s, who had sworn that their sons would go into mining "over their dead body", such was the strength of feeling over the dangers and low wages.

That attitude did begin to change somewhat from the 1950s when conditions, training, safety standards and pay scales improved significantly under the NCB and miners' lives began to change out of all recognition thanks to mechanisation and automation. Tempted by the national advertising slogan 'a job for life', young men once again began to be attracted to the profession.

Among the riskiest hardships in any mine were those experienced by the brave men whose task it was to pull out the props to allow the roof to collapse in goafs and other worked-out districts. Even with the use of a Sylvester apparatus on the end of a long chain, this was no job for the faint-hearted!

Any young 21st century reader doubting that conditions and risks in some mines were as bad as described need only look at this picture to be convinced. It was taken in a British colliery in the NCB era and shows a miner crawling through coal-blackened water as he negotiates his way through a 2ft seam. Only three dubious-looking wooden pit props protect him from the millions of tons of rock above him. Enduring similar situations in earlier times, his Victorian predecessors wouldn't even have had the relative 'luxuries' of helmet, cap-lamp, overalls, gloves and knee protectors.

'Like a mental picture of Hell'

MINES AND miners have fascinated people from many different backgrounds, particularly writers and poets. In the 1930s, author George Orwell, an Eton-educated southerner, visited collieries in Wigan, Sheffield and Barnsley to gain material for his book The Road to Wigan Pier, and gave a graphic description of the life he found there: "When the machines are roaring and the air is black with coal dust … the place is like Hell, or at any rate like my own mental picture of Hell. Most of the things one imagines in Hell are there — heat, noise, confusion, darkness, foul air and, above all, unbearably cramped space."

Orwell, a tall man, told how he started off walking in a slightly stooped way but then had to crouch, squat and finally crawl as the height of the roadway gradually reduced from six feet to three. By the time he reached the face, he was in agony in his knees, thighs, back and head, which he had grazed numerous times on the jagged stone roof.

"Before I'd been down a mine, I had vaguely imagined the miner stepping out of the cage and getting to work on a ledge of coal a few yards away," he wrote. "I had not realised that he may have to creep through passages as long as from London Bridge to Oxford Circus."

Despite the hardships, he noted how proud the Northerners were of their industrial heartland and that the miners of Lancashire and Yorkshire treated him with a kindness and a courtesy that were even embarrassing. "If there is one type of man to whom I feel myself inferior, it is a coal miner," he wrote.

CHAPTER 6

1947-2015: Nationalisation to privatisation

The NCB and British Coal

OR THE majority of miners, the NCB was the prom-ised land. After so many years of struggle against private owners, they would at last be working for themselves, stewarded by a Labour Government that 'spoke their language' and understood the reasons for their previous strife.

The company's motto *E Tenebris Lux* — Out of Darkness Cometh Light — articulated their hopes while the signs that went up at every mine on January 1, 1947 — 'This Colliery is now managed by the NCB on behalf of the People' — set the tone for the monumental industrial and social changes that followed the horrors of the Second World War.

New Year's Day 1947, known throughout the industry as

Vesting Day, was perhaps the most significant moment in the entire history of British coalmining. Overnight, the NCB became the largest non-communist industrial undertaking in the world, with 850,000 employees and just under a thousand collieries, some of which were enormous undertakings in their own right, utterly dominating their local communities. In Wales, the coal board was the largest single employer in the principality.

The whole exercise cost the nation's taxpayers the then immense sum of £394,365,176, including mineral rights, royalties, assets, stock and plant, but people on both sides of the political spectrum accepted that state investment was the only realistic response to worn-out infrastructure,

Many mines in the post-war era grew to enormous sizes and covered areas almost as great as small villages. This is a section of the extensive surface complex at Welbeck Colliery in north Nottinghamshire. ROBIN STEWART-SMITH

Typical of the pits inherited by the NCB was Penallta Colliery, in Wales's Rhymney Valley, pictured here in the early-1940s. The large message stating 'search yourselves' was a reminder to miners not to attempt to take cigarettes, matches or any other contraband below ground where it could cause an explosion. The headstocks and power house of Penallta Colliery still stand in 2021 but are derelict.

A fresh start: The sign that went up at every colliery on New Year's Day 1947.

poor management, bad industrial relations, demoralised workers and shortage of capital.

In addition to the 958 collieries, there were 323 small licensed mines, 75 coking and smokeless fuel plants, 1,803 farms, 275 shops, 141,000 houses, a cinema, a holiday camp, hotels, swimming baths, brickworks, railways, ships and even a slaughterhouse.

The NCB didn't actually take legal ownership of the licensed mines, which were allowed to remain in private hands if they employed 29 or fewer underground workers each. Most were tiny drift mines and a fair proportion produced fireclay rather than coal. Between them, they represented a mere 1% of national annual coal output.

Where coking plants and brickworks were concerned, the owners could negotiate to remain outside NCB ownership if they wished, and several took that option.

The most obvious benefit of nationalisation was a cash injection far beyond what the old firms could collectively

Hundreds of railway stations in Britain, both urban and rural, possessed a coal yard for domestic supplies. In this scene from 1968 – the year British Rail drove a nail into the coffin of its fellow nationalised industry by finally ridding itself of its steam locos – the coal yard at Woodley station, near Manchester, was doing a brisk trade as 8F class 2-8-0 No.48115 passed with coal empties from Heaton Mersey. DAVID ROSTANCE/RAIL PHOTOPRINTS

have afforded, but control by a single authority also brought logistical advantages not immediately apparent to the general public, one being that it was no longer necessary to leave coal in the ground where the boundaries of private company properties had met. Indeed, where two neighbouring collieries had been under separate ownership, it would now be possible to work them more efficiently. Other benefits were the ability to instigate a nationwide training scheme, a centralised system of maintenance and repair workshops and a co-ordinated pumping and drainage scheme.

The NCB's first headquarters was Lansdowne House in Berkeley Square, London, under chairman Lord Hyndley,

and the company was divided into eight divisions, sub-divided into areas. Although the South Western Division, which contained South Wales, had the most collieries (230), the largest division geographically was the Northern, which had 222 mines, ten areas and contained the counties of Durham, Northumberland and Cumberland.

The total national coal output at the time was just under 200m tons a year with all but 10m coming from deep-mining. Of that total, Britain's railways alone consumed 14m tons and domestic heating accounted for 30m tons, most homes having open coal fires.

At local level within the NCB little changed straightaway because many of the managers were simply the old private

Heading for the pithead baths in NCB days, miners leave both levels of the shaft cage simultaneously at Desford Colliery, west of Leicester. Note how the men are handing their brass tallies to the banksmen standing on the left.

company officials wearing a different badge, but the board set about building up a technical management team and gradually began to get to grips with the neglect and lack of investment that had characterised the years of depression and war during the 1930s and 40s.

The UK needed coal to help fuel the huge national reconstruction programme after the war, so one of the first acts of the new board was to open a series of drift mines as a short-term measure while it prepared a massive programme of deep mine redevelopment as part of a root-and-branch reconstruction of the whole industry.

Modernisation, mechanisation and safety were the key components in the NCB's armoury and no expense was spared by the Government-backed board in instigating the necessary improvements.

Among the priorities in this brave new world of jack-pot-style spending were fully-mechanised coalfaces, deeper shafts, locomotive haulage roads, trunk conveyors, skip-winding of coal from pit bottom to surface, new coal preparation plants, new coke ovens and greatly improved facilities in the way of showers, changing rooms, canteens and, above all, personal safety.

From the miners' point of view, nationalisation had another benefit as it gave them, through the recently-formed National Union of Mineworkers (NUM), a greater say in their own industry. Production soared as a result: In 1947, the

The concept of 'Merry-Go-Round' trains was introduced by BR and the NCB in the 1960s and revolutionised the power station supply business. In this mid-1980s scene, a long rake of loaded MGR 32-tonne hopper wagons is being hauled through Leicestershire by BR Type 5 diesel No.56089, one of a fleet of locos designed for such work. The branch line curving to the right would later serve Asfordby Colliery. JOHN CHALCRAFT

average daily output per man-shift had been 17.4 hundredweight but within the next 14 years it would double to 34.7cwt with men at some of the modernised pits each producing more than 50cwt.

Miners also had more freedom to move to different parts of the country, although in practice many stayed in the communities in which they'd spent their lives. There were enough changes going on as it was with frequent boundary amendments and constant management upheavals. The NCB's 'county' districts, for example, bore little relation to real shires, with internal border changes resulting in the Nottinghamshire pits around Worksop coming under the Yorkshire district.

As mineworkers and industry observers of a more cynical nature might have guessed in 1947, the "increased efficiency" trumpeted for nationalisation with regard to the working of neighbouring pits turned out to be more akin to rationalisation as duplicated collieries were shut down and workforces merged.

Communities were torn apart as small, antiquated and run-down pits were condemned and mining villages lost their prime *raison d'etre*. The closures were largely tolerated by the unions in the 1950s because they could see that they were an inevitable part of the huge inward investment in their industry and there were in any case plenty of new jobs for displaced miners to move to.

Wages for those who remained in work were rising in the 1950s too and, by the end of that decade, face workers could earn £20 a week, putting them at the top of the blue collar wages league — a marked contrast to the 1930s. Many employees benefitted from relatively high disposable income and it even became possible for them to afford cars, making it easier for them to take jobs in neighbouring towns and counties if they wished.

The NCB also improved the industry's poor safety record by expanding research into such matters as illness (particular pneumoconiosis) and dust control. Head protection was also greatly improved with soft caps being replaced by helmets made of compressed fibreboard and later of tough plastic.

The chairman of the NCB from 1971 to 1982 was Sir Derek Ezra, seen here in the company of good-humoured miners during one of his many underground fact-finding visits.

The industrial and munitions requirements of World War Two had disguised the fact that demand for exported coal had slumped, so in 1950 a bold and far-reaching document entitled 'Plan for Coal' was published. Its main objective was to increase domestic production in an effort to rejuvenate the shattered British economy, but although it brought about a massive mine modernisation programme, it failed to take account of developments elsewhere – completion of the Trans-Arabian oil pipeline, for instance, which would later unleash billions of gallons of cheap petrol and heating fuel into the UK.

In 1951, the socialist Government that had ushered in nationalisation of the mines and railways was replaced by a Conservative administration, but – somewhat contrary to their traditional free-enterprise philosophy – the nation's new rulers decided not to reverse Labour's efforts. Instead, they merely created a situation in which the coal board was exposed to increased market competition from the electricity, gas and solid fuel sectors.

This enabled the NCB to continue with its huge mechanisation programme with the result that the 1950s was generally a good decade for 'King Coal', so much so that domestic consumption reached an all-time peak in 1956.

The money-no-object mentality and rather lax attitude taken to return-on-investment in those heady early years of state ownership did, however, have something of an 'Alice in Wonderland' feel about it and matters weren't helped by the introduction of the Clean Air Act and launch of nuclear power generation in that watershed year of 1956. By the end of the decade, a major decline in the use of coal as a domestic fuel, coupled with a faltering economy, had brought the NCB to a crisis point and it wasn't long before the coal and rail businesses both found themselves being run by hardline chairmen, the railways by Lord Beeching and the coal board by Lord Robens.

Beeching's tenure saw thousands of miles of branch lines closed and thousands of steam locomotives sent to the scrapheap in a bid to stem losses. Robens presided over the closure of 406 mines and the loss of more than a quarter of a million jobs between 1961 and 1971 (ironically, more under Labour than the Conservatives), but he introduced mass mechanisation of cutter/loading and, for those men remaining in work, he achieved 40% extra output, improved wages and a 60% reduction in the number of fatal and serious accidents. His 'axe' may not have been as infamous as its Beeching equivalent, but it was just as devastating – or effective (depending from which political and economic standpoint it is viewed).

Robens' tenure coincided with a rise of the militant Left in the NUM, prompting him to make the thought-provoking comment: "One of the ridiculous aspects of the extreme left-wing in trade unions has always been their enthusiasm for strikes, whereas in the Soviet Union and other Iron Curtain countries, strikes are illegal." In 1969, the NCB was rocked by an unofficial dispute in which the men at almost half of its 307 pits walked out, losing 2½m tons of coal production.

Some of Robens' decisions were seen as bizarre. For instance, Kirkby Colliery was closed in 1969, just three years after proudly hoisting the union flag for breaking the million tons a year barrier. The chairman's reasoning was connected with over-capacity; his executives were urging

the closure of old, inefficient pits in Wales, Scotland and west of the Pennines, but he was aware that the NUM was, in some ways, a loose federation of nominally-separate area lodges. So, in order to secure acceptance of the cuts, he decided that each area should lose one pit, even though the Midlands and East Yorkshire had no really inefficient ones at the time.

This resulted in seemingly 'crazy' situations such as that at Kirkby – where contractors were still building a multi-million-pound coal preparation plant while NCB accountants were actively seeking tenders for its demolition! Also at Dyffryn Rhondda in 1966 where the shafts were deepened at enormous expense, only to be immediately filled in and capped as the colliery was demolished – and at New Lount mine in Leicestershire, where a brand new pneumatic stowing plant was still being painted on the day the pit closed … the fresh paint later clogging the nozzles of the demolition crew's burners as they cut the equipment up!

Most pits closed during that period were, however, inefficient and the policy improved overall productivity, although thousands of miners were thrown onto the jobs scrapheap

Snowdown Colliery, one of the principal mines in the isolated and politically-militant Kent coalfield, was one of the deepest and also one of the hottest in the country. Note how it featured a mixture of conventional and friction-style headgear in this photograph taken before its 1987 closure. NICK PIGOTT

The transition from NCB to British Coal – basically a name change only – took place in 1987 and saw the signage modified at all mines. Left: the old order at Maerdy Colliery in 1985 (note use of the Anglicised spelling) and (right) the newer look at Annesley Colliery in 1993. Left: NICK PIGOTT. Right: ROBIN STEWART-SMITH.

in communities that could offer little else in the way of alternative employment.

Despite all the cuts, the slimmed-down industry was, by the late-1960s, still absolutely huge compared with what it was to become by the end of the century. It employed approximately half a million miners at 483 facilities and produced 177m tons of coal a year – but that period saw both the end of steam traction on British Rail and the start of the North Sea oil and gas revolution. With millions of households switching away from coal and towards central-heating systems as a result of smokeless zone legislation in many towns and cities, the industry was under threat from all angles … even the coal board itself was replacing its (cheap to run!) steam winding engines with electric equivalents.

Fortunately, relief was at hand. Coal was still needed in huge quantities for electricity generation, so British Rail and the NCB worked together in the 1960s and 70s on a massive project to streamline the flow from pits to power stations. Known as the 'Merry-Go-Round' system (MGR), it saw construction of rapid-loading facilities at several modernised pits and the installation of continuous-unloading hopper systems at the nation's major coal-fired power plants – especially those in the East Midlands and Yorkshire.

BR locomotives were fitted with radio control and slow-speed apparatus to allow them to haul 1,000-tonne hopper trains through the power stations' automatic unloading bunkers at the required pace without the need for uncoupling, and large track loops were laid down so that trains could continue around the circuit without the need for shunting.

The MGR operations gave the coal industry a new lease of life that was to last well into the 21st century, but it

didn't stop the overall decline in the size of the NCB. By the mid-1970s, the number of deep mines was down to 240 – just a quarter of its 1947 total – with a workforce of less than 300,000. Productivity had increased 70% during Robens' decade but annual output had fallen to 114m tonnes and North Sea oil and cheap imports from the Middle East oilfields were beginning to take effect.

Robens was succeeded in 1971 by Sir Derek Ezra, who was to remain in charge for the next 11 years, steering a shrewd political course that maintained a reasonable balance between Government and unions.

As was the case with many of Britain's major industries in the 1970s, the decade saw union leaders taking a much greater role in the way the coal mines were run and the NUM had become one of the most powerful unions in the land. Compared with the private-owner days prior to nationalisation, the boot was on the other foot for colliery managers.

The year 1972 had been hit by the first official national miners' strike since 1926, after which the Conservative government of Edward Heath was obliged to accept wage demands that made the miners the highest-paid nationalised workers in the country. When a further pay demand was made just two years later, Heath put the country on a three-day week in a bid to conserve coal supplies and reacted to the start of another miners' strike by calling a snap general election, which, to the surprise of many, resulted in a change of Prime Minister.

This union victory had given the country a Labour government again, but it had unwittingly laid the foundations for the industry's ultimate demise, for those on the right-wing of British politics were determined that the NUM would never again be able to wield so much political power that it could effectively bring down an elected government.

It seems odd now to think that some of the more antiquated coal mines remained in operation long enough to be served by BR's smart new Class 60s, which weren't fully introduced until the 1990s. This is BR Coal Sector-allocated No.60057 *Adam Smith* at Bolsover Colliery in 1993, the final year of the nationalised industry. NICK PIGOTT

The 1970s strikes had also made businesses and householders realise just how dependent the country had become on coal to keep lights on, homes heated and the wheels of industry turning. Many individuals and companies began planning to switch to gas and oil — but just as they began doing this, the coal industry received an unexpected boost caused by a quadrupling of oil prices as a result of an Arab-Israeli war.

No longer could the UK rely on seemingly endless supplies of cheap imported oil while deliberately running down its mining industry. North Sea oil supplies were still in their infancy, so the decline in indigenous coal production, which had been continuous since the mid-1950s, had not only to be halted but reversed.

This resulted in a landmark decision in 1974 to re-invest in home-produced coal and one of the prime beneficiaries of that policy was the proposed Selby coalfield project in North Yorkshire — an exciting development of five new mines (primarily shafts only) that would tap seams as thick as 11ft and be linked by 124 miles of underground roadways. A series of drifts connected each mine to a huge central distribution facility at Gascoigne Wood, a few miles

east of the traditional West Yorkshire pits. The project was inaugurated by the Duchess of Kent in 1976 in a ceremony described as "restoring King Coal to his throne".

While the Selby complex was being constructed (it didn't fully open until the mid-1980s), a long-term contractual relationship was established between the NCB and the Central Electricity Generating Board (CEGB) for power station coal and the collieries of the UK began to enjoy a renaissance that was to last the best part of a decade.

Barely a week went by without some workforce somewhere being able to proudly pose for the *Coal News* cameraman next to a banner declaring that the all-time weekly, monthly or annual output record for that pit had been broken. High morale, coupled with ever-improving technology, was bringing massive advances in productivity and efficiency.

Once the Middle East crisis had abated, however, the steady decline in the industry's fortunes began to resume and it reached a low point when a bitter confrontation over subsidy withdrawals and threatened pit closures resulted in the even longer and more aggressive miners' strike of 1984/85 (see Chapter 22).

Once the men had been forced back to work after a stoppage that had lasted almost exactly a year, the retribution began with a vengeance. The initial closure programme was not only implemented but massively accelerated and within months there wasn't a single mine left in the Rhondda valley in Wales. By the end of the decade, there were only two left in the whole of Scotland.

"British Coal and the Government are not interested in whether collieries can produce coal efficiently or cheaply," stormed Barnsley Central MP Eric Ilsley in 1987. "They are simply closing mines as part of a short-sighted strategy to reduce costs as quickly as possible." He blamed the situation on a government decision to impose capital charges on individual collieries — charges and financial targets they simply could not meet on their own.

In one classic mid-1980s case in Yorkshire, construction of a coal preparation plant was supposed to have its £106m cost spread across a dozen mines in the area, but the rapid closure of nine of those pits suddenly meant the full cost being borne by the remaining three. Unsurprisingly, that put their paper accounts into the red — providing justification for closure. 'Creative accounting' examples such as that turned economic pits into uneconomic ones overnight.

In the interests of balance, former NCB managers have since pointed out that many of the older mines were genuine long-term loss-makers and would have closed eventually anyway, regardless of union activity. The board had also encountered great difficulties trying to manage at a time of restrictive workplace practices and massive liabilities in terms of pension fund and subsidence claim settlements.

Looking back on the nationalised era, there is no doubt that the state-owned company brought great benefits to the mining industry as a whole, but it had to take many unpalatable decisions in order to run the business

Sending coal by sea from coastal collieries in the North-East dates back many centuries and the tradition was still being practised by the NCB when this picture was taken in May 1985. BR diesel shunter No.08747 gingerly edges towards the end of the loading staithes at Blyth with a load destined for a Danish vessel. COLOUR-RAIL

efficiently and profitably. Some of those decisions were seen by the miners and by the public as scandalously wasteful – on a par with the worst excesses of British Rail which, in the 1960s, began scrapping not only old obsolete locos but perfectly good ones that had been built at huge cost only five or six years earlier.

The BR controversy was caused by a decision to withdraw steam rapidly to meet an arbitrary deadline and a parallel can be drawn in the coal industry in the rush to close and demolish allegedly inefficient pits, some of which were relatively new. Woolley Colliery, in Yorkshire, had a staggering £116m spent on it in a mid-1980s refurbishment, only for it to be closed in 1987! Neighbouring Redbrook, which had cost £29m to rebuild in the early-1980s and whose new structures opened in 1985, was condemned just 24 months later.

In January 1987 the NCB's title was altered to British Coal in a somewhat cosmetic revamp designed to give a modern look to reflect the streamlined, slimmed-down industry, but apart from a wholesale replacement of signage outside colliery buildings and some increased private sector involvement, the organisation remained basically the same and continued to be run from Hobart House in London's Grosvenor Place, the successor headquarters to Lansdowne House.

Until the 1980s, Britain had been an exporter of coal to power stations in France, Denmark, Portugal, Sweden and West Germany, but what remained of the overseas market was largely lost as a result of the strike and the situation gradually began to reverse, with more and more coal being imported.

Once natural gas joined the list of competitors and new houses were built with central heating systems instead of fireplaces, the NCB accepted that the domestic market was as good as lost and began to concentrate on power station supply. Electricity became known as 'coal by wire'.

In 1992 controversy raised its head again. The Government (by then under the control of Conservative Prime Minister John Major) decided to implement a privatisation programme similar to the one it had announced for the rail industry. The remaining unprofitable pits would be shown no mercy in order that those offered for sale would be attractive to private investors.

The announcement was made in the House of Commons by Trade & Industry Secretary Michael Heseltine, who said he "felt pain" over the proposed closure of 31 collieries. This prompted an ex-miner to write to the *Barnsley Chronicle* stating: "It's not pain but guilt. Pain is when a mother is told that her husband, son or father is dead in a pit disaster or when a wife is told her husband is in hospital and will

never be the same again."

By the time British Coal was sold off at the end of 1994, fewer than 30 deep mines remained in the whole of the UK and the total number of miners was down to a paltry 7,000, compared with 1.2m in the 1920s.

Privatisation became reality with the passing of the Coal Industry Act 1994 and the administrative and residual functions of British Coal were transferred to a new body, the Coal Authority, based in the Nottinghamshire mining town of Mansfield. The pits were handed to private ownership in January 1995, although the need to clear up some of the remnants meant that British Coal wasn't officially wound up until January 26, 1997.

RJB Mining, owned by industrialist Richard Budge, paid £815m to buy the majority of the collieries (including the Selby complex and more than a dozen opencast sites), with Coal Investments plc snapping up another half a dozen mines, only to go bankrupt a year later. Tower Colliery, the last deep mine in South Wales, was bought by an employee buy-out team with Celtic Energy taking the majority of opencast sites in the principality. Mining (Scotland) Ltd purchased the last colliery north of the border (Longannet), along with nine opencast sites, and a company called Midland Mining acquired Annesley Colliery and applied for a licence to mine under historic Newstead Abbey. The application was refused after complaints from all over the world!

The £815m paid by RJB was the value of the surface assets only – nothing was paid for the underground plant. Some of Budge's fellow directors were property speculators and very little allowance was made for mining development, leading to claims that the mines were being bought for short-term exploitation of reserves rather than for long-term investment.

Certainly, the new owners did not possess the financial clout of the NCB and if a mine encountered serious geological problems or ceased to make a profit, it was simply shut down. The casualties included the virtually brand new mine at Asfordby and the Selby pits, but for the handful that were retained, substantial sums were spent on modernisation, automation and the driving of new underground roadways to open up fresh coalfaces.

Collieries that benefitted from such investment included Kellingley, Daw Mill, Maltby and Harworth, which had a massive modern tower winder erected as late in the day as 1996.

Roof bolts had been in use in the US and Australia for several years but they weren't adopted on a wide basis in Britain until the late-1980s. They were 70% cheaper than the traditional arch type and enabled roadways to be built much faster. Harworth (where RJB also had its

Hatfield Colliery, near Doncaster, was one of the few that survived into the latter part of the privatised era, not closing until mid-2015. Following the end of nationalisation, four-wheeled MGR wagons were phased out in favour of 75-tonne capacity high-sided bogie vehicles operated by privatised freight companies such as English, Welsh & Scottish Railway. In this July 2008 scene, a train of such vehicles, headed by No.66173 passes Hatfield loaded – ironically – with imported coal from Immingham docks to Ferrybridge power station. Hatfield's headstocks and rapid loader still stand, having been saved following an 11th-hour intervention. JOHN CHALCRAFT

headquarters) broke a world record in the mid-1990s by driving through a mile of solid rock in just 24 weeks, but such development work required vast sums of capital. In the nationalised era, the NCB could arrange for neighbouring mines to increase production while an adjacent pit was shut for modernisation or redevelopment. The new private companies didn't have enough collieries to be able to do that and so they had to ask for Government subsidies.

Richard Budge left RJB Mining in 2001 and the firm was subsequently renamed UK Coal. Budge went on to form a company called Coalpower, which bought Hatfield Colliery, near Doncaster.

Modernisation and automation highlights aside, the first decade of the new millennium saw total deep mine coal production fall to fewer than 10m tonnes a year ... meaning that it was overtaken by the nation's opencast mines for the first time ever.

UK Coal soldiered on and as recently as 2013 it planned to open up new faces at its Thoresby, Kellingley and Daw Mill sites, but a huge underground fire at the latter resulted in the premature closure of that mine that year and when the Government refused the company subsidies for development of the other two pits in 2015, saying they did not represent value for money compared with cheap imports, the deep mining industry was condemned.

The only other colliery to survive into 2015, Hatfield, was by then owned by a miners' consortium but that too couldn't survive the drastic drop in world coal prices that resulted from the dumping of cheap Chinese coal onto the international market. Reeling from a triple blow in the form of a spoil tip landslip in 2013 and a rise in UK carbon tax, it closed suddenly in the summer of 2015 and was partly demolished, although its headstocks and winding house were saved by a preservation order just 24 hours before they were due to be toppled.

Kellingley Colliery lifted its last piece of coal on December 18, 2015, after which only imported and opencast supplies were available to supplement the other forms of energy – biomass, gas, wind, solar, fracking, oil and nuclear – in the constant quest for cheap, safe, reliable electricity generation in Britain. (This subject is dealt with in more detail in Chapter 28).

A MODERN BRITISH COLLIERY

This exploded diagram depicts and explains the components and operation of a typical British coal mine of the 1950s. The upper half of the drawing depicts the surface buildings and the lower half the mine itself. The method of coal-getting deployed in this example is the advance system associated with a longwall face and the method of transport is a combination of conveyors (face and gate) and rail tubs. The large white arrows indicate the flow of ventilation air. Most of the components and functions illustrated are described on other pages of this publication.

KEY TO MOVEMENT OF COAL
1) Coal seam, 5ft thick. 2) Coalface. 3) Position of future cuts. 4) Undercutting machine. 5) Compressed-air supply. 6) Face conveyor. 7) Props and roof supports. 8 & 9) Stone packs. 10) 'Goaf' or 'Gob' showing collapsed roof. 11) Coal-cutting machine. 12) Undercut coalface ready for filling. 13) Manual filling of face conveyor. 14) Face conveyor. 15) Gate, containing gate conveyor. 16. Stone and shale roof. 17) Gate conveyor delivering coal to tubs ('trams') waiting on main haulage roadway. 18) Full tubs en route to shaft. 19) Onsetter's office. 20) Full tubs entering cages and pushing empties from the surface out the other side. 21) Empty tubs. 22) A 'Paddy Mail' train bringing miners 'outbye' (i.e. back to the shaft).

KEY TO VENTILATING SYSTEM
23) Downcast shaft and air supply. 24) Air doors (ventilation doors) to help separate downcast and upcast air; tubs pass through one door at a time. 25) Downcast air travelling up main roadway. 26) Downcast air travelling along tail road. 27) Downcast air travelling along gate road. 28) Upcast (return) air travelling along tailgate. 29) Main upcast return air road. 30) Return (foul) air to upcast shaft. 31) Upcast air being drawn out of the mine by surface-based fans.

KEY TO OTHER NUMBERS
32) Tub sidings. 33) Haulage machinery. 34) Cage guides. 35) Brick-built rooms. 36) Steel-arched roadway with wooden battens. 37) Water sump.

KEY TO SURFACE STRUCTURES AND OPERATIONS

1) Downcast shaft. 2) Upcast shaft. 3) Cage in raised position. 4) Full tubs ('trams') being pushed out of cage by empties. 5) Tubs gravitate towards screen building. 6) Weighbridge. 7) Tippler. 8) Empty tubs hauled back to cage by cable. 9) Cage in upcast shaft. 10) Full tubs on way to screens. 11) Tippler. 12) Empty tubs returning to shaft. 13) Conveyor belt for sizing large coal and picking out stone, shale, slate etc. 14) Ditto for 'cobbles'. 15) Ditto for 'nuts'. 16) Ditto for 'smalls', which go straight to the washery. 17) Conveyor to rail-loading hopper. 18) Railway wagons. 19) Loaded train awaiting departure. 20) Smalls washery (coal preparation plant) with water/clarifier tower. 21) Washed smalls hopper to wagons. 22) Aerial ropeway for waste to spoil heap. 23) Spoil heap. 24) Downcast shaft headgear. 25) Banksman's office. 26) Winding drum, electric motor and control desk. 27) Ventilation tunnel from upcast shaft. 28) Fan house and evasse. 29) Upcast shaft headgear. 30) Upcast winding house. 31) Boiler house. 32) Power house, containing air-compressors, pumps and turbo-generators. 33) Pithead baths and canteen. 34) Cycle store. 35) Lamp room and medical centre. 36) Steps up to cage. 37) Tub maintenance dept. 38) Workshops. 39) Through roads. 40) Screen loading roads. 41) Sidings to stores and crippled wagons.

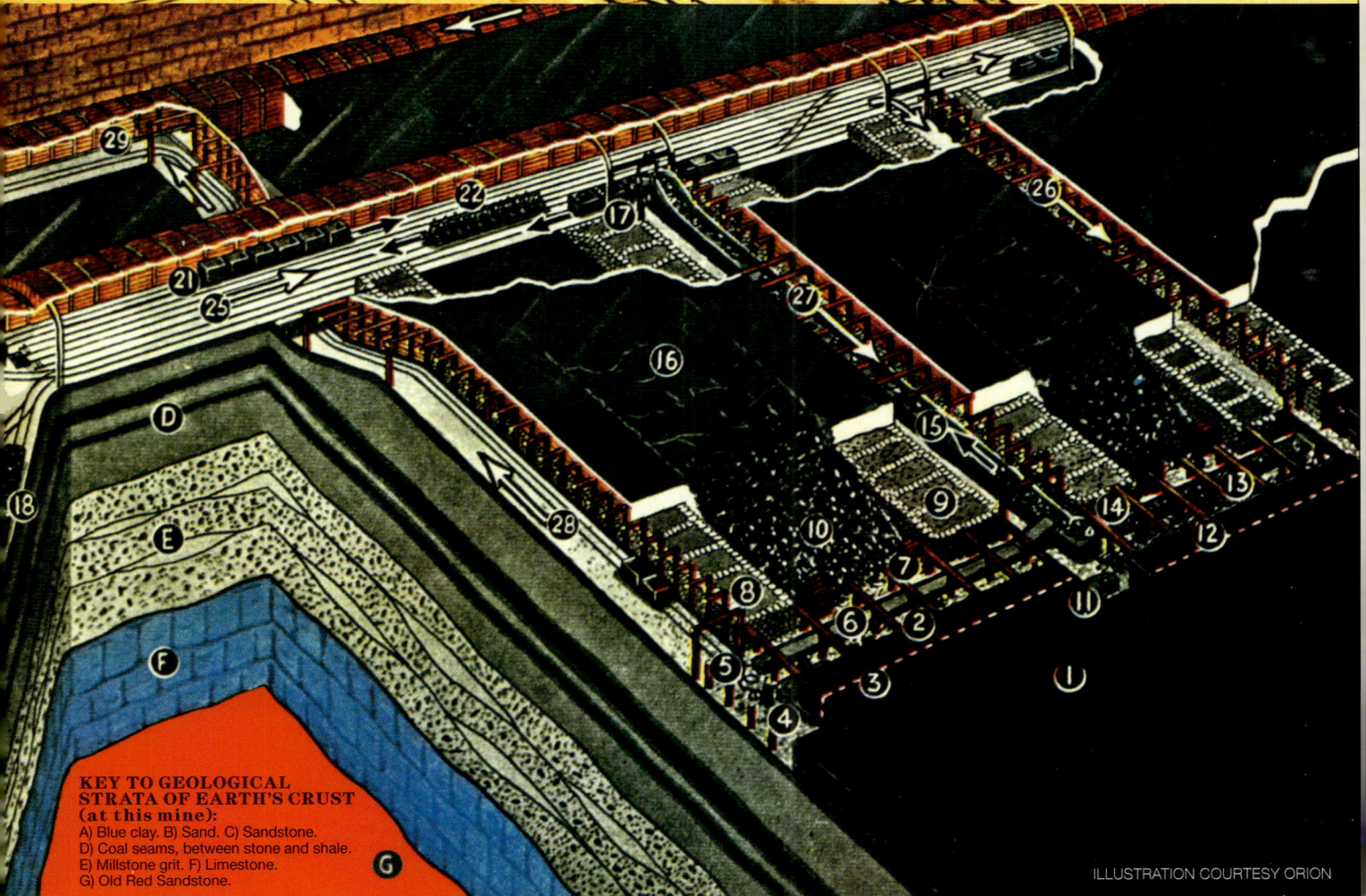

KEY TO GEOLOGICAL STRATA OF EARTH'S CRUST (at this mine):

A) Blue clay. B) Sand. C) Sandstone. D) Coal seams, between stone and shale. E) Millstone grit. F) Limestone. G) Old Red Sandstone.

ILLUSTRATION COURTESY ORION

CHAPTER 7

Headstocks and shafts

The ups and downs of mining

T HE INTERNATIONALLY recognised symbol of coal mining is the winding tower, also known as the headstock, headgear or headframe. Topped by huge spoked pulley wheels called sheaves, they were used for winding coal, men and materials up and down the shafts.

Before the 1800s, headstocks were constructed of timber, having evolved from the rudimentary windlasses erected over shallow bellpits, but as shafts became deeper and loads heavier, the height and strength of the gear had to increase too.

Deep mines of the type we are familiar with today began to appear in the late 18th century once the problem of water pumping had been overcome. Until then, shafts had rarely descended more than 300ft, but by 1801, a depth of 993ft had been achieved at Howgill Colliery on the Cumberland coast.

The downcast and upcast shafts of the preserved Woodhorn Colliery in Northumberland showing the difference between the open and enclosed types of headgear. Woodhorn is open to the public and also houses the Northumberland county archives.

Among the largest and most impressive examples of headgear in Britain were the two huge 'A'-frame towers at Lea Hall Colliery, Staffordshire. Opened by the NCB in 1960, these incorporated ground-mounted friction-winder systems with four pulleys each and produced coal for Rugeley power station, which adjoined it. The power station closed in 2016 and the colliery has been replaced by a huge distribution centre for the Amazon online retail firm. In this 1989 photo, one of the towers dwarfs a Hunslet surface shunter. GORDON EDGAR

A good place to see different designs of headgear is Chatterley Whitfield Colliery in Staffordshire, which possesses more winding towers than any other surviving site in the UK. Three of the four structures are visible in this image. NICK PIGOTT

As technology improved, it became possible to sink shafts to much greater depths and, for some years, the deepest in Britain were those of Parsonage Colliery in the Wigan coalfield, at around 3,000ft. They were later overtaken by a number of others, including Hem Heath (3,186ft) and Harworth's No.2 shaft in Nottinghamshire, which reached 3,297ft (just over a kilometre and roughly equivalent to England's highest mountain, Scafell Pike). To put that into context, the deepest part of the entire London Underground system is a mere 220ft.

At some modern collieries, coalface workers toiled at even greater depths as a result of long, and usually very steep, subterranean drifts descending from the shaft bottom (see next chapter). As a matter of interest, the deepest British vertical shaft of all is at Boulby potash mine in Cleveland—4,600ft (1,400m).

There were several types of headgear over the years, with some of the modern friction-winder designs erected at NCB superpits in the 1950s and 60s bearing more resemblance to concrete and glass blocks of flats than traditional steel towers.

Headstocks were either 'downcast' or 'upcast', depending on which direction the subterranean ventilation air passed through them, and it was usual for No.1 shaft to be the

Shaft-sinkers were a breed apart, usually employed on a contractual basis and travelling from coalfield to coalfield as new mines were opened across the country. Note the waterproof over-garments and wide-rimmed hats and hoods designed to deflect the water that cascaded down the shafts. The men even measured the depths they worked at in fathoms – equivalent to six feet – and in some places this maritime tradition was continued even after the shaft was in use.

would be made all around the surface in order to provide surveyors with a 'picture' of the underground bed and seams — the purpose being that faults and folds in the earth's structure could give a misleading impression and lead to the shaft (or perhaps even the entire mine) being an expensive folly.

To make a test borehole for a typical modern deep mine, a hollow cylindrical drill with a diamond-tipped or saw-toothed bit would be progressively driven into the ground by machine with additional sections continuously screwed on to it at the top until the desired depth was reached. Cores or 'plugs' of earth, rock and coal entered the hollow cylinder sections, were brought to the surface and then laid end-to-end on the ground for analysis by geologists.

Once the decision to go ahead was taken, a specialist team of shaft-sinkers would be brought in to dig into the soft overburden and sub-soils. A temporary headstock would then be erected above the cavity for lowering and raising muck and materials in a huge bucket known as a 'hoppit' or 'kibble', in which the sinkers would also ride themselves.

As they worked their way down through the water-bearing measures (usually the first 750ft or so of strata depending on the local geology), the sinkers would encounter varying volumes of water from subterranean aquifers, which would have to be pumped out as they progressed. The amount could vary from a highly manageable 20 gallons a minute to a fast-flowing torrent of several thousands of gallons a minute. Assuming the waterproof-clad men could keep the flow stemmed to a manageable level, they would insert cast-iron bolted segments known as 'tubbing' into the shaft to form a watertight seal. In the 20th century, this process was sped up by technological improvements such as cementation or even temporary freezing of the ground around the shaft.

This they would achieve by bringing in a surface-based refrigeration plant to freeze the rock, soil and sand and make it 'dry' long enough for the waterproofed shaft linings to be installed and secured. The system worked by cooling brine to below the freezing point of water and then injecting it into the ground to form walls of ice around the shaft. Once the tubbing had been inserted, the refrigeration plant could be switched off.

Depending on the surrounding ground conditions, the permanent lining would normally be formed either with bricks or by pouring concrete behind reinforced shutters known as coffers. Where bricks were used, a kerb-ring would be placed around the shaft wall on which to lay the bricks. Once the cement had set, the kerb-ring would be lowered about three feet and another set of bricks laid

downcast and No.2 the upcast, although there were exceptions. With the tower-mounted friction-winder types there was little visual external difference between the two, but with the lattice steel-frame designs, it was usually easy to tell which was the upcast, as it was normally clad in some form of air-tight shuttering, which was made of wood in the early days but concrete or metal in later years.

The shuttering was to ensure that the extractor fan fixed close to the top of the upcast shaft drew fresh ventilation air down into the workings via the downcast shaft and that the air didn't instead get drawn through the top of the upcast shaft and then short-circuit straight back to the atmosphere.

Air will always take the route of least resistance and so the cladding around the outside of the headstock tower created an airlock to ensure it followed its intended route through the underground network. Air-doors in the roadways helped direct the flow to where it was needed (see Chapter 14).

Before any new shaft could be sunk, numerous boreholes

A view down into a shaft a few days after sinkers had started work. Water ingress was a common problem, but from the late-1950s, mechanical 'cactus' grabs like this began to speed up the task considerably.

by men working from a temporary suspended platform. Ferro-concrete was normally the lining of choice in earth likely to remain wet.

Once the water-bearing measures ended and the 'rock-head' was reached, explosives had to be used to enable sinking to continue. The blasting was undertaken in stages; holes would be drilled for the charges, all equipment would be sent to the surface to protect it, and the men would exit the shaft themselves. They would then detonate the charges remotely before re-entering the shaft to remove the broken rock.

Before the invention of remote-controlled devices, the shot-firer had to remain in the shaft long enough to light a very long fuse before clambering into the hoppit and being hoisted quickly to the surface. You found out who your mates were in situations like that!

This procedure would be repeated hundreds of times over a period of months or years until the desired depth was attained. In the case of some collieries, it could take as long as three years before the first seam of coal was even located, although the introduction of high-capacity 'cactus' grabs in the 1950/60s sped the process up.

The long length of time it took led some shaft-sinking companies to go to quite elaborate lengths by erecting over the top of the shafts temporary structures that were almost as tall as the permanent ones that would follow. Vane Tempest Colliery in County Durham was particularly noted in the 1930s for a trinity of church spire-style structures clad in timber.

As each shaft grew deeper, fresh air would be sent down to the men using a surface fan and canvas ducts or tubes to prevent the air becoming stale.

It was a perilous occupation and there were numerous accidents over the years, one of the worst occurring at Bilsthorpe in 1927 just as No.1 shaft was about to reach the end of the water-bearing measures at a depth of 828ft. A heavy assembly of iron pipes carrying pumped water to the surface collapsed and plunged down the shaft, killing 14 sinkers. Other tragedies over the years included hoppit failures, platform falls and rising floodwater.

Once a shaft had been completed and was fully lined, permanent headgear would be constructed on the surface to enable the mine developers and their equipment to go down in cages and begin building the haulage roads that would access the various coal seams. A substantially wide pillar of unworked coal would always be left at the base of the shafts to ensure their long-term stability.

Once the ventilation system had been installed and the mine was in operation, the downcast shaft carrying fresh air into the workings would usually be used for conveying men and supplies, with the upcast shaft utilised for movement of coal to the surface, although the method varied from colliery to colliery, Bilsthorpe, for example, being one that used its No.2 shaft for man-riding.

The effectiveness of the airlock in the upcast shaft was not compromised during the constant coming and going of cages. In fact, in some large modern superpits, a separate shaft would be sunk some distance from the main buildings and be used for nothing other than ventilation (except in emergencies). Two downcast shafts would be provided at such a mine, one primarily for man-riding and supplies and the other for coal-winding.

Timber-clad temporary structures erected by shaft-sinkers at Vane Tempest Colliery in County Durham.

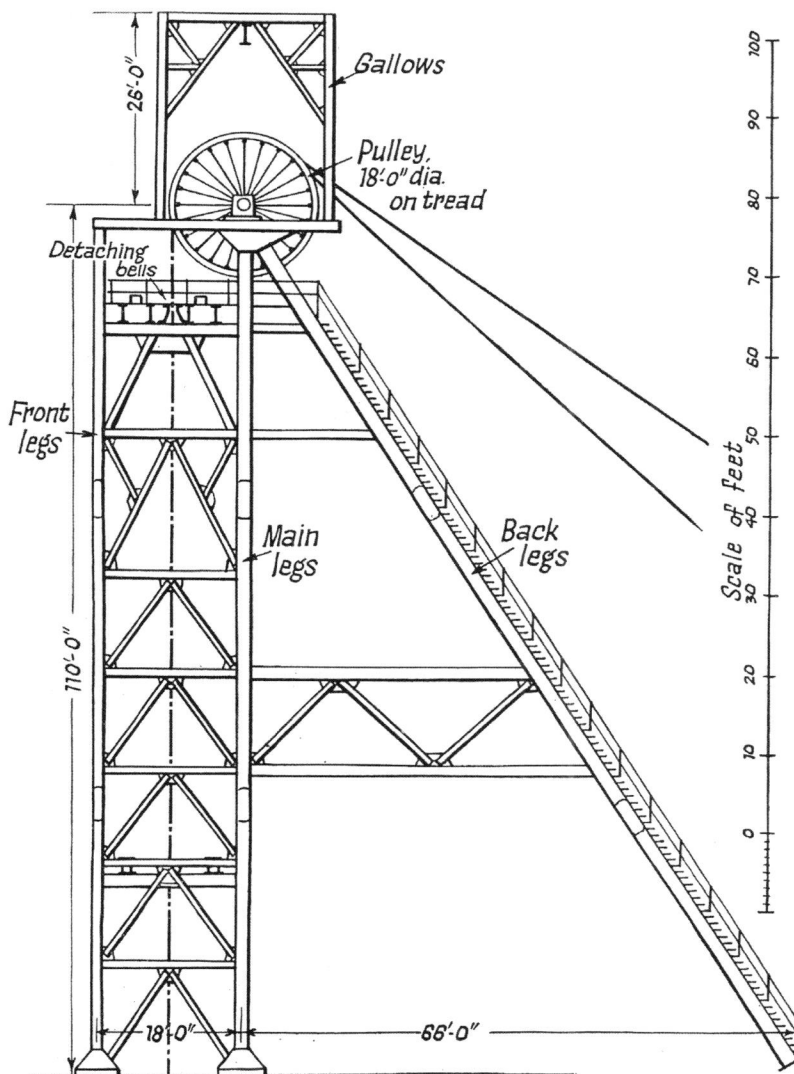

Diagram of a classic steel joist headgear illustrating the main components and average dimensions.

Before the 20th century, most headframes were made of timber — usually oak or pitch pine — and erected in a tandem arrangement with two narrow shafts sharing a set of ropes, but if anything happened to the rope or the winding engine, both shafts would be out of action and there would be no escape. So, after the Hartley Colliery disaster of 1862, in which the cast-iron beam of the mine's pumping engine snapped and fell down the shaft, trapping 204 men — all of whom died — an Act of Parliament was passed requiring collieries with more than 30 men underground at the same time to have a minimum of two separate shafts or other linked means of escape. Hartley had possessed one shaft separated into two compartments by a wooden brattice.

Half a century later, the Coal Mines Act of 1911 decreed that new mines, employing more than 30 people, had to have headframes built of non-inflammable materials. That led to a rapid increase in the lattice girder (and later rolled steel) types that became such familiar landmarks in the coalfields of Britain. In very small mines a few pitch pine structures remained in use into the 1950s.

Shafts weren't only used for bringing up coal, moving men and supplies and providing ventilation; to cleats on their inner sides were also affixed pipes for water and compressed air, cables for electricity and wires for telephones and other means of communication. In order to visually inspect and repair such equipment or the shaft walls themselves, special 'pitmen' were employed to descend the shaft while standing on top of the cage.

Shaft collars and pit banks often had sloping surrounds so that rain and other fluids would run away from them, but water and sludge nevertheless accumulated in a sump at the foot of the shaft and had to be frequently removed.

In operation, systems of bell codes or hooter sounds

Following an 1862 Act of Parliament requiring a minimum of two shafts or means of access/egress per mine, tandem headstocks became more commonplace. This set at Brinsley Colliery, near Eastwood, was built in 1872 and survived the mine's 1934 closure in order to provide ventilation and emergency egress for the nearby Underwood and Moorgreen collieries. By the time it came out of service in 1970, its historic importance was recognised and it was taken to the National Mining Museum, which at that time was based at Lound Hall, near Retford. When the museum vacated those premises, it was returned to Brinsley and re-erected as a monument in 1991 as part of a heritage theme based around author and poet D H Lawrence.

were used by banksmen, onsetters and winding enginemen to signal when cages — also known as chairs — were ready to be raised or lowered, or when the top half of a double or triple-decker cage needed manoeuvring up or down. The sheaves at the top of each headgear rotated in opposite directions as the winding ropes passed over them.

The speeds at which the cages and skips could be wound could reach 90ft per second (about 60mph), so it was sometimes necessary for shafts to be widened at the halfway point to reduce air pressure when two passed each other at speed. In practice, the normal velocities were about 60ft per second for coal and 30ft per second for men.

Without exception, a group of miners interviewed in the 1990s agreed that their very first trip to the pit bottom had been terrifying. Said one: "As soon as the gate was clanged shut on the cage and the banksman stood back and rang the signal, we dropped like a stone. About halfway down,

your ears suddenly went as though you were deaf and it seemed as though you were coming back to the top. But then I saw a light flash by and realised we were still going down. I was frightened to death."

At busy collieries, the coal-winding engines would run virtually non-stop 24 hours a day. Modern shafts were up to 30ft in diameter and capable of taking 30-tonne skips, or triple-deck cages containing as many as 120 men at a time, but many as small as 8ft diameter remained in use into the 1960s and in relatively shallow mines in the early years there had even been a number of 'corkscrew' shafts, up and down which men walked on a spiral path instead of riding in a chair.

In the early years, winding engines were steam-powered but the NCB converted almost all to electric during the 1950s-70s period. New mines such as Harworth had electric winding engines from the start, but so did a few older pits

A view up through the superstructure of a headstock from the cage entrance, showing the multiple rope system required to operate a shaft with two cages. This example is at Blaenafon Colliery, which utilises a drift as its other means of exit.

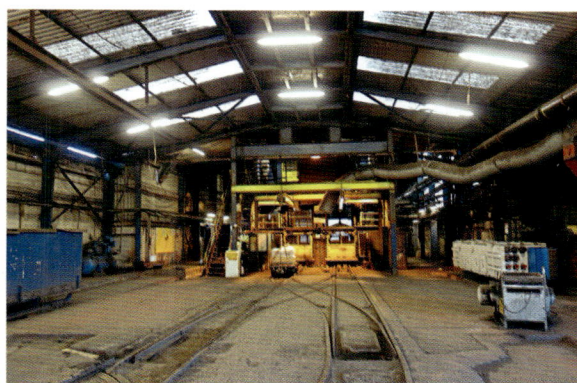

Pit banks of downcast shifts were hives of activity when miners entered or left the cages, but between shifts they were often much quieter than their constantly busy coal-raising upcast neighbours. This was Kellingley Colliery's downcast pit bank showing a wagonload of supplies waiting to descend.

such as Thoresby and Betteshanger.

The majority of UK shafts were equipped with two cages or skips secured to separate ropes. To enable men to escape up a skip-winding shaft in an emergency, most modern skips had a small auxiliary cage mounted above the coal-carrying section.

Any item of machinery too large to fit into a cage would either be dismantled into components first or – in the case of long locomotives and suchlike – be suspended vertically from the underside of the cage in a sling and then be brought round to the horizontal at the bottom for off-loading (see Chapter 20). It was a tricky operation and explains why so many locos, shearers and other large forms of equipment were abandoned underground upon the closure of a mine.

Headstocks were built in dozens of different shapes and sizes (see photo-spread at the end of this chapter for a selection of styles), but in later years they were basically of two main types: The first, the traditional steel winding tower, contained two sheave pulley wheels linked by cables to a separate winding house on the surface (one house for each tower). The cable drums within the winding house were operated by large stationary steam engines in the early years and then by electricity and were each manned by a skilled driver who normally had to work in isolation so that he would not be distracted by conversation or events going on around him. Safety devices were improved over the years, but total concentration was necessary to prevent the risk of a fatal over-wind (see next chapter).

The second type of headgear was generally known as the Koepe friction-winding type. Named after their German inventor, Friedrich Koepe, these were installed at many of the new or refurbished superpits in the NCB era. The system did not use a conventional winding drum but instead utilised the weight of the ropes, cages and skips to assist the grip of the ropes on the sheave wheels. The

cages were secured to opposite ends of the same single (or multiple) rope, which was then passed over surge pads on a smaller drum, the drive being transmitted to the rope(s).

In a modern Koepe headstock, the sheave wheels (which included a deflecting pulley) were not usually visible but enclosed in concrete or metal cladding. The reason was that the electric winding engine and controller's cabin were usually located at the top of the tower, rather than being in an adjacent building (although there were several examples of ground-mounted Koepe friction winders too, including the huge 'A' frame structures erected at certain NCB superpits).

Friction types were ideal for very deep mines as the drums needed by other systems would have been too large and the cables too long and heavy. They also required up to 30% less power and space. The first to be installed in Britain was at Northumberland's Plenmeller Colliery in 1914, but the system did not become more widespread in Britain until some years later.

A third and older type of winding tower, examples of which were prevalent in the Great Northern Coalfield, was known as the lever-type vertical winding engine. Patented by Newcastle engineer Phileas Crowther in 1800, it utilised a vertical steam cylinder to drive a large flywheel above it, which in turn drove the shaft pulley wheel by rope. This negated the need for a separate horizontal-cylindered engine in a separate building, but the concept didn't spread much beyond County Durham. Half a dozen engines of this type were still in operation in the mid-1950s and one is preserved in working order at Beamish Museum.

There was a fourth type – the water-balanced winder – which in former years was popular in relatively shallow collieries, especially in South Wales. The cages were fitted with water tanks beneath their floors. At the top, water would be let into the tank and the weight would cause

The tallest headstock in the UK until its April 2016 demolition was the Koepe tower winder at Harworth superpit, south of Doncaster. This 220ft high monolith had been constructed as recently as 1989 and had clearly been built to last, for it defied attempts to demolish it by explosives and had to be brought down by manual means. This scene makes an interesting contrast with the early-1920s view in Chapter 4.

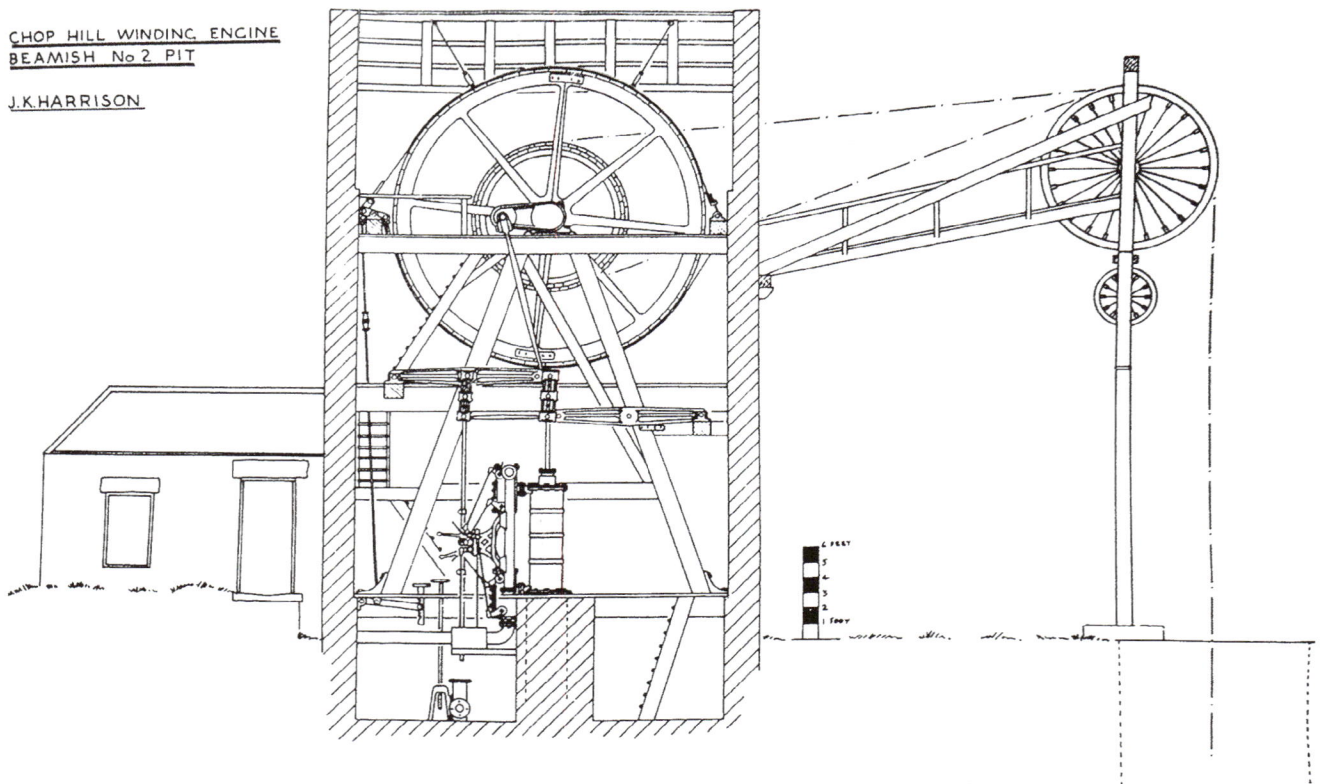

A type of headstock found in County Durham, but very rarely, was the vertical-cylinder winding engine, which used a steam-powered lever system to rotate a flywheel, which in turn worked a shaft pulley sheave via ropes. The last working example of this Victorian design can be seen in operation at Beamish Museum.

A water-balanced headstock preserved at Blaenafon, and (below), a diagram explaining how such winding gear functioned.

that cage (containing an empty tub or tram) to descend while the cage in the other shaft, whose water tank had been emptied at the bottom, would ascend with a full load.

With such an enormous number of collieries in Britain, it was inevitable that there would be exceptions and permutations to the types of winding gear. For example, one of the large modern shafts at Hem Heath Colliery, near Stoke-on-Trent, had two winders in one shaft—a standard electric winder on one side, operating down to the 1,836ft level, and a ground-mounted Koepe electric winder operating down to the 3,186ft level. Another Staffordshire colliery, Lea Hall, had a German-inspired twin headgear set with four sheave wheels serving two shafts on each of its two huge 'A'-frame structures. The 200ft high headstocks of Nottinghamshire's Clipstone Colliery, also of German design with exposed frames were, at the time of their construction in 1953, the tallest in Europe.

Most collieries possessed a minimum of two towers but some large mines—Chatterley-Whitfield, for example—had four or more separate sets of headgear on one site, depending on how many underground seams were being worked. Some smaller mines had only one winding tower, but in those cases there would either be a drift or other means of egress as well.

Preservation has left us with several examples of lattice steel headframes in the UK, including at least one friction-winder type, but there are now no examples of the

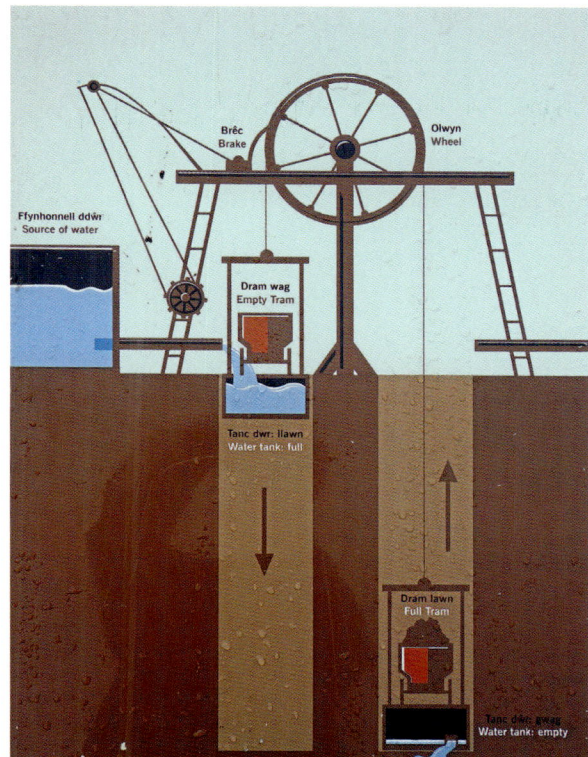

enclosed Koepe variety following demolition of those at Castlebridge, Harworth and Kellingley. Constructed as recently as 1989, the Harworth one depicted on the facing page bit the dust on April 11, 2016 after defiantly resisting an attempt to blow it up the day before.

Skip-winding

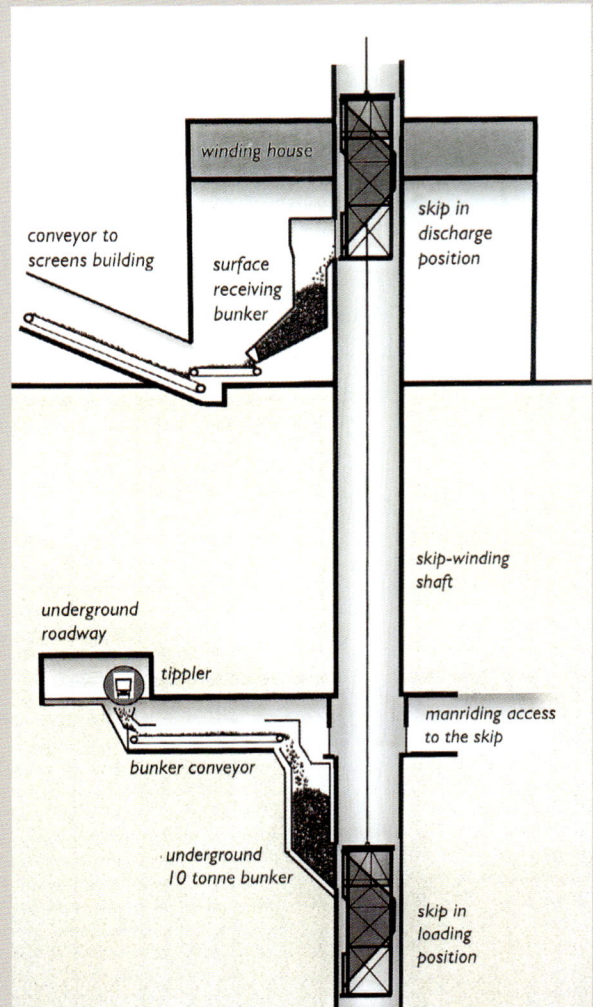

SKIP-WINDING WAS introduced in modern mines to increase the speed, volume and frequency of coal-raising in association with underground and surface conveyor belts. Before then, rail-borne tubs and mine cars had to be laboriously conveyed to the surface in cages and sent down again when empty.

Most skips were installed in upcast shafts, the main reason being that the huge clouds of dust thrown out as their loads were discharged would not be drawn back down into the mine by the ventilation system, thereby causing potential fire and breathing hazards. There were a few exceptions, however, usually depending on factors such as the hardness of the coal or the most conveniently-placed shaft for delivery to the preparation plant on the surface.

The main problem for mine operators has always been the need to maintain air-tightness in upcast shafts. At collieries that used them for man-riding, the miners simply walked through airlocks on their way into and out of the cages and potential problems only arose at shift-change times anyway, but skip-winding in the upcast shaft of a busy colliery meant constant disturbance to the air flow every few minutes throughout the day.

To get round this, engineers ensured that the skip-unloading system was designed in such a way that the airtight door in the shaft's cladding would spring open for just a few seconds before snapping shut again, giving enough time for the coal to shoot down the skip's steeply-inclined base but not enough time to disrupt the air flow. By the time the next skip load was due, the powerful fans would have compensated for any loss of pressure.

Picture above left is an example of a large skip on display at Caphouse Colliery museum (note the emergency man-riding cage at the top) and on the right a diagram showing how the system works.

Pillars of the community

To ROUND off this chapter, we present a gallery of photographs showing the wide architectural variety of traditional colliery headstocks in Britain. A selection of enclosed concrete tower winders of the type erected at superpits can be seen in Chapter 18. All colour photographs have been taken by the author unless stated.

Left: Rossington Colliery in 2007. These tall friction winders south-east of Doncaster have now been demolished... but those of Nottinghamshire's Clipstone Colliery (right) – the highest lattice steel towers in the country – enjoy protected status and in 2021 there were hopes they would become the centrepiece of a proposed mining museum-cum-leisure facility.

The upcast headstock of Tower Colliery – the last deep mine in South Wales. It was closed by British Coal in 1994 but was bought by its workforce and continued to work until 2008 when it shut for the last time. Part of the colliery yard is now used as the base of a zip-wire experience on an adjacent mountainside.

Many headstocks featured a metal or concrete frame above the sheaves. This was a frame hoist, also known as a gallows or gibbet, and was used whenever the pulleys or ropes needed changing. This example is at Lady Victoria Colliery in Scotland. In later years, several were removed as the height, reach and capacity of road-based mobile cranes increased, although in certain designs of headgear, the frames also acted as an additional safety device in the event of an over-wind.

Bestwood Colliery was once a huge sprawling industrial complex. Today all that remains is the headgear, winding house and a small building surrounded by neat lawns in a country park, but it nevertheless makes for a friendly and interesting visit.

The winding gear of Kiveton Park Colliery was visible to passengers in trains running along the Sheffield-Worksop main line. It is seen shortly before closure in 1994. GAVIN MORRISON

The collection of buildings around the base of a winding tower is collectively known as the heapstead and the most impressive and solidly-built survivor can be found at Pleasley Colliery, near Mansfield. The museum there houses an array of mining memorabilia, two beautifully-maintained steam winding engines, a brace of headstocks and a tall smokestack.

Saved at the last minute... the two classic towers at Hatfield Colliery ceased winding in 2015 and were due to suffer the same fate as those of three other mines closed in the 2010s (Daw Mill, Thoresby and Kellingley), but conservationists managed to get them listed as structures of historical importance. Sadly, salvation did not come soon enough to protect against the demolition of some of the buildings surrounding them.

Barnsley's last mine: The headstock and winding house of the former Barnsley Main Colliery, preserved but daubed with graffiti.

Painted in distinctive red oxide, the headgear at Big Pit Colliery in Blaenafon stands out among its South Wales valley setting and acts as a fine advertisement for the Welsh National Mining Museum.

One of the smallest preserved headstocks in Britain can be found at Foxfield Colliery at Dilhorne, Staffordshire. Built of concrete, it is one of two on the site, the other also being concrete but of much taller and more conventional appearance.

The 'blues': Haig Colliery at Whitehaven, Cumbria was, until 2016, preserved and open to the public. Now, ironically, there are proposals to mine coal in the area again. A picture of Haig in its prime can be seen in Chapter 2.

Another concrete design... the friction winder at Shirebrook Colliery, seen here in 1988, was partly encased in a concrete tower but with an exposed top section. The site of this mine is now occupied by a national sports goods distribution centre. Robin Stewart-Smith

CHAPTER 8

Coalfaces, seams and roadways

'The hardest work under heaven'

THE PHRASE 'working at the coalface' is known throughout the world as a reference to the core task in any operation, regardless of whether the business concerned is in heavy industry or merely office-based.

Few jobs carried such a globally respected reputation for hard work and high risk and few were surrounded by such mystique ... for the vast majority of the world's inhabitants have never been down an operational mine and thus have only a vague impression of what the conditions must have been like.

The nature of deep coalface work in Britain changed out of all recognition during the last few decades of its existence, culminating in a well-lit, high-roofed and fully mechanised environment in many major collieries. A century and a half ago, it was, as Derbyshire miner William Wardle described it, "the hardest work under heaven".

As some of the photographs and drawings in this book show, coalface work between the 18th and mid-20th centuries could be horrendous. The seams were often extremely thin and after crawling along rough terrain in virtual pitch-darkness for perhaps a mile or so to reach the face, the men would have to spend the whole shift on their knees or lying on their side in order to hew the coal with a hand-held pick.

Where high-quality coking coal was required, some pits in the North-East were still working seams of less than 2ft in height and width as late as the 1960s. As a pan shovel was almost 2ft long, this meant that a miner who accidentally took a shovel into a narrow opening the wrong way round would have to take it back to the gate road just to turn it over!

In the worst situations, a collier would have to lie in two or three inches of foul black water that splashed over him every time he wielded his pick — all the time living in fear of a sharp piece of rock falling and slicing through his neck, waist or leg. Experienced colliers learnt to tell where and when falls were likely to occur, but even they were sometimes caught unawares by a sudden collapse.

Even if they were not killed outright by such a fall, their route to safety could be blocked by tons of rock or they would occasionally see a workmate killed just feet away and would have to live with the memory for the rest of their lives. There was no such thing as trauma counselling in those days!

Small wonder that psychological, lung, back and muscle complaints were rife, yet such men had no option but to carry on working as there was usually no sick pay.

Undercutting — also known in the old days as holing-out or kirving — was the means by which a thin slot had to be created at the base of the coalface in order to encourage the main body of coal above the slot to come crashing onto the floor ready for shovelling into tubs. Short wooden props known as sprags or nogs were used to bear the weight of the coal during the holing-out process but, as can be imagined, it was an incredibly hazardous job. To make it worse, the miners had only cloth caps to protect their heads. Sadly, falls of coal were commonplace in the Victorian and early 20th century eras, frequently causing injury or death.

The greater use of ponies underground after 1842 helped ease conditions in some collieries as the roadways had to have their height increased to enable the animals to walk, but the districts nearest the faces themselves were often still very low.

In the early years before mechanisation, colliers undercut

LIMESTONE STRATA

DRILLING STONE FOR BLASTING CHARGE

PACK

WASTE

PACK

MEN GETTING THE COAL USING THE PRESSURE OF THE STONE. LARGE FLAKES ARE REMOVED BY CROWBAR

IN SIX SHIFTS OF 8 HOURS 22 MEN MOVE FORWARD 5 YARDS ON FACE OF 60 YARDS

WHEN PROPS ARE REMOVED THE MASS OF STONE COMES GRADUALLY DOWN ON THE PACKS AND FILLS THE WASTE BETWEEN

COAL FACE 5½-FOOT SEAM

PROPS

WASTE

ADDITIONAL HEADROOM FOR THE GATE IS MADE BY BLASTING OUT THE ROCK TO 8 FEET

TURNTABLE FOR TRUCKS

PACK

ROOF SUPPORTED BY BEAMS AND PROPS

GATE 12 FEET

PACK 12 FEET

MEN BUILDING PACKS FROM THE STONE WHICH HAS SUBSIDED ON REMOVAL OF PROPS

LIMESTONE STRATA

WASTE 24 FEET

PACK

This illustration from the early 1920s shows what would be seen if it had been possible to remove the millions of tons of earth above a non-mechanised longwall coalface. It shows how the gate approaches the face at a right angle and how the goaf or 'gob' (the void created by the most recently-hewn coal) is filled by hand with packs of stone and other waste to support the roof once the timber props are removed. This face was being worked by the advance method; in later years many mines would switch to the retreat method (see main text).

One part of Britain that didn't need to worry about increasing height for the ponies was Staffordshire, whose thick seams could be 15ft high in places and this made it possible to undertake the room-and-pillar method of mining with the emphasis on 'room'! Miners crawling through 2ft-high gaps in the thin seams of Lancashire and other areas could only dream of such spacious working conditions.

and prepared their own sections of coalface prior to hewing. In larger collieries, such tasks were taken over by kirvers until the advent of shot-firers, whose job it was to drill holes in an undercut face and insert sticks of explosives. Having checked no gas was present, they would then retire to a safe place to detonate the charges and bring the coal down for shovelling into tubs or onto conveyors. Shot-firing was a highly-skilled job in more ways than one, for the object in those days was to fracture the coalface into lumps, not to shatter it.

Very occasionally, a detonator or charge would fail to go off and it was not unknown for them to explode later in domestic fireplaces or even in the fireboxes of steam locomotives!

To advance or retreat? As mentioned earlier, mining was originally carried out by the pillar & stall method, but in England, towards the end of the 17th century, the concept of longwall mining was developed. Sometimes known as the 'Shropshire' method, it basically involved all the coal being taken from a single face, leaving a large void known as the 'goaf' or 'gob'. There were basically two methods of longwall mining — advance and retreat.

In the first, coal-cutting would begin at the shaft or drift end of a new mine and advance into the coal deposits, with the lengths of the accompanying access roads or gates keeping pace with the face as progress was made.

In the far more modern method of retreat mining, the roads were built first and extended all the way to the far boundary of the panel or district to be mined. The men and machinery would then start cutting the coalface at that far end and work their way back towards the direction of the shafts.

The retreat method was developed in the late 19th century but it didn't become widespread in Britain until the 20th century due to the high initial costs. It had several advantages, the main one being that the void behind the face didn't need to be supported beyond the section being cut at any particular moment and could simply be allowed to cave to a greater extent than had been the case with advance mining. (Most such collapses occurred far too deep to have a noticeable subsidence effect on the surface). It also meant that the gate ends were much less cluttered with roadheaders and other bulky equipment.

The main gate of a longwall coalface would typically be the intake airway and the tail gate the return airway, carrying away the coal dust and gases. The main gate, also known as the loader gate or mother gate, was usually the one through which the coal was conveyed to the shafts, while the tail (or supply) gate was used for taking in materials.

To loosen the coal at the face in the early years of mechanisation, compressed air tools were used to drill holes for explosive charges. It was safe to detonate such shot-firing charges as long as stringent tests had been made by an official beforehand to ensure no pockets of 'firedamp' were present. The second photograph, taken at Eckington half a century later in 2016, shows that this aspect of mining had stood the test of time.

It might seem illogical for the coal to be taken out at the fresh air end of the face, but there were fewer chances of interruptions to the all-important coal production flow with that method, as machinery exposed to foul air in the tail was more suspect to temporary shutdowns in the event of high methane levels and suchlike. Arrangements did vary from mine to mine and even from seam to seam, with some managements preferring to concentrate switchgear and other electrical equipment in the main gates to reduce the likelihood of problems.

Unless a face was particularly dusty, it was safe for men to work and travel in return airways, as long as the oxygen content remained above 19.5%.

As big modern collieries had numerous faces in simultaneous production, the transport of coal from each one

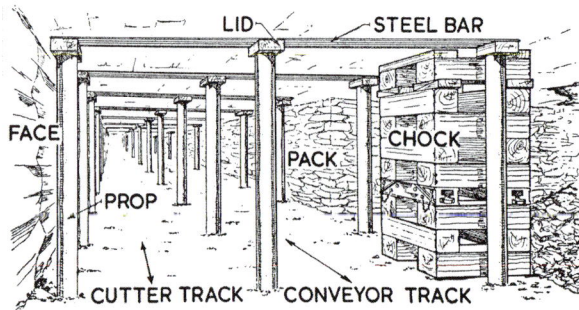

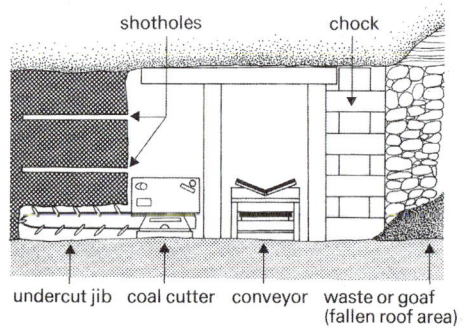

Seen in conjunction with the picture on page 87, this view (left) along a traditional longwall coalface worked by the advance method, shows the permanent pack and also a temporary chock made of timber beams to provide additional support to the roof while packs, props, lids and steel bars were being erected. The diagram on the right from the early years of mechanisation shows the relationship between the various components.

through the various gates and roadways to the shaft bottom required careful planning and co-ordination. Even with computerised monitoring in later years, things didn't always go as planned so, to even out the flow of coal to the shaft in the event of interruptions, huge bunkers containing hundreds of tonnes were often positioned at strategic points along main roadways. The largest, at Kellingley, was capable of holding 15 double-decker buses!

Retreat mining had further major benefits in that any geological problems or areas of spontaneous combustion could usually be identified before production began, thus minimising hold-ups and expensive mistakes. It was also much faster and more efficient once coal-cutting had started – but the driving of complete roadways and gateways before any income could be earned from the coal required major capital outlay and was therefore expensive. For that reason, private owners post-1994 often required state subsidies to develop new faces and when that funding dried up in the 21st century, the end of deep mining in the UK was inevitable.

The dreaded term 'geological problems' was in itself a 'minefield' and covered a multitude of sins. (In fact, many miners considered it a euphemism deployed by owners as an excuse to close an otherwise sound pit.) We shall never know now whether such cynicism was always justified, but many pits definitely did suffer from serious instabilities – Hucknall No.2 for example, which was struck by a sudden massive intrusion of sandstone in 1986.

The earth's crust is constantly restless and although roof falls were usually the result of insufficient prop support, the floor of a mine would often move too, being thrust upwards by tremendous forces of nature. In such cases, miners would have to restore the floor to a reasonably level state by a process of cutting and smoothing known as 'dinting'. In later years, special machines were devised to perform this function.

Constant maintenance and repair of roadways – a process known as 'back ripping' – was necessary as the weight and crushing effect of the strata surrounding them in some areas caused roof arches to contort and the height of the roadway to reduce. In areas prone to such pincer-like convergence, regular setting of new steel arches (rings) had to be factored in by colliery managers for it was not unknown for ground settlement to reduce the height of a thin seam from, say, 2ft to 18in over the course of a single weekend. In a bid to counteract this, telescopic arches were introduced that automatically adjusted to the earth's movement.

Earth thrust that had occurred in prehistoric times left some coal measures almost vertical and those were known as edge seams or 'rearers'. In 1972, a seam of 1-in-2 (as steep as the roof of a house) was opened at Arkwright Colliery, Derbyshire, and required special regulations to enable men to work up and down it safely. At Bilsthorpe Colliery in neighbouring Nottinghamshire, a short but gruelling

Even in the safest and most modern mines, reminders of the immense pressure being brought to bear on the roof were never far away. This picture was taken 2,200ft below the ground at Thoresby in 2015 and shows how steel arches in a roadway had bent under the weight and how traditional timber props had been brought in to help support the roof. NICK PIGOTT

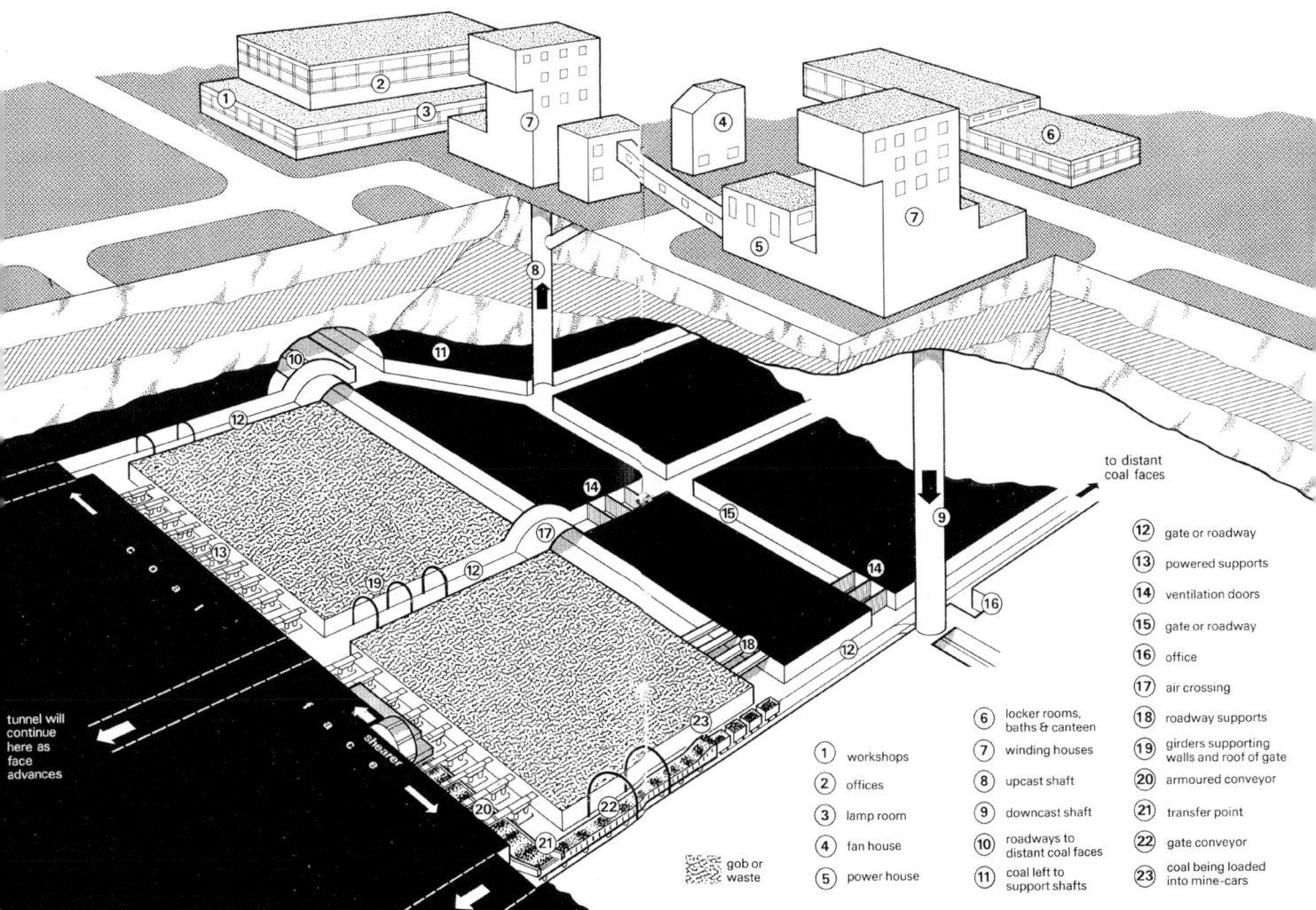

1	workshops
2	offices
3	lamp room
4	fan house
5	power house

6	locker rooms, baths & canteen
7	winding houses
8	upcast shaft
9	downcast shaft
10	roadways to distant coal faces
11	coal left to support shafts

12	gate or roadway
13	powered supports
14	ventilation doors
15	gate or roadway
16	office
17	air crossing
18	roadway supports
19	girders supporting walls and roof of gate
20	armoured conveyor
21	transfer point
22	gate conveyor
23	coal being loaded into mine-cars

gob or waste

A cutaway view into a mine which, although relatively modern and partly mechanised with shearer and conveyors, is worked on the advance method with the coal taken to the shaft in mine cars. In later years, a trunk conveyor would replace the mine car transfer point and the coal would be raised to the surface in a skip rather than a cage.

1-in-2 gradient caused by an anticline in a seam gained the local nickname "Cardiac Hill" because of the number of heart problems men suffered having to walk up it in 90° heat every day.

Geological problems also embraced strata faults. They could cause huge differences in seam depths, the Top Hard seam at Newstead Colliery, for instance, being located 484 yards deep in No.1 shaft but only 426 yards in No.2. Until the science of geology was better understood, major faults made hewers in the Middle Ages believe mistakenly that they'd found two different seams (see diagram in Chapter 1).

Faults have had a big bearing on the internal layouts of mines and have often dictated where shafts and roadways are built. Flooding also fell under the heading of geological problems. Many mines, especially older ones whose shafts did not extend beneath the local water table, suffered terribly from fluid intrusion and had to have powerful pumps in continuous operation. Even after the merger of collieries

for economic reasons in later years, otherwise-redundant shafts and headstocks would often be retained to pump water out of the combined workings.

Until the advent of steel archway supports and hydraulic roof supports (see next chapter), all methods of mining required timber pit props in the roadways and at the face. Oak examples discovered in an old room & pillar mine at Coleorton, Leicestershire, have been carbon-dated to the 1400s, but most collieries used Scottish or Norwegian spruce tree props due to their combination of strength and elasticity.

The props and their timber lids or caps enabled many thousands of miles of tunnels to be driven, yet the word 'tunnel' was not used in coal-mining parlance as often as might be expected. The preferred terms were 'roadway', 'gate', 'heading', 'drivage' or 'haulage road', depending on size and usage.

Strictly speaking, a tunnel has to be open at both ends,

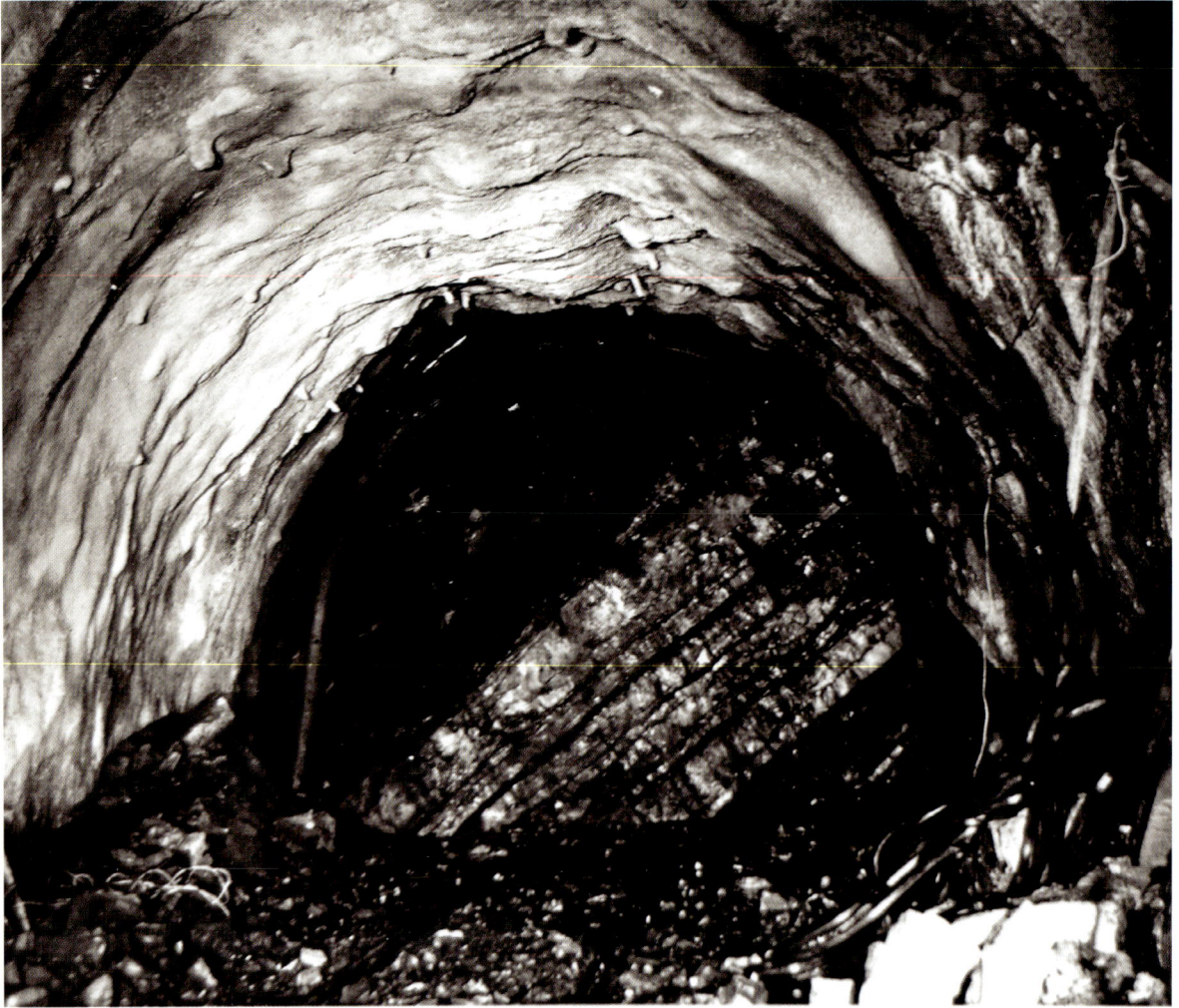

Coal seams affected by geological faulting can be sharply inclined, some almost vertically. Such seams were known as 'rearers'.

A view inside the workings of the now-closed Eckington Colliery showing timber props and lids supporting steel girders. NICK PIGOTT

but the word does nevertheless occur in official mining documentation, especially when used as a verb, and some large roadways in modern mines were driven by cylindrical tunnel-boring machines in exactly the same way as railway tunnels are constructed, so there was a considerable terminology crossover between the two disciplines. Dawdon Colliery, in County Durham, was one mine in which a full-face tunnel-borer was deployed in the mid-1970s.

Tunnel was also the name used for a subterranean connection (often bored through solid rock) between two previously independent mines. Such a joining of neighbouring collieries was known as a 'thirl' and Trentham and Florence pits in Staffordshire were joined by such a link in 1979. Many of the mines in the Dukeries area of Nottinghamshire were joined underground too, a small team of men being detailed to make the long underground walks from village to village every week or so to ensure there had been no blockages and that they could still be used in the event of an emergency.

The coalfaces in Warwickshire were among the thickest in the country and this enabled Daw Mill Colliery to enjoy the rare luxury of a high, wide, well-lit roadway containing no fewer than three rail tracks. Such roadways were sometimes known by miners as 'motorways', although 'main lines' would have been more appropriate.

The greatest thirl network of all in Britain was the Selby complex, which at its greatest extent, totalled 472 miles of underground roadways connecting the coalfaces of its five collieries with their preparation and loading point.

Adding the workings of mines together resulted in some enormous lengths of subterranean tunnels, but of course such labyrinthine networks benefitted from the ventilation systems of one or more collieries. It was a different story where dead-ended headings were concerned, for simply extending them ad-infinitum would have meant losing the ability to ventilate them efficiently. Eight or nine miles from pit bottom was thus generally considered a limit, with those under the sea at Ellington and Easington in the North-East being among the longest in Britain.

A roadway was known as such even if it contained only railway tracks, but in such cases it would often be referred to as a 'locomotive road' because underground workers surprisingly didn't use the word 'railway' very often either, the preferred terms being 'haulage road', 'haulage way',

'Paddy' road or 'tub track'.

In all mines, travel in the direction of a coalface was known as 'inbye' and travel back towards a shaft was referred to as 'outbye'.

In latter years, special roadheader machines were built to rip out roof stone but before that it had been a case of drilling, blasting and shovelling to construct a roadway. The men who did that were even more prone than the miners to lung problems and eye injuries due to the dust and shards thrown up from the rock and, in later years, they were allowed to wear protective masks and goggles.

In more recent times, the task of road-building was sped up by the introduction of roof-bolt technology. Basically, long holes of 10ft or more would be drilled into a newly-excavated roof or wall until they reached a strong layer of rock that could support its own weight. The holes were packed with quick-setting resin, long bolts were driven in by a special machine and then tightened to pull and bind the whole lot together. Heavy-duty steel mesh netting

Roadways were extended in the mechanised era by compressed air and electrically-driven 'road-header' machines, which used a rotary drill bit on the end of a movable jib to rip out the stone.

held in place by the bolts covered the roof and walls as an additional safeguard.

Roof bolts were much quicker to fit and enabled roadways to be built higher and wider than previously. Given the fact that with fast retreat mining methods the total life expectancy of roadways wasn't much more than a year, it made sense to mine owners to opt for the cheaper method rather than expensive arches, but the bolts did require a very strong strata and many miners disliked them as they didn't consider them to be as safe as the older system.

Another development was known as 'horizon' mining. The customary method when working inclined measures was to follow the undulations of the coal seams via underground roadways, but that often resulted in severe gradients, making mine car haulage along them difficult.

With horizon mining, level roadways (hence the name horizon) were driven from the shafts to the extremity of the area to be mined and were designed to intersect the maximum number of inclined or faulted seams as often as possible. At the points of intersection, headings were

driven into the seam to extract the coal and short shafts, known as staples, were driven up or down to connect two or more levels. As with retreat mining, a major capital outlay was required, but the advantages outweighed this once production began, as much longer trainloads could be taken to the shaft.

The NCB laid horizon lines in some of its superpits during the early years of underground rail haulage of coal, but their construction produced vast quantities of waste rock and they were really only suited to large takes of virgin coal in new mines. There became less call for them as conveyor belt technology and capacity improved.

Another cause of steep underground gradients in later years was the tendency for drifts to be driven down from the bottom of shafts in preference to extending the shaft itself. The No.2 pit at Bilsthorpe Colliery was such a case, ending at the 1,502ft (458m) level, whereas the No.1 shaft went down to 2,267ft. To reach the lower seams, five deep drifts were driven, three at a gradient of 1-in-6, one at 1-in-5 and another at 1-in 4. The latter was fitted with a cable

The modern way of building roadways was to do so with roof-bolts rather than with props or metal arches. Long bolts and quick-setting resin were inserted into self-supporting rock by special machines such as this and protective steel mesh was fitted to prevent small stone falls.

Beams from the cap lamps of miners and deputies pierce the gloom in this atmospheric longwall coalface scene. Note the circular cuts made by the shearer and also the hinged drop-down shields, an additional feature of modern hydraulic roof supports. NICK PIGOTT

Stacks of timber props were a common sight in the stockyards of collieries in the days before mechanised roof supports were introduced. This large load was photographed at Ayrshire's Auchincruive Colliery (also known as Glenburn) as ex-LMS 2-6-0 No.42739 passed by in April 1965. COLOUR-RAIL

belt and used for coal haulage, the 1-in-5 was used as a man-riding conveyor and one of the others featured a rope man rider.

British mines were typically divided into underground areas known as districts and miners working in quiet, or worked-out districts, would sometimes report being able to hear the machinery of a nearby colliery working at a level above or below them.

In the very early days, the more unscrupulous miners or coal owners had not been above taking coal from seams belonging to a neighbouring company and claiming ignorance if caught out, but that practice was abolished in the late Victorian era when it was decreed that all underground plans and boundary demarcation details had to be deposited with the Mines Inspectorate.

Overlapping of roadways had been occurring since the very earliest years of coal mining, with the difference being that in the old days they often weren't aware that neighbouring workings existed. There is a report of an Edwardian-era collier who suddenly fell through into a gallery that had been abandoned almost a century earlier and found the skeleton of a young child — a victim of the times when women and children were employed underground.

In 1948, a miner working in the Lower Fenton seam at Rockingham Colliery found a newspaper dated 1912. Looking up, he saw it had fallen through a small hole from

Timber props were also being used in big mines well into the mechanisation era, as evidenced by this huge stockpile at Littleton Colliery in 1993.

the abandoned Upper Fenton seam, which was sealed off, not having been used for years. Both men were fortunate that no water or methane had built up during the intervening years.

It became necessary to make test boreholes well in advance of the coal or rock that was about to be cut, to ensure that unrecorded old workings or deposits of gas or water were not lying in wait. This was particularly important in coastal locations, where workings often extended miles under the sea. Collieries with sub-marine roadways included Ellington in Northumberland, Point of Ayr in North Wales and Haig in Cumbria.

Mechanisation and automation

The machine age

O NE OF the greatest priorities for the NCB upon its formation in 1947 was the modernisation of the collieries — and that meant mechanisation.

A number of wealthier and more progressive coal-owning companies had been investing since the end of the 19th century in labour-saving devices, such as compressed air-driven drills and saws, but even in the peak production year of 1913, only 8% of output was machine-cut.

Compressed air equipment was essential in 'gassy' mines where it was unsafe to use steam or electrical machinery underground. Some companies piped steam from surface-based boilers down the shaft, but condensation in the long pipes and pressure-drop at the point of use affected power output. Compressed air machinery was far more efficient, involved no ignition and helped dilute toxic gases, but even that required enormous steam-driven compressors on the surface with air pipes up to a foot in diameter in the shaft.

Electricity had first been tried underground in the 1880s but suffered a temporary drop in popularity after the Senghenydd disaster of 1913. During the 1920s and 30s, machine-cut output rose to more than 30% and most major collieries benefitted from some form of coalface machinery (much of it by then electrical), but many owners put improvements on hold due to the Great Depression, the Second World War and the knowledge that nationalisation was pretty much inevitable.

With huge teams of men still using shovels to hand-load coal into horse-drawn tubs or crude conveyor belts, only a radical programme of modernisation and mechanisation could save the industry.

Soon after winning the 1945 election, the Labour Government set up a body under Sir Charles Reid, of the Fife Coal Company, to visit the US and report on the mechanisation of the mines there. In addition to recommending a switch to more modern coal-cutting and loading machinery, the Reid Report advocated the widespread use of locomotive-operated railways on the basis that there's no point in mining coal faster than it can be taken to the shaft.

Over the next decade or so, expensive new hardware was purchased and installed at many of the NCB's 'premier league' mines:

- More longwall coalfaces were set up to make the most of the new cutter/loaders.
- Wooden pit props on the faces were replaced by hydraulic versions.
- Shafts were enlarged and equipped with faster, more powerful winding gear.
- Some coal-raising shafts were deepened and converted to skip-winding rather than cages and tubs. In other cases, surface drifts were driven for the installation of conveyors.
- Flame-proofed electrical machinery was introduced to replace compressed air equipment.
- Horse-drawn and rope-hauled underground transport was gradually replaced by trunk conveyors, gate conveyors and locomotive-powered rail systems.
- In mines that were not equipped with conveyors, half-ton tubs were replaced by two-ton or four-ton mine cars.

The trunk conveyors were also used later for the speedy movement of men to and from the coalface in districts where there was no rail transport available.

A longwall coalface in a modern British mine, showing the shearer/loader in action, the armoured face conveyor and the self-advancing powered roof supports. Note how far the longwall extends into the distance (some could be several hundred yards in length) and the fact that the operator is wearing a face mask, ear defenders, eye protectors and shin guards, as well as the traditional helmet.

A late-1940s advertisement for a 'mechanical coal miner'. Cutting in both directions and eliminating the need for explosives, it would have been state-of-the-art at the time, but such machines would soon be superseded by shearer/loaders.

When it came to the use and manufacture of mechanised coal-cutting equipment, the US was a world leader, thanks in part to the pioneering efforts of inventors like David Joy, whose name is still well-known in the mining world today.

Apart from the first rudimentary disc-type undercutting machines of the late- Victorian and Edwardian periods, one of the earliest forms of large underground equipment was a coal plough, which in its basic form was literally dragged along the face by a chain and guiderail, slicing off coal as it went, but it required reasonably soft coal, so it could not be used in all locations.

In the early days of mechanisation, cutters were hauled along the face by a steel rope or, later, a chain anchored at the end, but a number of serious accidents were caused by chains breaking and ropes 'whipping' along the face. A broken rope would thrash about for several seconds until its energy was dissipated, whereas a chain would kick just once when snapped and then lie still. Although a flying broken link could still kill anyone standing nearby, chains were considered less hazardous — but both methods were eventually replaced by safer systems, such as rack & pinion.

From those early cutters were developed the various forms of cutter-loader, which delivered the freshly-cut coal

Adjustments being made to the top section of a trepanner-type coal cutter and (below) a trepanner on display at Caphouse Colliery showing three separate cutting devices. The small ones on top were roof cutters.

Mechanisation of coal-cutting at the face was only part of the story... the ability to quickly develop new headings to keep pace with ever-increasing demand was also vital and, in this regard, roadheaders such as this Dosco-built machine proved indispensable. The movable arm supporting the rotating picks enabled high, wide roadways to be created, with the conveyor blades around the lower part ensuring rapid removal of the ripped stone.

straight onto an armoured coalface conveyor to eliminate the need to gather it up by hand.

There were two basic forms of cutter – a trepanner (rather gruesomely so called because of its similarity to a surgical instrument used to drill small cylindrical holes in skulls) and a shearer, which worked more like a bacon slicer.

Trepanners had been popular in the 1960s because they produced large lumps, but once the market moved away from railway/industrial/domestic in the 1970s and power stations began requiring crushed coal for blowing into furnaces, shearers became more popular. The development of double-ended ranging drum shearers that could cut high or low in either direction instead of having to return to the start each time was a major breakthrough and virtually doubled production.

Longwall mining techniques such as these also eliminated the need for drilling and blasting of the coalface and, in some cases, a machine was able to cut and load more coal in a few minutes than miners with picks and shovels could in a whole day, although at first, allowances had to be made for the time it took to prepare each end of the face for the next cut. Until the introduction of self-advancing roof supports, it was also a labour-intensive operation to manually move the hydraulic props and conveyor forward each time.

In 1947, 187m tons of coal had been produced by 707,000 miners (264 tons per man) and by 1973, 130m tons were produced by 268,000 miners (485 tons per man). That shows the effect of mechanisation.

Across the industry as a whole, job losses were inevitable; what would have taken 50 men in 1947 was being done by perhaps five by the end of the century, but remote control/monitoring did at least make it possible to remove humans from areas of potential danger.

This was particularly important given the unfortunate propensity of the early cutter/loaders to exacerbate two of the ever-present hazards facing coalminers, one being the huge clouds of dust they threw up. Even with water jets on, it was so bad that men had to retreat to fresher air now and again, yet even so, some still chose not to wear breathing masks or goggles.

The second was the noise. The machines kicked up such a racket in confined spaces that they nullified one of the miners' most valuable senses. No longer could the experienced men hear the roof 'talking' to them – the tell-tale sound of a wooden pit prop beginning to split, the ominous dribble of a little bit of dirt from a roof, a low groan somewhere from the bowels of the earth. All would warn the miner to retreat to a place of safety.

tunnel will
continue
here as
face
advances

1	workshops
2	offices
3	lamp room
4	fan house
5	power house

6	locker rooms, baths & canteen
7	winding houses
8	upcast shaft
9	downcast shaft
10	roadways to distant coal faces
11	coal left to support shafts

CHAPTER 9

Above: Hydraulic roof supports on display in the coalface section of the Scottish Mining Museum at Lady Victoria Colliery. Each chock can weigh up to 40 tonnes. Below: The four stages by which a hydraulic roof-support advanced itself towards the coalface in relation to the armoured face conveyor and the power-loader coal-cutting machine.

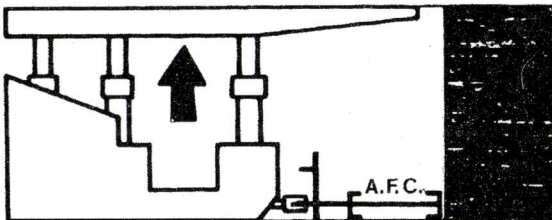

STEP A
The vertical supports are extended to bring the roof beam into contact with the newly exposed roof.

STEP C
The vertical supports are lowered.

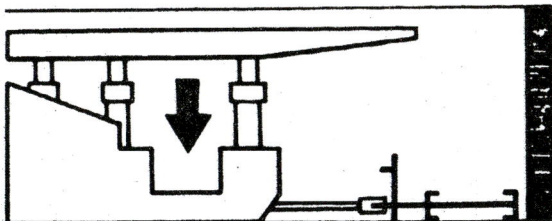

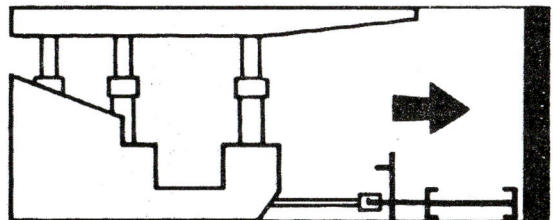

STEP B
The power-loader has passed on the loading run and the double-acting ram is extended, pushing forward the conveyor.

STEP D
The ram is set into reverse and the support is drawn up to the new face line. It is then reset to the roof (step A).

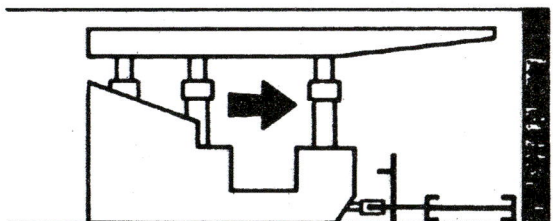

'Distance no object' proclaims this advertisement in a 1960s colliery managers' yearbook. This particular model was a world-beater at the time, using just one drive unit to send coal four miles from face to shaft bottom.

Not for nothing, therefore, did those early machines begin to attract nicknames such as 'the widow-maker'.

In South Wales some drift mines were classified as 'naked light' as they had no gas problems and could thus experiment with early electric machines. A 1920s description of one of the first US-built electric coal-cutters to work in Britain tells us it was powered by a long thick high-voltage cable and drawn by a steel rope travelling at about a yard a minute. Its size made it too wide for pit props to be placed as close to the face as in former days (powered props had not then been introduced) and if it did accidentally touch one of the timber posts, it would chew it to matchwood in seconds and possibly bring tons of rock crashing down.

Such a fall would not damage the machine, as it was heavily armoured with steel plate, but it was extremely hazardous for the miners, who were unable to take avoiding action quickly enough. Lives lost as a result of the 'widow-maker' were partly for that reason and partly because of the huge clouds of dust it threw up in the days before face masks became readily available. On top of that, the falling stones sometimes damaged the high-voltage cable, leaving the risk of a lethal electric shock for anyone who

accidentally came into contact with it.

Seemingly oblivious to the effect on its employees, the mine owners loved the machine's greatly-increased productivity and extended the cutting target from 150 yards a day to 500 yards (it had been a mere 12 yards when cut manually).

Imagine visiting the coalface when such a 1920s cutter was in operation. The machine's roar would be amplified in the confined space, the coal would be splintering and crashing, the operators would be shouting to make themselves heard above the din and if there was no loading belt in use, as many as 30 men would be shovelling coal into tubs, which would be rumbling along the rails behind horses. It was bedlam and it caused many old miners from the much quieter manual days to leave the industry or seek work on the surface.

They had been brought up in a time when miners had a professional respect for the coal and worked it in a skilled and neat fashion – not by "roughly dragging it out by the scruff of its neck".

Overall, however, the advantages of mechanisation massively outweighed the disadvantages and completely revolutionised the industry. Some of the benefits hadn't been immediately obvious; take Blaydon Burn Colliery, for instance, which in the 1950s had a seam of fine coking coal just 14in thick. This was virtually inaccessible until it was found that a remote-controlled device could scrape 100 tons a day from the seam onto a conveyor belt running at right angles to it.

Away from the face, other processes were being sped up too. The 'Lambton Worm' in the Great North Coalfield worked on the principle of a roller-coaster, with a heavily twisting track causing a fast-running train of mine cars to turn upside down so that the coal fell out of each one into a bunker or conveyor before they were returned the right way up again.

The conveyors themselves became wider, faster, stronger and steeper and, on the surface, automation in the coal preparation plants (CPPs) meant they could be left to operate all day with only minimal supervision. The development of new roadways was also sped up by the use of caterpillar-tracked roadheader machines loading onto conveyors and doing away with much of the time-consuming blasting and hand-hewing methods of old.

A perhaps unplanned consequence of the early moves to mechanised cutting and loading at the face was the removal of check-weighing staff (see Chapter 4), for the indiscriminate ripping down of rock and dirt with the coal meant there was no longer any need for tubs or mine cars to be checked for payment purposes.

The new machinery introduced did, however, bring

into existence a new breed of mine worker – the electrician – and by the middle of the 20th century those skilled and qualified men were considered by management and miners alike to be among the most valuable and respected members of underground teams; in fact, once the major mines had been fully modernised, they were almost totally reliant on the repair and maintenance skills of the electricians to keep them running smoothly.

By the 1960s, the world was entering an era of increasing energy alternatives with the growing popularity of gas, oil and nuclear power, and the NCB and its political masters decided that the only way to restore coal's competitiveness was to reduce costs by further mechanising selected large collieries and closing small or high-cost pits that were not considered to be worth modernising. This involved enormous capital investment by the Government of the day, for even in the 1960s and 70s the development cost of a single face could run into seven figures.

By that time there were even nucleonic-steered shearers that could sense automatically the difference between roof stone and coal and thus reduce the amount of waste rock sent to the surface with the coal. These worked by using a cobalt power source to emit particles towards the roof and then measuring the back-scatter to gauge the thickness, as the amounts reflected by coal and stone are different. A small computer in the shearer adjusted the cutting head accordingly. However, after several years of experience, the system was adjudged to be more trouble than it was worth.

As such devices were not common anyway, mechanisation of thin or disturbed seams meant that as much as 30% dirt and stone was being loaded with the coal, a problem particularly prevalent at some Lancashire collieries following mechanisation, hence the need for CPPs to replace less efficient screening methods (see Chapter 11).

The modernisation programme nevertheless enabled massive improvements to be made. As an example, an investment of half a million pounds in South Yorkshire's Wentworth Silkstone Colliery in the early-1950s saw it gain a CPP and a trunk conveyor system linking the face with the plant. This resulted in a huge increase in efficiency almost overnight and its annual output more than doubled from 160,000 tons to 345,000.

Even more successful was the modernised Linby Colliery, in Nottinghamshire, which was recognised as the most efficient in the whole of Europe at one time. It had a workforce of only 1,100 but it was one of only three mines in the UK producing more than a million tons a year in those formative NCB days.

Perhaps the most significant development of the

Record breaker

As if to show his new masters at the NCB what an individual miner could do with only minimal mechanised aids, 37-year-old South Wales miner Edwin Slade, of Pontycymmer, created a world record in 1947 when he won 120 tons of coal during a six-day week shift at International Colliery, Blaengarw, using a hand-held pneumatically-powered pick working a 4ft seam. To achieve that, he also had to shift 20 tons of 'clod' (waste).

modernisation programme, however, was the way the roof was supported at the coalface. Traditionally, timber props had been placed under the roof and tightened with wooden lids knocked into place with sledgehammers; then came hydraulically-operated metal props and, finally, self-advancing powered supports.

The hydraulic mechanism on the latter could be operated so that they would move themselves towards the face after the shearer had passed, and also so that their roof-supporting cantilevers could be elevated to take the strain of the rock above. One machine on its own would not have been able to bear such a weight, but by lining up dozens and dozens of powered roof supports alongside each other, an entire section of newly-exposed roof could be supported, providing a 'corridor of steel' up to 1,000ft in length to protect the men working beneath it.

Although the shields of the hydraulic chocks reached well forward, they could obviously not support the narrow strip of roof above the shearer machine itself, so the approval of the Mines Inspectorate was required before trials could be conducted with the new equipment. It was found that the shearers moved along the face fairly quickly and could be controlled remotely from a position of safety on the goaf side of the conveyor.

So, the strip was unsupported for only the few minutes it took a miner to operate the hydraulic advancing mechanism. As each individual cantilever was lowered and moved, the weight of the roof was taken by the supports either side of it.

The only other thing the operators had to do once the shearer had passed was to move the armoured flexible conveyor by hydraulic ram towards the newly-exposed part of the face, the conveyor being composed of loosely-linked sections so that it could be 'snaked' into position. With modern roof supports, this part of the operation is undertaken automatically as part of the advancing procedure.

The fact that both the cutters and the conveyors were heavily armoured meant they would not be damaged if any part of the roof did happen to fall. Developed by the German mining industry, armoured face conveyors were appropriately known (by the NCB as well as the men) as 'Panzers'.

Automation of the cutting-and-loading process was known as continuous mining and was so successful that coal became competitive on the world markets again.

By the mid-1970s, more than 90% of all Britain's coal was being won by cutter/loaders. Three-quarters of the nation's coalfaces used shearers, 22% used trepanners and the remaining 3% mainly used ploughs. Hand-winning of coal, which had accounted for 99% of output in 1900, had thus been totally eradicated everywhere, except in a tiny handful of small privately-owned drift mines.

Following the installation of such machinery in large NCB pits, outputs of a million tons a year per colliery became reasonably frequent. The British mine that hit the magic million tons in the shortest time was Bentinck, Nottinghamshire which, in 1969, achieved it by July 25, not much more than halfway through the year.

Automation allowed coal preparation plants to be left to run virtually all day without human involvement and huge reductions even became possible in the size of teams at the coalface, where a single powered roof support could have as many as three micro-computers managing its auto-mated functions.

In fact, if desired, the entire underground environment could be monitored from a surface-based control room, enabling critical factors such as gas concentrations, venti-lation levels and temperature readings to be checked and adjusted remotely if necessary. In practice though, many mine operators preferred to keep a human presence at the 'cutting edge' and that remains the case today in many countries.

Mechanisation began in a small way but by the end of the 20th century it had grown to such an extent that it had completely changed the way many coal mines looked externally. In place of the traditional look typified by the images on pages 30 and 45 came a maze of covered conveyors rising and falling in all directions, as typified in these views of the modernised collieries at Ollerton (top) and Kellingley.

CHAPTER 10

Working above ground

Life on the surface

A BIG COLLIERY in the heyday of mining was effectively a self-contained industrial plant, employing its own fitters, mechanics, electricians, engineers, welders, joiners, blacksmiths, bricklayers, plumbers, farriers, stable lads, loco crews, shunters, cage-smiths and wagon repairers, not to mention administrative staff such as managers, deputies, surveyors, accountants and clerks.

The nationalised era saw much of the routine overhaul of machinery transferred to central workshops, which served several mines – but the pits themselves retained a surprisingly high number of surface-based disciplines, particularly those of electricians, fitters, shunting crews and office staff.

Photographs of collieries in the early half of the century often show plumes of steam emanating from various parts of the site. In addition to the winding engines, there were steam-driven compressors for underground equipment and steam-driven turbines for machinery on the surface. Many early ventilation fans were also steam-powered and in winter months, large braziers would be used at the top

Collieries in the heyday of mining a century or so ago had a characteristic look about them, almost invariably distinguished by myriad plumes of steam from various boiler houses. Tall smokestacks, private-owner wagons and piles of coal completed the image, as typified in this view of International Colliery at Blaengarw, depicted on one of many postcards made popular from the Edwardian era onwards.

Following the introduction of 'Merry-Go-Round' (MGR) deliveries of pulverised coal direct from colliery to power station, huge rapid loaders were constructed. BR Coal sector-allocated Class 58 No.58004 takes a train through the loader at Bentinck Colliery in January 1994. RAIL PHOTOPRINTS

of the downcast shaft to warm the air before it entered the mine to prevent the pipes in the shaft from freezing.

All those steam-powered machines were fed by boiler houses, some of which were absolutely immense and could house as many as 16 'Lancashire-type' stationary boilers with their attendant pipework and staff. Most boilers would naturally be fired by coal but some were adapted to burn excess methane captured from the mine workings.

Some pits also had steam or electrically-driven capstan engines for shaft maintenance and rope-changing. If a main winding engine was out of action for any reason, central workshops would have a lorry-based, diesel-powered emergency winder that could be taken to any colliery in the area that required it.

In the years before the National Grid, collieries generated their own power, which they mainly did via large stationary steam engines, but from the late Victorian period onwards, several became self-sufficient to the point of possessing small power stations and electricity networks. They were able to do away with those once the National Grid had been fully established in 1938, but the last few self-contained NCB electricity networks weren't discontinued until the 1970s.

Power stations at some of the larger collieries could generate currents as high as 2,200v AC, stepped down through transformers to much lower strengths for colliery machinery purposes, and several even had sufficient capacity to supply their local village with electricity...but to prevent abuse or wastage, some had a system whereby if a householder attempted to have more than three 60W bulbs on at the same time, a switch would kick in and flick the lights on and off until the load was reduced!

In 1882, Pleasley, near Mansfield, became the first colliery in Britain to have electric lighting at the pit bottom and 1910 saw the country's first all-electric mine – Britannia, in Monmouthshire. Electric generators and dynamos didn't simply allow use of electric tools and winding gear, they generated power to operate compressed air equipment too.

The amount of separate surface buildings to be found on a typical coal mine site was impressive. Perhaps not immediately springing to mind for most people asked to make a list of such buildings would be the powder magazine (explosives store). These were always located well away from the other surface structures and kept securely locked when not in use. When underground, explosives and detonators were almost invariably kept apart from each other and were carried in specially-modified drams or wagons.

In areas where the coal was suitable, many large mines also had a coking works attached to them (see Chapter 16). Others, especially in the Midlands, might be accompanied by a brickworks. Bricks became cheaper to make when coal,

The superbly preserved and presented pit bank at Lady Victoria Colliery, south of Edinburgh. The two loaded mine cars in the middle are posed as though they have just left the cage and the two in the foreground are on the 'tub circuit' heading for the washery screens.

rather than charcoal, was used to bake them and, in some cases, the clay was produced from the mine. In others, an opencast clay pit might be dug nearby.

The NCB inherited 85 brickworks in 1947, producing about 400m bricks a year. The company itself consumed about 25% of the bricks made by its collieries, using them for the construction of new mine buildings and for lining shafts and pit bottom areas. By 1973, only 19 such works remained and they were sold that year to the private sector, but a reminder of the old days can still be found by the presence of a brickyard on the site of Desford Colliery, near Leicester.

Because the sheer volume of large heavy equipment required at the bottom of a mine was so great – especially while new roads were being driven and new faces opened up – it was normally necessary to have a large open-air stockyard compound on the colliery premises in which to store roof-supporting arches, spare items of machinery, lengths of railway track and, in former years, freshly-delivered timber props and so on. These large areas were in addition to the colliery stores building, where small items were kept.

One of the largest buildings at a traditional major colliery would have been the workshop for repairing, maintaining and even manufacturing equipment. The district's railway locomotives would sometimes be overhauled there too.

Tall factory-style chimneys were a common sight at traditional mines and one of their prime uses was to create a draught for the boilers. The steam winding engines exhausted separately (or their steam was condensed and the water re-used). Stale air exhausted out of the mine workings by the ventilation fan exited through a wide-rimmed, tapered concrete or metal tower called an evasee. It was important to keep the gassy air and coal dust extracted by the fan separate from any other form of chimney due to the risk of an explosion.

Grimethorpe (few names summed up southerners' perception of a colliery location better than that!) was one of many gassy mines with a methane-drainage system that recovered burnable gas for the boilers. Piping the gas to the surface also reduced its concentration.

Methane-exhausting pipes can still be seen on the sites of several demolished collieries to this day, even in the midst of some modern housing estates – and there are two black pipes near the car park of Sunderland Football Club allowing methane to escape from the workings of the old Wearmouth Colliery, on whose site the stadium has been built.

Another common sight at collieries, particularly older ones, would be settling ponds, normally in a row of three

Among the many items of machinery found on the surface of a traditional colliery were stationary boilers. These were used for the heating or powering of plant and were of several types – 'Egg-ended' and 'Lancashire' types being the most common. Four of the latter are seen at Staffordshire's Chatterley Whitfield Colliery in September 2015.

The upcast winder cable drum at Pleasley Colliery, seen during an open day in September 2015. Both the steam winding engines at this mine near Mansfield have been preserved.

The stock yards of major collieries were almost businesses in their own right, holding and supplying replacement parts for the thousands of different components used above and below the ground. This was part of the sprawling yard at Markham Colliery in March 1993. NICK PIGOTT

Mineworkers were renowned for their sense of humour, as evidenced by this sign at Rufford Colliery in 1992.

or four at slightly descending levels, which helped separate slurry and water. Many of these remained even after the installation of sophisticated coal processing plants. For fresh water purposes, a well or borehole would exist wherever the water-bearing measures were found to be suitable.

In addition to the headgear, some modern mines possessed other tall concrete structures, similar to silos. These were pit top bunkers that could be used either for blending coal of different qualities (a process known as 'sweetening') or for regularising the coal flow to the preparation plant so that if a delay occurred on the surface, the storage facilities could be brought into play and the winding of coal would not be affected. At its peak in the 1960s Calverton Colliery was operating nine faces at once, hence the need for storage and blending bunkers. Some large mines had additional bunkers underground too.

Among other large concrete structures on the surface were rapid-loading bunkers of around 5,000 tons capacity for depositing coal into main line railway wagons, conical-shaped water/slurry towers, screens, washeries and power stations for providing electrical energy for the mine

Lagoons and settling ponds were common sights at collieries in their heyday, but although Pleasley Colliery has escaped demolition, this view from April 1984 is no longer possible, as the reservoir has been filled in. ROBIN STEWART-SMITH

A main line train driver's view of the rapid loading bunker at Kellingley as a Merry-Go-Round service arrives to collect another load in the 1990s. This scene is absolutely typical of the way colliery surfaces turned to morasses of grey slurry every time it rained. DAVE DARWIN

An aspect of surface working now long disappeared is the rope haulage system, which enabled standard gauge wagons to be worked on far steeper inclines than would be possible with locomotive haulage. This example was photographed at Kilmersdon Colliery in the Somerset coalfield in 1970. COLOUR-RAIL

(and sometimes for the local village too).

Smaller surface structures included locomotive sheds, fan houses, timber stockyards, lamp rooms, pump houses, stores, blacksmiths' forges, joiners' shops, electricians' and fitters' cabins, administrative offices, fire stations, medical and ambulance centres, shower and canteen blocks and, in later years, a maze of elevated, covered conveyers linking numerous parts of colliery infrastructure.

The advent of computerisation enabled remote control and digital equipment to be installed on the surface to automatically operate underground conveyers, bunkers, pumps and fans. At some collieries whose coal-raising shafts were equipped for skip-loading, even the headgear was automatically controlled.

Add the omnipresent spoil tip, more often than not towering over the scene like a brooding mountain, and it was not uncommon for some larger collieries to extend over a mile in length.

CHAPTER 11

Washeries, screens and preparation plants

Making the coal fit to sell

THE COAL that came up to the surface was referred to as 'run-of-mine' and in the mechanised era it was usually mixed with shale and other forms of non-flammable rock from the strata above and below the coal seam.

In order to make it marketable, it had to be cleaned and graded and this is where screens and washeries came into play. Almost every colliery in the 20th century had some form of screen building – or at least the use of one within a short distance – and from the middle of the century onwards, the major modernised mines began to have their washeries replaced by larger, more sophisticated installations known as coal preparation plants (CPPs).

A CPP improves marketability by removing stone and dirt and by sizing and grading the product to ensure that a higher proportion is saleable. It also improves profitability by reclaiming small pieces of coal that would otherwise have ended up on the waste tip.

The old form of screens basically comprised a large elevated building on strong steel, concrete or timber stilts straddling a row of sidings on which would stand main line railway wagons. Most buildings contained rudimentary washing facilities and some form of conveyor known as a 'picking belt', beside which would stand workers who hand-sorted the coal and identified the shale and other rocks – quickly lifting them off the belt and throwing them on to a waste pile.

Such visual separation of unwanted minerals was to continue at some collieries for many years, but the sizing part of the process soon began to be semi-automated by the introduction of vibrating shaker screens and different-sized sieves, allowing the smallest pieces to fall through, while the largest continued until reaching the widest apertures.

In each case they would fall by gravity into waiting wagons below – a row of vehicles for each size.

Anything that didn't go into the wagons was sent to the spoil tip, usually by internal-user wagons, a conveyor belt or an aerial ropeway. Depending on how efficient the washery building's exterior cladding was, a thick pall of dust could often be seen hanging around the outside of the structure whenever the screens were in operation, making driving conditions hazardous if there were any public roads nearby.

Removing waste from run-of-mine (ROM) coal was important as it reduced impurities and thus increased the value of the product by making it more attractive to customers. By taking out heavy stone, it also reduced transport costs.

There were many sizes of coal marketed by coal merchants or supplied to specialist users, the main categories being: large cobbles, cobbles, trebles, doubles, singles, nuts, beans and peas. A cobble would typically measure about six inches by four (15cm x 10), a nut about two inches by one, while anything gravel-sized would be grouped under terms such as smalls, grains or slack. Particle-sized specks were known as fines, but as the majority of customers in the early years wanted only large lumps for domestic or industrial use, there wasn't a great deal of commercial need for the tiny sizes.

In fact, some coal owners in the Victorian era refused to pay their self-employed or piece-rate colliers anything for small coal, even though the men still had to hew it from the coalface! Forks rather than shovels had to be used in some mines to ensure no smalls got into the tubs. The advent of large coal-fired power stations in the second half of the 20th century changed all that, as most required pulverised coal.

In the years when the engines on the surface were all

The coal preparation plant, clarifier tower and rapid loader at Bilsthorpe Colliery in 1993 – a far cry from the early 20th century picking belt scene on the right, with ten pit brow lasses and three men doing their best to spot and remove stone from the coal as it moves quickly past them on a conveyor. Photo left: M THURLOW/COLOUR-RAIL

driven by steam, fines were sometimes mixed with dried slurry effluent recovered from the washery and fed into boilers, but otherwise small pieces simply ended up on spoil heaps.

Many of the picking table workers in the pre-mechanisation era were females, displaced from their duties underground as a result of law changes in the Victorian era (see Chapter 5), and they were supplemented by lads aged about 14 to 16 and former miners, some of whom had perhaps suffered a serious injury in the past and were no longer fit enough or young enough for heavier tasks. It was boring, repetitive and demanding work that required constant attention, but it provided regular employment.

A coal preparation plant, on the other hand, was a totally different beast altogether and the NCB built about 200 of these huge structures between 1947 and 1956, following that with modernisation of less sophisticated ones it had inherited at 170 or so other pits.

In a CPP, automated machinery and complicated technology took the place of humans, sorting or crushing the coal to the required sizes, reducing waste and making the mine far more efficient and profitable. Not only did it take the laborious manpower out of coal separation and sizing, but it retrieved the tiny particles of fines and dust that had previously been allowed to go to waste.

Designs of CPP differed depending on the manufacturer, but a great many British collieries were equipped with the Baum system, based on a design by German engineer Fritz Baum and later improved upon in what became known as the 'dense medium system'. Its principle of operation hinges on the fact that coal has a lower density and specific gravity than shale and other rock and will thus 'float' in certain liquids.

After passing under a powerful electro-magnet (to remove bits of wire and scrap metal that may have been picked up underground), the mixed minerals enter a large 'washbox' whose water has been made denser by the addition of sand or a pulverised iron oxide such as magnetite. Bursts of compressed air are sent through the liquid and the pulsations cause the mixed coal, shale and dirt to become separated into different layers as they are jigged about. The heaviest pieces of stone sink immediately and are removed from the plant.

The coal and middle-sized pieces of waste then pass into a secondary compartment, from where the dirt drops through a screen to be discarded, while the clean coal flows out over the top of the tank and is taken for classifying.

This process is linked with another environmentally-friendly procedure — the recycling of water. As the dirty liquid leaves the washbox, it is pumped to the top of a Baum tower, a conical-shaped concrete settling and clarifying tank. There, the solids are allowed to slowly sink to the bottom and form a slurry, while the clear water at the top is piped to the washbox for re-use.

In pre-CPP days, the slurry and the large quantities of fines it contained would have been sent to settling lagoons, from which the slurry would eventually be removed by grab-crane, but under the more sophisticated process, the fines are moved to what is known as the 'froth flotation process'. This is an ingenious system in which an oil-based frothing agent is added to the water to form an emulsion and create air bubbles. As the bubbles rise to the surface, the minute particles of coal are persuaded to stick to the outside of them by means of surface tension and effectively 'hitch a ride' to the top. The specks of dirt and shale, being a fraction heavier, remain behind.

The coal-laden froth is then skimmed off and moved to a bath beneath a large, hollow rotating metal drum, inside which a partial vacuum has been created. As the drum slowly rotates through the froth, the vacuum causes the

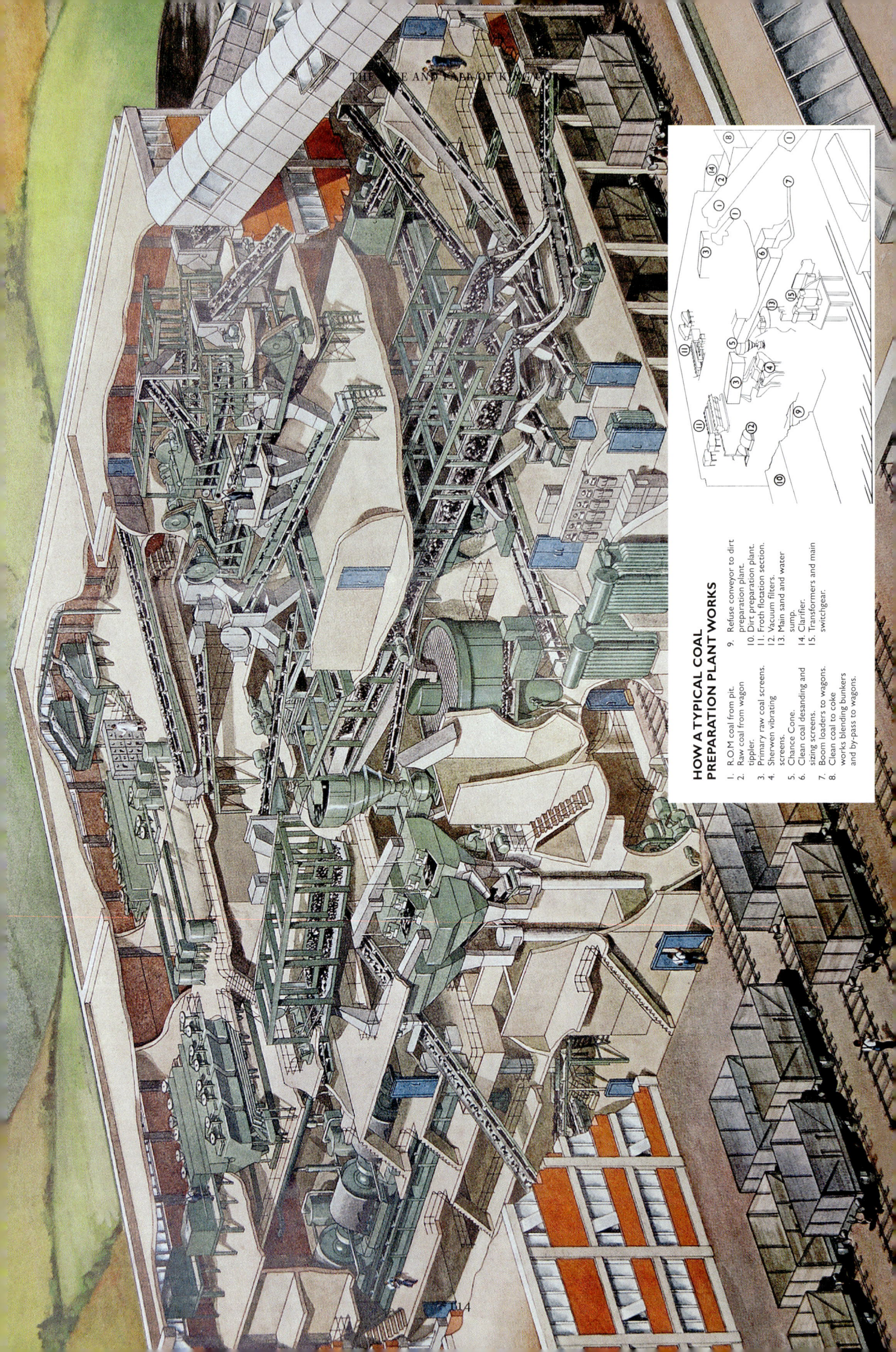

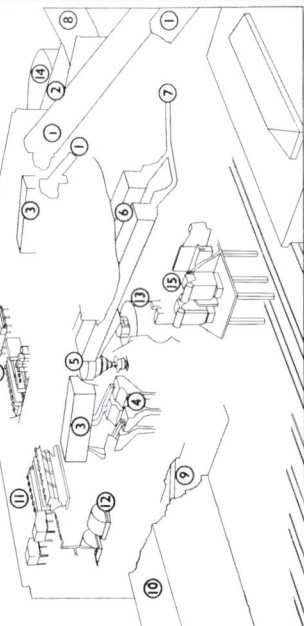

HOW A TYPICAL COAL PREPARATION PLANT WORKS

1. R.O.M coal from pit.
2. Raw coal from wagon tippler.
3. Primary raw coal screens.
4. Sherwen vibrating screens.
5. Chance Cone.
6. Clean coal desanding and sizing screens.
7. Boom loaders to wagons.
8. Clean coal to coke works blending bunkers and by-pass to wagons.
9. Refuse conveyor to dirt preparation plant.
10. Dirt preparation plant.
11. Froth flotation section.
12. Vacuum filters.
13. Main sand and water sump.
14. Clarifier.
15. Transformers and main switchgear.

A rarely-seen view taken from the top level of a full-size gravity-fed coal preparation plant in operation showing the water rushing through the washbox far below. A description of the coal washing and reclamation process can be found in the main text. NICK PIGOTT

particles to adhere to a belt around the drum, forming a filter cake, which is then blown off by air and collected.

The rejected particles (known as 'tailings') then have a chemical re-agent added to make them flocculate into clumps and are sent to a thickener tank, where they are churned by revolving rakes and sink to the bottom to once again leave clear and reusable water on top. The sediment is then sent to a de-watering press from where it is safely disposed of while the liquid is pumped back for re-use. This effective closed-circuit ensures that no polluted effluent finds its way into natural water courses.

It might be wondered why so much effort has been invested in retrieving particles of coal almost too small to be seen by the naked eye, but power stations require pulverised coal as it is blown into their boiler furnaces and a big 'prep plant' could recover 100 tons or more of particles a day. When all that material is added together over the course of a year, it can amount to 50,000 tons of profitable energy-generating coal. In earlier years, when most colliery output had to be in the form of large chunks for railway, industrial or household use, slurry-processing wouldn't have been necessary.

The other reason, of course, is that without CPPs it was difficult to get water clean enough to recycle efficiently into the system, meaning that collieries would constantly have to be paying for fresh water supplies if they didn't have access to a well, borehole or river. A further advantage is that processing helps reduce harmful emissions by removing impurities.

Preparation plants have traditionally been large tall buildings with multiple levels to maximise the use of gravity flow, but towards the end of the deep mining industry there was a trend towards single-level facilities with more of the slurry being moved by pumps instead of gravity. Following the 2013 closure of Warwickshire's Daw Mill Colliery, UK Coal moved an example of this more modern type to Nottinghamshire to replace a life-expired multiple-level facility at Thoresby.

Although Britain's deep shaft mines have all gone, a handful of washery preparation units remain in operation at surface mines, where the more productive but less selective nature of opencast excavation makes it difficult to produce coal clean enough for sale without processing. By 2025, those too are expected to have disappeared.

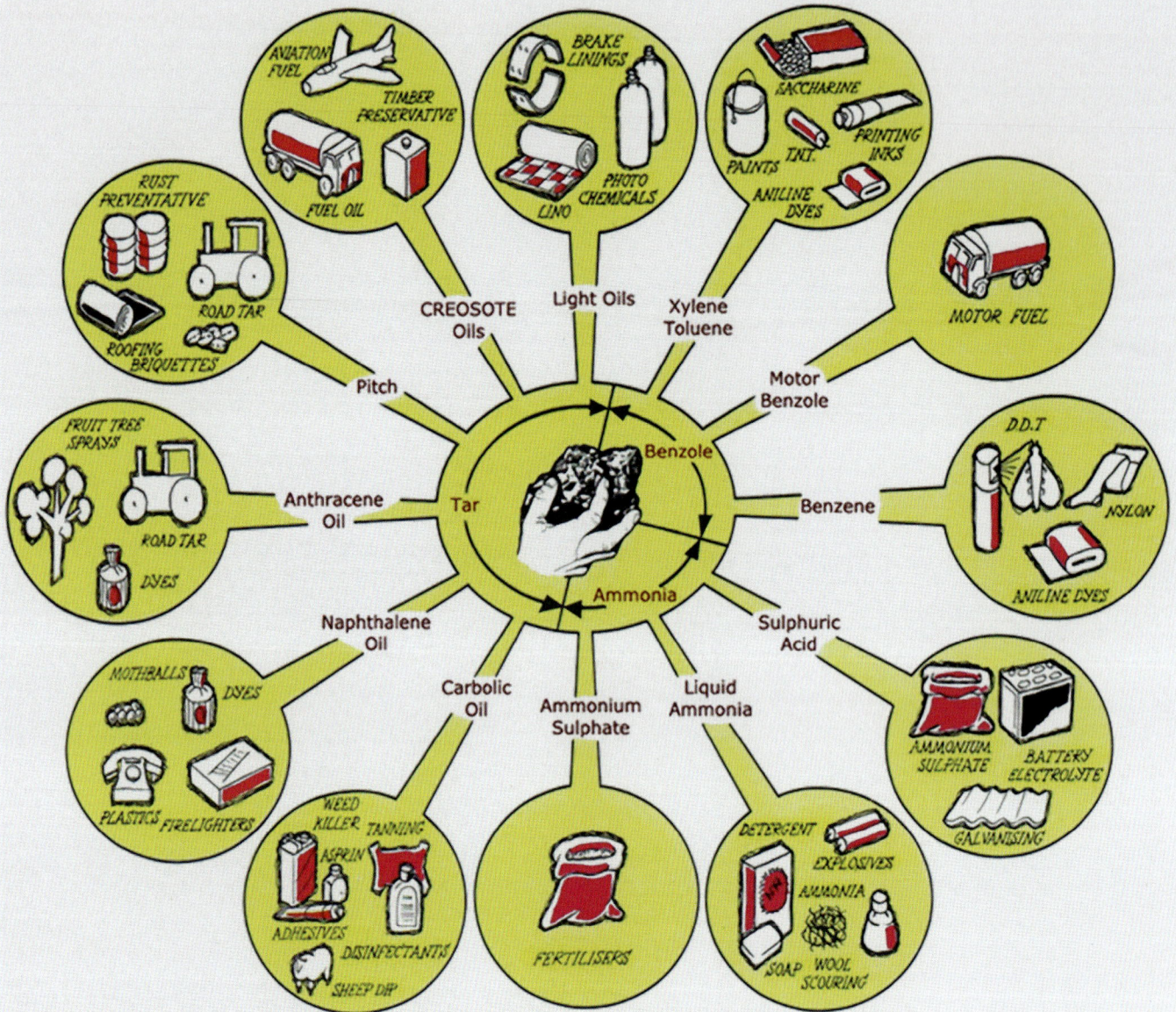

The many uses for coal

A SURPRISING VARIETY of everyday household products are created from coal and there are many other uses to which the by-products of coal and coke have been put to, once they have been processed (some indirectly).

The main by-products are benzene, ammonia and tar, and from those, combined with other ingredients, can be gained the following: margarine, washing powder, baking powder, soap, mothballs, nylon, linoleum, aspirin, saccharin, waxed toilet paper, wax oil, fertilisers, sheep dips, weedkillers, insecticides, disinfectants, sulphuric acid, road tar, dyes, explosives, firelighters, adhesives, plastics, motor fuel, aviation fuel, creosote, brake linings, battery electrolyte, rust preventative, fruit tree sprays, ammonia, photo chemicals, golf balls, clay pigeons, inks, paints ... and even perfume!

The diagram shows some of the many remarkably-varied uses to which coal and its by-products can be used.
Courtesy Healeyhero.co.uk

An aerial view of Snibston Colliery, Coalville, in the 1980s, demonstrating how much larger and higher the modern coal preparation and loading plant (centre) was compared with the original mine buildings on the right. History has turned full circle here... the CPP is no more and the now-preserved colliery is back to its original size.

When things go wrong!

THOSE WORKING in the washery buildings of collieries in the old days did a grand job of screening out unwanted objects, but it was inevitable that a few 'foreign bodies' would slip the net.

In the years when mechanical coaling plants were in use on Britain's railways (1920s-1960s), whole wagons were often hoisted bodily up the tower-like plants so that their contents could be tipped into hoppers for dropping into the tenders of main line steam locomotives.

It was inevitable that items of colliery waste would end up in tenders along with railway dross such as firebricks and loose wagon planks, but nothing could prepare the staff at London's Cricklewood engine shed for the day a loco fireman spotted some coalface detonators in a tender just as he was about to shovel them into the fire!

No-one knew how many more explosives had been accidentally tipped out of the coaling tower, so panic-stricken managers had to spend the next hour or so desperately trying to track down which engines had been dispatched from the depot with the means to kill or maim unsuspecting firemen and drivers. Fortunately, the miniature bombs were all found before they could explode.

On another notorious occasion, an outlet chute jammed open on the Exmouth Junction tower and buried a 'King Arthur' class 4-6-0 under 300 tons of coal! It took three days to retrieve it.

The screens at Mansfield Colliery, seen in 1989, were a good example of the large multi-tracked type found at many major collieries in earlier decades.
ROBIN STEWART-SMITH

A rare peep into the top of a high-level Baum tower containing unclarified liquid. In the background can be seen Eggborough power station and in the far distance, Drax power station

In recent years, coal preparation plants became smaller as pumps took over from gravity feed for movement of the fluids through the system. This one at Thoresby Colliery in 2015 had been at Daw Mill until two years earlier, being moved in component form and re-erected at its new location.

Beamish Colliery is one place where traditional colliery screens can still be seen. Lewin 0-4-0ST No.18 is pictured underneath them with a rake of chaldron waggons.

CHAPTER 12

Spoil heaps

Man-made mountains

IN THE Wigan area of Lancashire in the 1930s, author George Orwell referred to a "lunar landscape of slag heaps" as far as the eye could see and recorded that they were often on fire.

"At night, you can see the red rivulets of fire winding this way and that. Overhead are steel pylons and cables where tubs of dirt travel slowly across the countryside."

His vivid description could have described almost any coalfield scene at that time, for the heaps towered over almost every colliery and told travellers for miles around that they were approaching a mining community. Even today, it is still possible with a trained eye to detect the sites of many former collieries from their tips, even though they've usually been landscaped or planted with grass or trees and turned into country parks.

The tendency of tips to smoulder or spontaneously burst into flames led during the Second World War to water having to be sprayed onto some to stop them giving the position of the mine away to crews of enemy bombers.

Spoil heaps are sometimes known as shale heaps as that's what many of them largely comprise. Other terms are waste tips, pit hills, muck stacks, batches or bings, the various terms emanating from different geographical regions, with bing being more widely used in Scotland and muck stack in Yorkshire.

Probably as a result of being popularised by Orwell, the term 'slag heap' is used extensively by the popular media, but is, strictly speaking, incorrect, as slag is a product of the ore-smelting industry. Few working in the coal industry would have used such a phrase, except perhaps as a slang term, and the words dirt, waste, reject, discard, rubbish and rock were more commonly used.

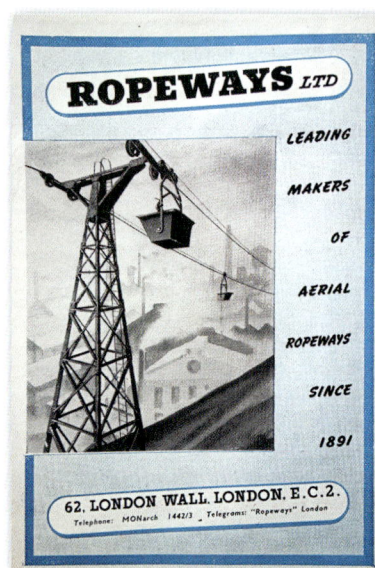

Some collieries, especially if in built-up areas or hemmed in by roads or railways, were cut off from their spoil heaps and so they sent the waste shale and dirt out by aerial ropeway, each container automatically rotated by treadle to tip out its contents. These twin-cable ropeways, some of which could be a mile or so in length, were quite common in mining areas at one time and although no colliery examples have survived in Britain, there is still one conveying shale to a brickworks at Claughton Moor, in Lancashire.

The aerial ropeways that sometimes linked the tips to the collieries also had a nickname, called 'Blondins' in some areas after the French tightrope walker.

Some spoil heaps can cover several acres and be more than a mile long and members of the public could be forgiven for wondering why so much waste was produced by the mining industry: it didn't use to be. When coal was worked by hand in the 19th century, colliers were paid less if they allowed too much dirt to enter their tubs, so it was

A highly nostalgic and evocative landscape portraying the coalmining industry in its NCB heyday. The year is 1966 and British Railways Class 4MT 2-6-0 No.43123 is running past Ashington Colliery's spoil heap with a train of loaded BR coal wagons as the mine's aerial ropeway goes about its business. Note the protective structure erected over the railway to prevent spillages of rock and spoil falling onto trains or even onto the nearby signalbox. On the right, a crane is loading a rake of wooden-bodied internal user wagons. RAIL PHOTOPRINTS

Many large spoil heaps were graded level on the top by earth-moving equipment, but some retained their characteristic cone shapes. This was Blaenafon Colliery in 1973. BRIAN SHARPE

in their interests to ensure as little wastage as possible was sent to the surface.

The waste stone was often used to fill the goaf and to build packs along the roadways – but in the mechanisation revolution of the second half of the 20th century, the whole seam, including dirt bands and adjacent stone, was wrenched off by machines and transferred directly to conveyor belts, so perhaps only 70 to 80% of what was wound to the surface was coal.

In fact, at Kent's Betteshanger Colliery (which didn't close until 1989), as much as two tons of dirt was produced for every ton of clean coal and it was said that the waste tip there was the largest ongoing civil engineering site in the county apart from the Channel Tunnel construction site!

As explained in the previous chapter, it was possible to compensate for this apparent flagrancy by enormous advances in coal washing and preparation techniques, with highly-efficient automatic screens and reclamation systems doing what huge teams of pickers used to do.

In the early-1960s, environmental issues began to see a change of policy at some locations, with ways being found to stow more waste in the goaf instead of it being taken to the surface. At Lewis Merthyr Colliery, the stone did actually come up the shaft but it was then crushed to fist size by a special hopper and sent back under the ground, where it was either blown into the goaf by compressed air or mixed with concrete to help build the side walls of new roadways. Stowing the stone that way was an expensive and time-consuming process, however, and it didn't make financial sense for many mines. In fact, it could make the difference between a pit being profitable or not, so most waste continued to be sent to the tips.

Britain's general switch from advance to retreat mining, in which the goaf did not need to be packed with stone for roof support, contributed to the increase in surface waste and, after the Aberfan tragedy in 1966 (see Chapter 15), new regulations stipulated that spoil had to be spread in thin layers by bulldozers or graders and be compacted before the next batch could be added. Kellingley Colliery, which opened in 1965 never had a large tip at all. Instead, its spoil went in fleets of lorries to nearby Gale Common to build embankments containing power station fly ash. The waste from Arkwright Colliery was used to fill a railway tunnel at Duckmanton, while Linby Colliery's was used to cover an entire disused railway marshalling yard at Annesley on the old Great Central main line.

Nevertheless, 'slag heaps' were back in the national media headlines again in 2013 when part of the vast tip at Hatfield Colliery slid down and undermined all four tracks of an adjacent main line railway, which had to be closed for several months while the spoil was removed and the line rebuilt.

Given the number of years mechanised operations dispatched waste to the tips – half a century or more in some cases – it's easy to understand why heaps grew to such enormous sizes, but most have since been landscaped, lowered or eradicated completely to reduce risks or simply to remove what many people considered to be an eyesore.

In 2013, the spoil heap of Yorkshire's Hatfield Colliery slipped and undermined an adjacent main line railway, throwing the tracks onto their side and closing the line for months. This incident should not be confused with subsidence (see next chapter). NICK PIGOTT

CHAPTER 13

Subsidence and surveying

Rolling country!

N EAR THE Staffordshire village of Himley is a pub whose patrons feel the effects of alcohol before they've even lifted a glass! It is the Crooked House and it's four feet lower on one side than the other.

The building was condemned in the 1940s but rescued by a brewery company, which used buttresses and girders to make it safe.

The inn's lop-sided appearance is caused by mining subsidence dating back to the 1800s when one of its previous owners, Sir Stephen Glynne, ordered his men to remove more coal from deep beneath the building than was good for it. It is a graphic reminder of what can happen in the mining industry when things don't go to plan.

In most strata, the amount of subsidence is relatively predictable and as most undermined areas were in the countryside, damage was usually limited to cracks in farm buildings or collapsed drainage channels in fields. In those cases, the mining company paid compensation or

The effects of mining subsidence can be seen quite clearly in this view of the Coalville-Leicester line alongside the former Ellistown Colliery. Negotiating the dip at slow speed in February 2015 are Type 1 diesel locos Nos.20107, 20096, 20132 and 20118 working a new London Underground train from Derby Works to a test centre established on the site of Asfordby Colliery, near Melton Mowbray. NICK PIGOTT

No, you've not been drinking! The Crooked House pub at Himley in Staffordshire really does lean at this drunken angle, a victim of ancient mining subsidence.

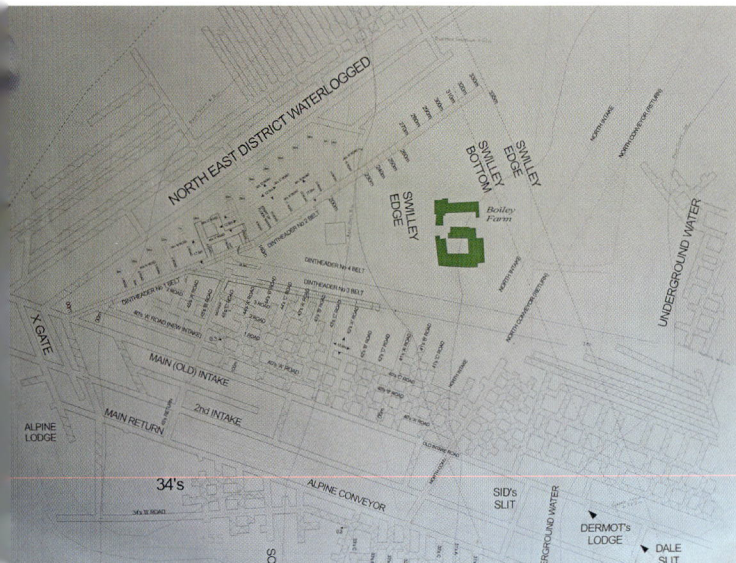

An example of a surveyor's underground working plan indicating the position of the main intake and return airways, the headings and gates, the waterlogged areas and any surface buildings that need to be avoided. Note also the 'pillar & stall' nature of extraction and the identification numbers of the various faces.

could, if necessary, be partially packed with stones before the roof was allowed to cave in, thus reducing the effect on the surface.

Where important buildings or strategic infrastructure such as railway lines were concerned, it was possible to prevent subsidence by leaving unworked pillars of coal underneath them; indeed, in former times, railway companies were able to purchase pillars of unworked coal under their property for precisely that reason. Surprisingly, few did so however, with the result that some routes were quite badly affected, the Leicester-Coalville line near Ellistown being a good example.

Something not always appreciated by laymen is that badly-undulating colliery branches could present drivers of long coal trains with perhaps as many as three changes of gradient within a single train-length. In the days of loose-coupled wagons, such situations called for exceptional skill and co-operation between driver and guard.

SURVEYING: There was an unusual accident in January 1969 when a new loading bunker at Sharlston Colliery in Yorkshire collapsed, destroying three British Rail wagons. The bunker had been built in the vicinity of an ancient mineshaft that had not shown up on old plans or been detected by preliminary boring.

That incident underlined the importance to the mining industry of surveyors. Theirs was one of the most important

undertook rectification, but it was inevitable that urban areas were affected too sometimes.

The reason there were relatively few claims compared with the vast tonnages of coal removed over the centuries was due to the packing of worked-out areas with stone and other waste to help support the roof. Even with the more modern form of retreat mining, the worked-out void

but unsung departments in a mine. Not only did they ensure roadways were driven in the right direction but they were responsible for constantly updating underground working plans (daily in some cases) and predicting when road-headers and coalface cutters were due to pass beneath important surface locations. By law, the plan had to be updated at least every 12 weeks or within 100 yards of underground progress, whichever came first.

Another important role of the surveyors was the charting of workings in areas where there was a likelihood of coal having been dug in an earlier century. This was to prevent miners suddenly breaking into a disused gallery or even plunging into one at a lower level.

Water was the big fear in this regard. As it wasn't always possible to predict exactly where ancient workings were, test borings had to be made to prevent men inadvertently cracking the wall of a water-filled cavity, as seven South Wales miners tragically did while shot-firing a coalface at Gleision Colliery as recently as 2011, four of them losing their lives.

An accidental breakthrough into the workings of a neighbouring mine could also alter the ventilation flows of both collieries, with possibly disastrous results for the men of both concerns.

Methods of surveying improved over the years, one way being for a seismic survey team to make small explosions on the ground. Based on the time it takes the shockwaves to travel through the earth, it is possible to tell what kind of rocks lie beneath.

Until 1942, when the state took legal ownership of coal and certain other mineral rights as a wartime measure, most owners of surface land owned the rights to what lay below and that caused untold problems for colliery owners and their surveyors; the Wigan Coal Corporation, for instance, once had to negotiate with no fewer than 1,200 different landowners and lessors, and deal with their relevant royalty claims, in order to extend a coalfield.

Fortunately for the advance of the industry, many colliery proprietors in the early years were noblemen who owned the surface estates anyway, but just one refusal could cause huge problems for surveyors attempting to plot straight roadways.

The potential risks of subsidence were at their worst in heavily built-up areas, as can be appreciated from this photograph of Bradford Colliery which, despite its name, was in the heart of Manchester.

CHAPTER 14

Ventilation

Too little air, too much heat

VENTILATION SOUNDS a straightforward enough subject, but it was one of the most important aspects of mining operation – if not **the** most important.

Air didn't just serve the vital purpose of keeping miners alive by supplying fresh oxygen; it also performed the role of removing methane, carbon dioxide and coal dust from the atmosphere, as well as partly compensating for the high levels of heat generated in the bowels of the earth.

Too little ventilation and those problems would all occur; too much ventilation and there was a risk in some mines of creating an environment conducive to spontaneous combustion.

The upcast and downcast air-circulation principle dates back to the days when bellpits began to be knocked through into each other and it was noticed that this had the effect of improving the strength and freshness of the flow, particularly when one shaft was deeper than the other.

As underground layouts began to expand in the 16th and 17th centuries, supplementary air was often pumped in using hand-worked bellows and ran through the galleries on its way to an exhaust shaft, but that meant that the men working at the far end of the mine received foul air, so mines began to be divided into districts by the use of air-doors to ensure that different sections all received similar amounts of fresh air. Without the doors, the air would take the shortest route from one shaft to another, leaving all other parts of the mine unventilated.

Downcast air (also known as intake air) is fresh and upcast (also known as return air) is foul or stale.

To create a draught for ventilation in the early years, a furnace would be lit at the bottom of the upcast shaft

and the hot air from it would rise, causing the colder and denser air in the downcast shaft to flow downwards through the mine's roadways and gateways. The problem with furnaces, of course, was that they created a large naked flame underground – the last thing needed with methane in the offing – so they were eventually phased out in favour of powerful electric extractor fans fixed close to the top of upcast shafts, but sadly not before several fatal explosions had occurred.

Fans capable of circulating 200,000 cubic feet of air per minute began to replace furnaces after 207 lives were lost in the Blantyre explosion of October 22, 1877. It is thought that a ventilation furnace there might have gone out overnight, causing air levels to fluctuate and allowing gas to build up.

As mentioned in Chapter 7, airtight cladding around the exterior top of upcast headgear was necessary to ensure that fresh air drawn into the mine by the fan was forced to enter the workings via the downcast shaft and not simply take the route of least resistance by going in through the top of the upcast shaft and short-circuiting straight back to the atmosphere. It was therefore necessary when building upcast shafts to ensure that the effectiveness of the ventilation flow was not compromised during the constant coming and going of cages. With man-riding cages, this was effected by means of an airlock through which the miners and tubs would have to pass on the way in and out. With the later skip-winding method, it was done by ultra-rapid mechanised opening and shutting of coal doors so that the shaft wasn't open to the atmosphere for more than a few seconds at a time.

Airlocks possessed a minimum of two or three doors with

There was no mistaking which was the upcast shaft at Annesley Colliery, as its white-painted cladding sported a huge 'A'. As Annesley-Bentinck, the mine survived into the 21st century, but it has since disappeared under a housing estate.

A close-up of the ventilation fan external housing at Rossington Colliery, near Doncaster, showing just how large some of them grew to be. The tapered structure at the top is the evasee, so shaped to ease and accelerate air flow.

Left: Photographic proof that miners in the hottest and deepest pits often had to strip down to their underwear in order to cope with the oppressive heat and humidity. This picture was taken at Tilmanstone Colliery in Kent.

men and tubs passing through one door at a time. Those through which trains had to pass were spaced further apart.

Return air was almost always considerably hotter than downcast air, providing a strange sudden experience for anyone passing between one flow and another while underground. At points where there was a chance of the two flows mixing or short-circuiting, air crossovers were installed and when it was necessary to prevent air passing into a disused part of a mine, a 'stopping' would be used to basically seal off the entrance.

Fans could be either 'extracting' or 'forcing', although most could be reversed to work either way if necessary, and in fact air currents within individual districts of a mine could be temporarily changed by officials depending on local requirements. The fans could be 15ft in diameter or more and the speed at which they ran was dependent on the weather; slower at times of high pressure and vice versa, making a barometer an unexpected item of colliery equipment. Nevertheless, in some mines, especially those with booster fans in the roadways themselves, the pressure and speed could be so great that air doors could only be opened by brute force, so a small regulator hatch would often be inserted to help equalise the pressure.

Parts of the workings that were particularly narrow or low-roofed became veritable 'wind tunnels' and for men trying to crawl along them it was like battling through a storm. "I got a shock on my first day at work," recalled one ex-miner. "It was blowing a gale down there!"

Better that than the alternative, though; the importance of proper ventilation was underlined at Wharncliff Woodmoor Colliery on August 6, 1936 when two airway doors were wedged open with bricks to facilitate the passage of tubs. That allowed firedamp to accumulate, which was then detonated by an electrical fault, resulting in an explosion that claimed the lives of 58 miners.

Fans thus had to be left on 24 hours a day, 365 weeks a year in many places to ensure dangerous levels of methane and heat did not build up (being lighter than air, methane tends to form in pockets along the roof). A stand-by fan would be necessary in case of breakdown, and during long strikes and other periods of inactivity it was important for fans and water pumps to be kept running if there was to be a mine left for the strikers to return to.

The other aspect for which fans were essential concerned heat. People who've never been down a mine might reasonably expect it to be cold in the ground and although men working close to the surface or close to a downcast shaft in mid-winter could well have suffered from hypothermia, the greater risks were actually from hyperthermia!

Temperatures underground are dictated by the

When a 'tweet' meant life or death

CARBON MONOXIDE is a poisonous gas with no smell or taste. In 1913, Scottish physiologist John Haldane — who had investigated tragedies in which colliers in poorly-ventilated districts had been poisoned because they'd had no warning of its presence — came up with the idea of placing canaries in coal mines.

He reasoned correctly that the faster metabolism, smaller lungs and greater sensitivity of the birds to carbon monoxide (seven times more so than humans) would lead them to become sick well before the miners, thus giving the men time to escape or at least put on respirators. A miniature tank of oxygen attached to each cage enabled the birds to be revived.

Aviaries were installed at collieries and a caged canary became an essential part of underground equipment, not finally being replaced by electronic methods

until the late 20th century. It was necessary to keep the birds' claws trimmed, however, as rigor-mortis could sometimes prevent dead ones from falling off their perches!

Illustrated is the canary aviary at Littleton Colliery in 1993. NICK PIGOTT

geothermal gradient, which rises by one degree Fahrenheit for every 70ft of depth (2.5°C for every 100m). On top of that, powerful machines generate heat, the bodies of hard-working men add to it and the oxidation of strata creates heat too.

The trapping of all that in a confined space explains why it gets so hot, with temperatures in some deep mines reaching 100°F (38°C) and humidity levels at an almost unbearable 98%.

"Working at the coalface is like sweating in a sauna for six hours," said one Hatfield miner in 2012. "They do their best to get fresh air to you but you're half a mile beneath the ground so it's going to be hot."

"It's like being abroad when you first get off the plane," commented a Kellingley man. "That sort of heat can make you quickly ill if you're not acclimatised and there can also be 98% humidity down there. They say it can take ten years off your life."

Mines with faces several miles from the pit bottom often had large booster fans positioned at strategic locations along roadways in an effort to strengthen and cool the air flow and keep it moving in the required volumes. There is a limit to how far along the roadways this can remain effective, however, and it is this, rather than any physical obstruction, why coalfaces are not extended more than eight or nine miles from the pit bottom.

As mentioned in Chapter 8, it is also necessary for the oxygen content of air to remain above 19.5% in order for men to breathe normally and the further the air has to travel, the harder it is to ensure adequate maintenance of such levels.

Good places to see (or rather hear) ventilation systems in action today are the preserved collieries of Caphouse and Blaenafon, but non-operational mines are actually quite chilly underground and, although fascinating to visitors, are physically incapable of replicating the atmosphere, sounds, smells and sensations of the real thing. This is especially true where heat is concerned … the dramatic change in temperature as one stepped through airlock doors from hot return flow to cold intake flow in an operational deep mine provided many a shock for the unwary.

Some of the hottest mines in the country were in Kent. Snowdown, despite its chilly-sounding name, was notorious and was known as 'the Inferno' because it was "hotter than Hell" 3,000ft below the earth's crust. Miners in most deep mines wore just helmet, boots and thin shorts while working at the face and headings, but it is said of the Kentish mines that even underpants were too hot to bear

As breathing apparatus became more reliable during the late-Victorian era, rescue teams were set up to serve the larger or gassier collieries. This one was based at Mauchline Colliery in Ayrshire in the 1950s. (Note the little canary cage with its own miniature oxygen tank for reviving the bird if necessary.) See the next chapter for more information about rescue teams.

and that tough face workers sometimes used to borrow their wives' briefs!

One of the questions most asked by the general public on mining museum tours concerns toilet arrangements underground. Sweating so much and eating only modest amounts of food meant that a miner didn't need to answer the calls of nature as often as most people, despite drinking up to eight pints of water per shift, but when he did ... it was a case of just finding somewhere private in the abandoned workings.

WATER: Fluids were essential to keep miners hydrated and alive, but, as mentioned previously, water could also be a killer. It could pour in enormous volumes from subterranean watercourses or from abandoned workings and the battle to keep flooding at bay was a constant one that taxed the ingenuity of the early mining engineers.

Water occurs naturally in the sub-strata and some pits simply had reputations for wetness right to the end of their lives; Westoe in County Durham, for instance, had to have 5.5m gallons of water pumped out every day and Northern United mine in Gloucestershire was raising 60 tons of water for every ton of coal when it closed in 1965.

There was so much pressure from water in the Kent coalfield that the shafts of Snowdown Colliery began to collapse within days of the pumps being switched off following the mine's closure in 1987. Even in the 2020s, pumps have to be used at preserved collieries to keep the subterranean sections dry.

Mineral water percolating from the upper measures was often pure enough to drink and many mines sank their own boreholes or wells, while others collected it in lodgements at the shaft side and sold the excess to the local water authority, those collieries unable to do so taking the water they required from local rivers.

On the other hand, some mines had problems with toxic water leeching into watercourses and there were organisations like the South Yorkshire Mines Drainage Board, whose sole occupation it was to keep pits dry. In 1943, that board installed the first submersible pump, which could be left to work unattended. Such machinery became very widespread in later years.

Not all water was unwanted, of course. In the form of a fine spray, it played important roles in the laying of dust and the cooling of powered cutting tools. Care had to be taken not to use excessive liquid, however, as that would turn the dust underfoot into a morass of black glutinous slurry, similar to the cloying conditions prevalent on any colliery surface whenever it rained heavily.

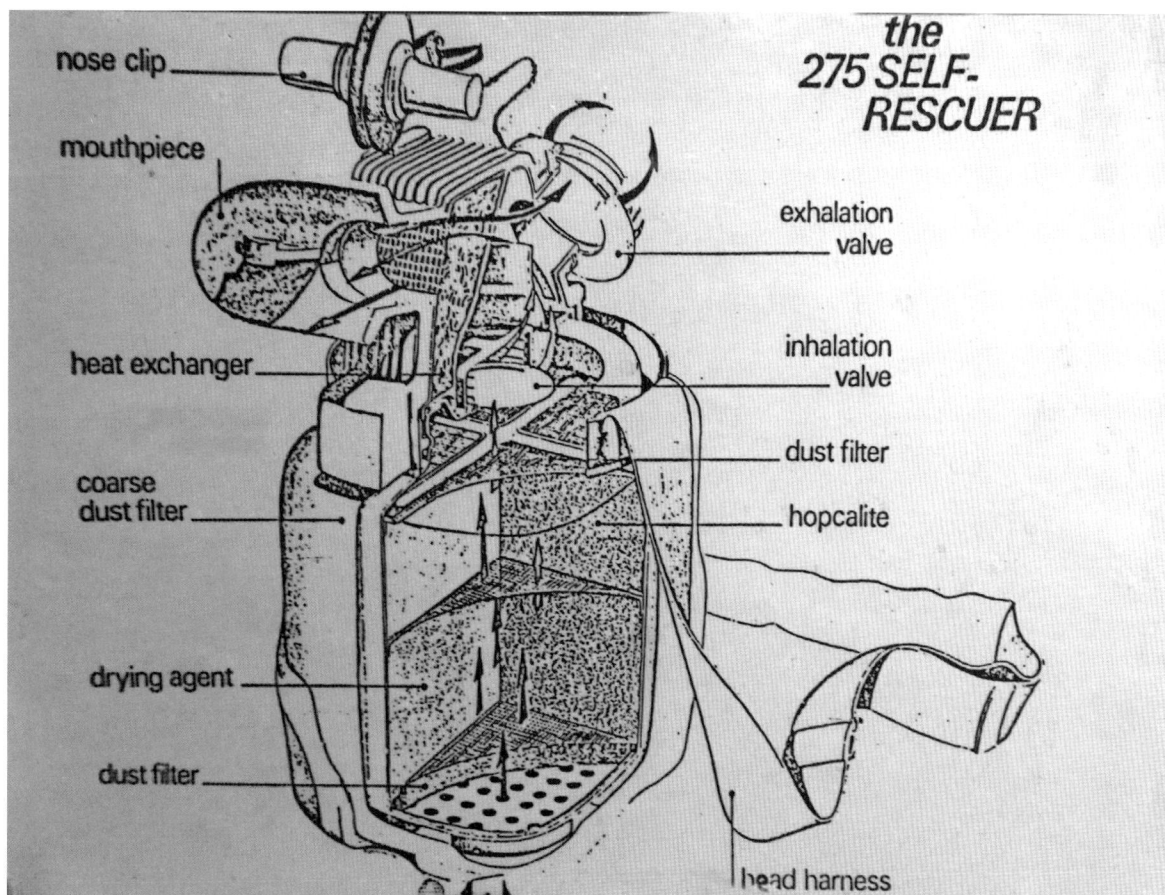

The introduction of 'self-rescuer' apparatus (see page 142) did much to transform underground safety whenever ventilation hazards arose. This diagram on display in the South Wales Miners' Museum shows the basic principle of operation.

CHAPTER 15

Disasters, hazards and safety

Too many ways to die

EVERY DAY, underground men went to work not knowing if they would return home that night. They faced death in numerous different ways.

To stress just how many ways a mineworker could perish, be crippled or become permanently ill, the main causes are listed below:

- Roof fall
- Shaft plunge
- Explosion of methane
- Explosion of coal dust
- Asphyxiation & suffocation
- Subterranean fire
- Subterranean flood
- Haulage accident
- Cage over-wind
- Pneumoconiosis

Until the horror of two world wars led people in western society to reappraise the sanctity of human life, many industrial proprietors viewed their workers as a dispensable means to an end with injury, mutilation and death simply being accepted as daily occurrences in mining communities.

The statistics speak for themselves: In the 30 years between 1880 and 1909 there were more than 1,000 fatalities a year in British coal mines — an average of three men killed every day.

In 1910, the national fatality figure for the year rose to a shocking 1,818. Of those, 501 died in explosions, 658 in roof or wall falls, 286 in accidents involving the transport of coal underground and 373 as a result of other types of misfortune. Injuries totalled 173,700 that dreadful year — an average of 470 a day!

The first recorded victim of a coalmining accident in Britain appears to have been a man by the name of Ralf

Ulger, who drowned while digging for sea coal in 1243 and although there would have been numerous fatalities after that, the first recorded death of an underground collier is that of James Townend, who was killed in a firedamp explosion at Barnsley in 1672.

The last man to join the grisly roll call was 49-year-old Gerry Gibson, who became British coal mining's final underground victim when he was killed by a roof fall at Kellingley Colliery on September 27, 2011. Two colleagues had died there since 2008, including Don Cook, whose mother summed up the remarkable affection in which colliers viewed their perilous jobs when she commented afterwards: "He loved being a miner. It's a wonderful culture and a wonderful life."

By a cruel twist of fate, September 2011 proved to be one of the blackest months in the history of modern mining, for a mere 12 days before Gerry Gibson's death, disaster struck at Gleision Colliery, near Neath. Although checked regularly by the Mines Inspectorate, the small drift mine was in some respects operated in conditions reminiscent of the Victorian era and, on September 15, an inrush of water and debris engulfed a team of seven men shot-firing a coalface 300ft below ground, drowning four of them.

Underlining the ever-present risks underground, even a preserved mine open to the public suffered a fatal accident in that dark year of 2011. The tragedy occurred in January when an experienced ex-miner helping to extend a subterranean roadway at the National Coal Mining Museum near Wakefield was crushed to death by a machine he was operating.

Even those recent incidents might not have been the end of the litany, for as late as May 2017 a collier had his back crushed in a roof fall at Danygraig drift mine near Crynant. His life was saved by a colleague who used a sledgehammer

This graphic artist's interpretation of an underground explosion is a well-known one in mining circles and says far more about the potential horror of life in the pits than a photograph ever could.

to break a half-ton lump of rock pinning him to the ground.

The final fatalities took the total killed in Britain since 1851 close to 100,000 – but even taking the comparatively accident-free second half of the 20th century into account, the figure has to be seen in the context of a vast workforce numbering at its peak almost one-and-a-quarter-million men spread over 3,000 collieries.

Probably the best-known person to die in a mine was England international footballer Walter Bennett, who played at the turn of the 20th century for Sheffield United (one of the top two clubs in the country at that time). He was killed in a roof fall at Denaby Main Colliery in 1908. In those days, even international players' earnings were insufficient to let them retire after they'd hung up their boots and he'd taken a job in the pits to make ends meet.

One of the rescuers involved in the following year's West Stanley disaster, in which 168 men perished, was Frank Keegan, grandfather of future European Footballer of the Year and England manager Kevin Keegan who, in 1995, unveiled a memorial to the deceased on the site of the colliery.

The even greater disaster at Lundhill, Yorkshire, in 1859 and others at that time appealed to the ghoulish Victorian tendency for sightseers to flock to the scene; thousands of 'excursionists' arriving by train from non-mining areas and creating something of a country fair atmosphere rather than one of mourning at a scene of great human suffering.

The Oaks Colliery explosion at Ardsley in 1866 was Britain's largest peacetime disaster since the Great Fire of London 200 years earlier. The bodies of more than 100 men remain entombed to this day. One of the blasts propelled a cage straight up its shaft and into the headgear. The flames eventually had to be extinguished by stopping up the shafts to starve them of oxygen. A total of 371 men and youths perished, including 27 members of the rescue team. Some of the survivors found jobs at other mines but by a cruel twist of fate, one of them was killed in a roof fall near Barnsley four years later.

The worst disaster of all in British coal mining history occurred at Universal Colliery at Senghenydd, near Caerphilly, on October 14, 1913, when an underground explosion claimed the lives of 439 miners.

Many collieries in the South Wales coalfield worked seams that contained high quantities of methane ('firedamp') and Universal was no exception. It had already suffered an extremely serious incident 12 years earlier when three subterranean explosions killed 81 men. The cause of the 1913 catastrophe was never established for sure, but almost certainly related to the high levels of airborne dust for which the pit was notorious. An initial methane blast, probably

The worst tragedies in British mining history

440 died at Senghenydd, Wales, in 1913

371 at Oaks Colliery, Yorkshire, 1866

344 at Pretoria Pit, Lancashire, 1910

294 Albion Colliery, Cilfynydd, 1894

268 Prince of Wales, Abercarn, 1878

265 Gresford, near Wrexham, 1934

207 Blantyre, Lanarkshire, 1877

204 Hartley, Northumberland, 1862

189 Lundhill, near Wombwell, 1857

189 Wood Pit, Haydock, Lancs, 1878

178 Clifton Hall, Lancs, 1885

178 Ferndale, Glamorgan, 1867

176 Llanerch, Monmouthshire, 1890

168 West Stanley, Co Durham, 1909

164 Seaham, Co Durham, 1880

155 Minie Pit, Staffordshire, 1918

143 Swaithe Main, Barnsley, 1875

142 Black Vein, Risca, 1860

139 Combs, Dewsbury, Yorkshire, 1893

136 Wellington, Whitehaven, 1910

120 Black Vein, Risca (2nd tragedy), 1880

119 Wattstown, Glamorgan, 1905

114 Cynmer, Glamorgan, 1856

112 Parc Slip, Glamorgan, 1892

104 William Pit, Whitehaven, 1947

102 Wallsend, Northumberland, 1835

101 Penycraig, Glamorgan, 1880

In addition, 144 lives (116 children and 28 adults) were lost in Aberfan in October 1966 (see separate panel). Almost half the above disasters occurred in Wales.

Flames shoot from the ventilation outlet at Lundhill Colliery, where 189 men lost their lives in an explosion in 1857.

caused by a spark from an electric bell signalling system, is likely to have been carried further into the mine by a chain reaction of explosions.

Those men not killed instantly died as a result of inhaling afterdamp, a poisonous mixture of carbon dioxide, carbon monoxide and nitrogen left after an explosion. Fire in the workings hampered rescue efforts and it took six weeks for most of the bodies to be recovered and the blaze to be fully extinguished. One rescuer died in the process, taking the death toll to 440.

Demands were understandably made by miners for the removal of electricity from all pits as a result of the Senghenydd disaster but such a drastic move would have been a serious impediment to progress. Instead, minds were focused on reduction of sparks and prevention of coal dust explosions.

The latter was eventually combatted by the introduction of stone-dusting measures, but troublesome electrical equipment continued to be one of the biggest scourges of 20th century mining and extremely strict regulations were put in place to minimise the risks. Machines and switchgear had to be made flame-proof, which usually meant enclosure of fuses, wiring terminals and switches in thick steel boxes secured by means of numerous tightly-fitted bolts.

The necessity for such equipment to be worked on and maintained only by trained staff gave rise to a new breed of subterranean worker – district electricians – and by the

Long lines of miners and their loved ones queue up at Senghenydd Colliery to await news following Britain's worst mining disaster in 1913.

second half of the century those skilled men were ranked among the most valuable and respected members of underground teams.

A tragedy at Cambrian Colliery in 1965 served to underline not only the importance of their role but the importance of underground communication, for electricians working under pressure to try to repair a broken-down coal-cutter motor had not been informed of an interruption to the ventilation system elsewhere in the district. The electrical fault in the motor was proving difficult to trace and required numerous brief testing sessions. Being under management pressure to get it working, the frustrated electricians are thought not to have fully tightened all ten bolts on the switchgear box between every session, assuming the ventilation flow to be sufficient for them to take that risk. The combination of that decision and the unseen build-up of gas caused an explosion in which 31 people died.

As early as the 1840s, philosopher Friedrich Engels drew attention to the risks inherent in coalmining when he wrote: "In the whole British Empire, there is no occupation in which a man may meet his end in so many diverse ways. The coal mine is the scene of a multitude of terrifying calamities … of evils which descend upon the head of the coal miner."

Examples of the many different ways in which mineworkers could lose their lives are given below:

Roof fall: At Bilsthorpe Colliery in August 1993, a block of sandstone described as "the size of a small asteroid" and weighing an astonishing 8,000 tons, plunged from a roof into a roadway, killing the three men working underneath.

The tragedy at the British Coal-owned pit was the result of a roadway being driven too close to an old coalface, exacerbated by the use of rock-bolts on what was known as a 'skin to skin' development with no roof props. Because no supporting pillar of coal had been left between the new and old workings, the roof-bolted heading was unable to bear the weight and collapsed.

That was one of the largest single falls, but it was typical of the hazards miners have had to contend with for centuries. So many roof falls took place, especially in the early years of mining, that there were hardly any collieries that didn't have at least one such episode in their histories and the various memorial gardens around the country are a sobering reminder of this fact.

Given the phenomenal volume of earth and rock above every subterranean gallery, it is a remarkable testament to the skill of the engineers and miners that so (relatively) few major roof fall tragedies have occurred, especially when it is considered how many hundreds of years mining has been undertaken in Britain.

Shaft plunge: One of the most horrible ways to die was in a cage that was either plummeting downwards or shooting upwards too fast to stop, for in such cases, the occupants knew what was happening and could only wait for the inevitable.

In 1886, an appalling accident occurred at Houghton Main Colliery, Barnsley, when a cage containing 10 men plummeted to the bottom of a 1,605ft shaft at a speed of more than 100mph. Taking 12 seconds to do so, it splintered into smithereens as it smashed into the sump at the bottom of the shaft.

At Rufford Colliery, near Mansfield, in 1913, there was a terrible incident when a winding engineman was temporarily unsighted by a tarpaulin sheet that fell on him while he was raising a seven-ton tank of water during a shaft-sinking operation. Without his hand at the controls, the tank hit the temporary headgear, broke loose and plunged back down the shaft. Fourteen men working near the bottom were killed by the force of the water and flying metal as the tank shattered.

In 1915, two cages at Bentinck Colliery, Notts, collided at the halfway point at a combined speed of 80mph. The wooden floor of the descending cage was dislodged by the impact and seven men plummeted 660ft to their deaths. Two more died of injuries sustained in the collision and some of the survivors were left dangling, one of them upside down suspended by his trousers, which had luckily snagged on a piece of metal. So mutilated were some of the bodies at the foot of the shaft that relatives had difficulty identifying them.

A relatively recent tragedy saw 18 men killed in a cage fall when the braking system failed at Markham Colliery on June 30, 1973.

Although it didn't directly involve a cage, the dreadful disaster at Hartley Colliery in 1862 was also caused by a shaft plunge, only in that case, it concerned the wooden ventilation brattice dividing the shaft into two, which was struck when the 42-ton cast iron beam of a steam pumping engine snapped and fell onto it. The resultant blockage, coupled with the damaged air system, caused the deaths of 204 men trapped underground, most of whom died of carbon monoxide poisoning caused by the ventilation furnace. Single shaft mines were outlawed by Parliament that same year and thereafter all had to be provided with a second shaft or alternative means of escape.

Gas poisoning: Miners' lives were plagued by several types of poisonous or asphyxiating gases that could be found in pits. The names of these were all characterised by the suffix 'damp' (a derivation of the German word 'dampf', meaning vapour).

Blackdamp (also known as Chokedamp or Stythe): A mixture of carbon dioxide and nitrogen that could cause oxygen deficiency. It is odourless and colourless and gained its name from the fact that lights wouldn't burn in it and hence darkness ensued.

Whitedamp: A toxic, odourless residual gas consisting primarily of carbon monoxide and so called because (unlike blackdamp), it allows lights to continue burning. To detect it, miners took caged canaries underground (see panel on page 129).

Stinkdamp: So-called because its principal content was hydrogen sulphide (which smells of rotten eggs). Unlike odourless methane, it was easily detected but was extremely poisonous. It might seem trivial, but some miners were reluctant to pack egg sandwiches in their lunch boxes for fear it would mask, or be mistaken for, the smell of stinkdamp.

Afterdamp: A lethal cocktail of carbon monoxide, carbon dioxide, nitrogen, hydrogen, oxygen and residual methane left in the atmosphere of a mine after an explosion of either firedamp or coal dust. It is not flammable itself but, depending on circumstances, has been known to kill more miners in the aftermath of an explosion than the blast itself.

Firedamp: Last but by no means least, this was the most common form of 'damp'. It comprised a highly combustible mixture of gases, the principal one of which is methane.

Methane is lighter than air and tends to accumulate in roof cavities. It is not poisonous but was the cause of thousands of mining deaths over the years due to its flammability. The first recorded death in Britain from a methane gas explosion was in Durham in 1621, but miners continued to use candles, oils and other naked flames for two more centuries.

Until the invention of safety lamps (see later in this chapter), there was little option but to rid the mine of methane by deliberately igniting it. For that job, a 'fireman' wearing a monk-like hood and thick water-soaked clothing would gingerly crawl forward with a naked light on the end of a long pole, keeping his head down so that the blast would hopefully pass over him, but jumping up immediately afterwards to avoid breathing the low-lying afterdamp. As can be imagined, people didn't last very long in that job!

Sparks from hand picks could potentially cause a methane explosion too, as could shot-firing, wiring faults and overheated machinery. Low barometric pressure encouraged methane to seep from the strata, exacerbating the risk.

Depending on the type of seam it is trapped in, methane

Daily Herald

No. 6390   FRIDAY, AUGUST 7, 1936   ONE PENNY

Barnsley Pit Explosion

57 MINERS HURLED TO DEATH IN A FLASH

ONLY ONE MAN KNOWS HOW IT HAPPENED

Wives See Bodies Brought Up

FROM OUR SPECIAL CORRESPONDENTS
BARNSLEY, Yorks, Thursday.

FIFTY-SEVEN bodies, some of them twisted and battered beyond recognition, are to-night being slowly borne from the Wharncliffe Woodmoor Colliery, shaken this morning by one of the worst mine explosions this county has known.

Along a private road at the back of the pit, ambulances are moving through the darkness to the quaint, disused church school of

⸺ GERMANY ARMS REBELS ⸺

SENDS CARGO OF PLANES

SECRET SHIPLOAD OF BOMBERS SHOCKS BLUM CABINET

FROM OUR OWN CORRESPONDENT
PARIS, Thursday.

NEWS reached French Ministerial circles to-night that a German steamer is now on its way to Spain with a cargo of 28 bombing planes aboard.

BROADCAST TO BRITISH SUBJECTS

3 Britons Die In Alps

From Our Own Correspondent
GENEVA, Thursday.

SWISS Alps claimed two more British victims to-day—making three within the past 24 hours.

How the Daily Herald broke news of the Wharncliffe Woodmoor Colliery explosion near Barnsley in August 1936.

is usually emitted at a known rate, which, while not eradicating the dangers, made risk assessment at any given colliery easier to manage. Statistically, the most dangerous seam in Britain was the Hutton seam in the Great Northern coalfield, which caused 37 explosions and killed 1,090 people between 1705 and 1883.

Although death through asphyxiation was more common, miners also faced death through suffocation, usually as a result of being trapped under or behind a roof fall.

Coal dust explosion: If there were large quantities of coal dust in the air at the time of a methane blast, a series of chain-reaction explosions could be triggered and tear along the whole length of a roadway, killing men far away from the source of the initial blast. The burning of coal dust also creates poisonous carbon monoxide and that too resulted in deaths.

In the 1870s, such a series of explosions killed 73 men at Udston Colliery, Hamilton. It was a dry, dusty pit and thereafter it became compulsory in the UK to liberally scatter limestone dust all over underground walls and roadways as it was found it had a preventative effect by diluting the concentration of coal dust. Shelves containing bags of limestone dust were also placed across the top of roadways at strategic locations. The force of a blast would blow the limestone off the shelves and snuff out the chain reaction.

This practice was continued until the very end of deep mining in Britain and is still carried out today at the preserved Blaenafon Colliery.

Subterranean fire: In addition to the many fires caused by methane explosions, blazes could result from other sources. In 1950, for example, a conveyor belt in the main air intake roadway at Creswell Colliery jammed and the resultant friction caused it to overheat and burst into flames, the rubber producing thick acrid smoke that trapped 80 miners. They all died of carbon monoxide poisoning. The roadway was sealed off as the only means of starving the fire of oxygen while keeping the rest of the pit operational, but several men did not go to work the next day as a mark of respect — a long-standing tradition in the mining industry.

The cause of the jammed belt was later found to have been extremely lax maintenance and fault-reporting methods, coupled with poorly-maintained fire extinguishers and water supply. It proved to be a watershed in mine safety, bringing about the introduction of a 'self-rescuer' breathing mask (see later in this chapter).

Spontaneous combustion: It may seem strange that a fire — which requires oxygen in order to burn — can survive underground, but in fact some subterranean conflagrations have been burning continuously for more than half a

THE RISE AND FALL OF KING COAL

century, defying all of man's ingenuity to extinguish them. In Germany there is said to be a coal seam fire that has been smouldering since 1668 despite numerous attempts to extinguish it.

Such phenomena are caused by natural spontaneous combustion and although serious outbreaks were relatively rare in Britain, they were most prevalent in the thick seams of Staffordshire, Warwickshire and South Derbyshire. The most recent in the UK broke out in the workings of Warwickshire's Daw Mill Colliery in 2013, doing so much damage underground that the mine had to close – a nevertheless shocking decision for what at the time was Britain's most productive pit and one that caused a deal of controversy.

The usual ways of combatting an underground blaze were either to starve it of oxygen by sealing it off, to flood the mine, as happened at Hucknall in 1867, or (in more recent times) to pump large quantities of the inert gas nitrogen into the workings. The latter method, however, is prohibitively expensive.

Spontaneous combustion has also been known to occur in large stockpiles on the surface. Coal stored in the open air slowly disintegrates under the action of weather, particularly frost, and this has the effect of breaking it into small particles which, in the presence of oxygen, can sometimes start a fire.

Subterranean flooding: Floods and water intrusions caused numerous tragedies over the years, including one at Yorkshire's Lofthouse Colliery in 1973 when water burst through a seam and trapped seven men 750ft underground. Rescue teams estimated where the men were likely to be and set up a drilling rig on the surface above that point to bore an air hole for them while frogmen from the NCB's underwater rescue team based at Hednesford, Staffs, tried to reach them. So great was the inundation that it took six days before the first body could be retrieved and all hope for the other six was then abandoned. They are entombed to this day.

Their funeral and memorial service was conducted by the Bishop of Wakefield, the Rt Rev Eric Treacy, a renowned industrial enthusiast who would sometimes visit his parishioners at work in the collieries and crawl on his belly through very thin seams to reach those working at the coalface.

Man-riding accidents: A surprisingly high number of deaths and serious injuries have been caused by derailments and by runaway mine cars, either pinning men against other tubs or trapping them against walls in narrow roadways.

At Silverwood Colliery in 1966, a train of materials crashed into the rear of a paddy train, killing 10 miners and seriously injuring 29 others. Seven men were killed

and 19 injured at Bentley Colliery, Doncaster, in 1978 when a train ran away down an underground incline. After that, speed retarders were fitted to the tracks in most mines.

Some miners' trains could be as long as 300ft and in the days before radio communication, several died when their train was being propelled (rather than hauled) towards a coalface. Unbeknown to the driver at the rear, a fire had broken out near the face and his passengers were being choked to death by thick smoke. The guard at the front is believed to have succumbed before he could use his warning whistle and the miners in the carriages had no way of telling the driver to reverse. By the time the driver realised what was happening and began hauling the train out, it was too late for those at the front. Safety improvements implemented as a result brought about changes in train operation.

In 1991, there was an unusual accident at Thurcroft Colliery when a conveyor on which miners were riding suddenly began to accelerate due to a faulty gearbox. As it reached speeds of 40mph, panic set in and lots of men jumped off, sustaining broken bones as a result of being thrown against steel girders and roof supports. More than 40 had to be ferried to hospital in a fleet of ambulances.

Despite continuing tragedies, the process of continuous improvement was such that by the late-1970s British mining had been able to declare itself "the least hazardous" in the world but, of course, it wasn't necessary to die for one's life to be wrecked in numerous other ways.

Eye and head injuries: In 1950 alone, there were 11,058 notifiable eye injuries in UK collieries, yet incredibly, it wasn't until as late as 1972 that the Protection of Eyes Regulations were introduced and for more goggles to be made available. The injuries from flying shards of coal and many other hazards were in addition to debilitating ailments caused by having to work for years in poor light over many years – nystagmus, for instance – which was a strange affliction resulting in rapid involuntary oscillation of the eyeballs.

In today's litigious society, safety helmets are compulsory for workers and visitors at industrial sites, even out in the open air when there's nothing above them but sky, but in the old days it was the opposite extreme. Miners were issued with no protective headgear and had to get by with nothing unless they provided a cap of their own. Around the middle of the 20th century, helmets made of compressed fibreboard became available but were really only useful in preventing cuts and grazes and it wasn't until NCB days that tough metal or plastic helmets began to be issued.

Lung diseases: Also stalking miners throughout their

A graphic poster warning miners not to travel on anything other than approved man-riding systems.

pneumoconiosis is almost unknown among younger ex-miners.

Also suffering terribly in terms of lung conditions were those whose job it was to drive headings through solid rock to open up new roadways. They were constantly breathing stone dust, but because that type of work meant they were continuously moving from mine to mine, they were never at one colliery very long. This enabled less-caring coal owners in pre-NCB days to deny that the disease, called silicosis, had been contracted on their premises. As a consequence, the men were unable to gain compensation and had to rely on parish funds to see out their final years. In later times, face masks were supplied for road-header operators.

Other sicknesses: Among the other afflictions faced by miners were emphysema and bronchitis (lung conditions), hyperthermia (over-heating) and 'white finger', the latter caused by vibration. It particularly affected men who cut coal from the face with pneumatic picks and other hand-held power tools driven by compressed air or electricity. In 2001, there were 19,000 outstanding compensation cases of white finger waiting to be resolved, along with 14,500 cases of emphysema and bronchitis – and 4,000 cases of deafness brought about by the noise of powerful machinery in confined spaces.

'Bad backs' have long been a reason for workers in offices and other professions to take a day off work, but where mining was concerned, it was plain to see why. In pre-NCB days, and even for some years after, it was frequently necessary for men to work in or constantly move through spaces that were barely 18in high. Even lying down on a conveyor whizzing along a low roadway at high speed could cause dreadful injuries if a man inadvertently raised his head or shoulders more than a few inches. "If you suffered from claustrophobia, you'd have gone stark staring mad," said one ex-collier. "If you panicked and tried to get off, there was no way out; there were umpteen men in front of you and behind you."

All this was in addition to the many other conditions associated with mine work – ruptures and further types of back ailments caused by heavy lifting, inflammation of the joints, head injuries in the days before helmets and so on … but there was another ailment peculiar to miners called 'beat knee', which was caused by spending year after year crawling or kneeling on jagged surfaces. 'Beat hand' was another recognised condition.

A fact not widely known outside pit communities is that some older miners bore tiny dark blue scars on their face and forehead and carried them to their deaths. This was due to coal dust entering tiny cuts and abrasions without the men realising it. As the new skin grew under the scab,

careers and retirements were illnesses and diseases found in few other walks of life. The most notorious and widely-known was pneumoconiosis (the miners' dreaded 'Black Lung'). One has only to look at photographs of colliers with black faces to realise how much coal dust must have been passing through their mouths and nostrils.

When underground, the beam of a cap lamp would pick up hundreds of thousands of tiny shimmering particles of dust suspended in the air – even in well-ventilated modern mines and often several miles from a coalface.

Many men chewed tobacco in an attempt to prevent the particles entering their lungs via the mouth, which is less able to filter them than the nose, but it was impossible not to inhale huge quantities and the specks that did get through caused scarring and clogged up the tiny air pockets in the lung tissue. The result was a slow lingering death for many thousands of older men.

Not all miners contracted pneumoconiosis, just as not all smokers contract lung cancer, but to help combat the problem, dust masks and other safety measures were implemented for underground workers in the 1970s. Water sprinklers were also introduced to help suppress the dust and to damp it down at points at which coal was either cut or transferred from one conveyor to another. As a result, it formed a permanent blue stain rather like a tattoo. If caught in time, the colliery nurse would scrub the coal out of the open wound, but it was an agonising procedure!

Yet — despite all the disadvantages listed above — coal dust was credited by many miners with great healing powers. The hardy individuals who in the old days considered a 'blue nose' to be a badge of honour would sometimes deliberately rub dust into wounds and grazes to heal them faster and a lot of men even sucked lumps of coal to ease their thirst. Countless others unwittingly ingested large quantities of it over the years simply by eating their sandwiches and suchlike in dusty atmospheres, yet still lived to a ripe old age.

At the end of the day, a miner's safety underground depended on the man next to him and the constant need for vigilance and loyalty — even with colleagues they might not have particularly 'got on with' above ground — formed a vital bond and sense of camaraderie that ran through their lives. Miners had to trust one another and individualism and indiscipline were effectively outlawed by the very nature of the task.

PREVENTION: Terrible though the disasters were, it has to be said that almost every one resulted in major improvements to safety as the tragic lessons were learned. The following are among the principal aids to accident prevention:

Safety lamps: Between 1813 and 1815, several designs

Don't go down in the mine, Dad

A MINING DISASTER in South Wales in 1907 inspired lyricists Robert Donnelly and Will Geddes to compose the following, published in 1910.

A miner was leaving his home for his work,
When he heard his little child scream;
He went to his bedside, his little white face,
"Oh, Daddy, I've had such a dream;
I dreamt that I saw the pit all afire,
And men struggled hard for their lives;
The scene it then changed, and the top of the mine
Was surrounded by sweethearts and wives."

Chorus:
Don't go down in the mine, Dad,
Dreams very often come true;
Daddy, you know it would break my heart
If anything happened to you;
Just go and tell my dream to your mates,
And as true as the stars that shine,
Something is going to happen today,
Dear Daddy, don't go down the mine!

The miner, a man with a heart good and kind,
Stood by the side of his son;
He said, "It's my living, I can't stay away,
For duty, my lad, must be done."
The little one look'd up, and sadly he said,
"Oh, please stay today with me, Dad!"
But as the brave miner went forth, to his work,
He heard this appeal from his lad:

Repeat chorus.

Whilst waiting his turn with his mates to descend,
He could not banish his fears,
He return'd home again to his wife and his child,
Those words seem'd to ring through his ears,
And, ere the day ended, the pit was on fire,
When a score of brave men lost their lives;
He thank'd God above for the dream his child had
As once more the little one cries:

Repeat chorus.

Selections of lamps – modern battery-powered types as well as numerous older safety lamps – can be seen in most mining museums and demonstrate various developments since the early 19th century.

were devised by the likes of William Clanny, Humphry Davy and George Stephenson. They not only provided safe (if dim) illumination but also showed whether methane was present. If it was, the shape and colour of the flame would change.

Methane makes a lamp's flame burn blue and change shape the more gas is present. Carbon dioxide, which is heavier than air, makes the flame go out through absence of oxygen.

Methane is only explosive when mixed with air at a certain percentage, being at its most dangerous at 9.4%, although each colliery had slightly varying safety ranges. When the level was outside the specified limit, it was safe not only for men to work but for otherwise potentially lethal activities such as explosive shot-firing to take place. When it entered the danger zone, electricity had first to be switched off and if it continued to rise, all men had to be quickly withdrawn from the affected district.

The Davy design, in which the flame was contained within a gauze screen, became the best-known type and over the ensuing years the efficiency of the various designs of lamps improved tremendously, not only saving lives but, by enabling miners to go deeper, making it possible for millions of tons of otherwise unrecoverable coal to be won. In that regard, the lamps did much to perpetuate the industrialisation of Britain and other coal-producing nations.

With the development of reliable battery power in the 20th century, electric cap-mounted lamps and battery packs were issued to every miner, but various types of safety lamps continued to be used in certain circumstances, particularly by deputies when checking for gas. If a miner's lamp went out during a shift, he had to find an official

equipped with a special re-lighter lamp.

Methane monitors: Unless a colliery was classified as a 'naked light mine' (a category that was done away with by the NCB in the 1950s), all electrical equipment underground had, by law, to be flameproof or 'intrinsically safe' to reduce the chances of a spark igniting a patch of gas. In modern mines, electronic hand-held digital monitoring devices have replaced safety lamps (although many deputies in mines around the world still choose to carry an older type as well). The monitors are carried on the belts of underground officials as they are the men who would order the workers to evacuate if necessary. In the early years of the NCB's film unit, movie crews working underground had to use clockwork-driven cine cameras, but intrinsically-safe equipment later made it possible to use low-voltage digital photographic kit incapable of generating an incendive spark. In operational mines in other countries to this day, deputies still mingle with miners around faces and new headings, constantly monitoring for gas.

Cap lamps: In the very early days before the introduction of safety lamps, colliers working in non-gassy mines with slow-moving air currents would sometimes strap a candle to their foreheads to illuminate what they were doing — something that was not possible with the relatively large and heavy Davy lamps. However, the invention of electric batteries in the early 20th century enabled lighting to return to its most sensible position close to the wearer's gaze once a way had been found in the 1930s to make the new power sources fire-safe. Rechargeable cap lamps soon became the norm, especially after improving technology allowed lamp room staff to tell how much charge each battery had left. The development of light-emitting diode bulbs and sturdier helmets with built-in fitments brought further improvements.

Self-rescuers: Even in the best-regulated modern mines, the threat from fire or gas remains ever present, so self-rescuer apparatus came into general use in the late-1960s/early 70s following a number of fires in which men had been killed by inhalation of fumes.

Self-rescuers are portable kits clipped to the belt of every underground worker for use in the event of gas or excessive dust. There are several types and filters, but they basically contain chemicals which, when activated, generate oxygen to convert carbon monoxide into more tolerable carbon dioxide. By means of a mask and nose-clip, they provide breathable air for about an hour, which was enough to give most men a fighting chance of getting back to the surface provided they weren't too many miles from the shaft bottom when the emergency occurred. The appliances were made compulsory for miners as a result of a disaster at Scotland's Michael Colliery in 1967.

Although self-rescuers saved many lives, the chemical reaction made the air inside them very hot and miners had to resist the temptation to briefly remove the masks for a gulp of cooler air. Such an action could prove lethal.

Also available at collieries for those who required them in the post-nationalisation era were ordinary face masks and dust masks, some incorporating a renewable filter.

Cage-arrestors: Following a high number of cage over-wind incidents in which men were killed or maimed, Nottinghamshire man John King invented the King patent detaching hook in 1860. In the event of an over-wind by an engineman at either end of a shaft, a hook would engage with the headgear, suspending the cage and releasing the rope. In the event of steam pressure falling too low in a winding house boiler, a solenoid with counter-balance weights would drop and automatically apply a caliper brake to stop the engine.

From 1917, headstocks had, by law, to be fitted with over-wind mechanisms, but most colliery managers still insisted on the winding engine man being able to concentrate fully on the job in hand and it was therefore often the case that his cabin would be kept locked to prevent colleagues from entering without permission.

Rescue stations: The year 1902 saw the Mines Rescue Service initiated and nine years later, central rescue stations within ten miles of every mine were established under the 1911 Coal Mines Act, which also made it compulsory for collieries employing more than 100 men to be provided with their own rescue teams. Ambulance stations and medical centres were thus established on the surface

A display case from Snibston Colliery containing examples of what miners were forbidden to take underground.

at most major collieries and the centre would always be staffed by at least one qualified nurse.

Once underground, the rescuers (kitted out with full protective clothing and breathing apparatus) would travel inbye, on Paddy trains whenever it was safe to do so, in order to reach the incident scene as soon as possible. Some railways had special ambulance carriages able to take a man on a stretcher to the pit bottom. In addition to a fire station on the surface, there would be fire-fighting apparatus and hoses at the pit bottom, along with men trained in their use. There would also be points in each district and coalface containing chemical extinguishers and bags of stone dust and sand.

The Mines Rescue Service (now known as MRS Training & Rescue) has survived the death of the industry it was set up to serve and has adapted to meet the needs of the health & safety market generally and to train employees of other organisations who work below ground, specifically water and cable firms and those engaged in non-coal mines.

Communication systems: In the early days of mining, communication was literally by word of mouth and could therefore take a long time to get from the surface and shaft to the working districts and vice versa. Once electrical devices became safe for use in mines, rudimentary signalling systems and then internal telephones and loudspeaker tannoys were installed and proved vital over the years in co-ordinating haulage, informing production teams of delays and, most crucially of all, giving directions and warnings that saved countless lives.

Protective clothing: In the early years, colliers had to provide their own attire and many went to work in old or second-hand jackets and moleskin trousers (as ordinary ones would be in rags within a few days). Unless working for a particularly beneficial company, miners had to wait until NCB days for safety gear to be made available. These included knee pads, shin guards, dust glasses, goggles, face masks, steel-capped boots, thick overalls and heavy-duty gloves.

Contraband searches: A miner could take a Mars bar underground but not a KitKat. Why?

It was all to do with the foil wrapping around the chocolate, for anything that could generate a spark was classed as 'contraband'. So strictly was this rule enforced that searches were frequently conducted at the pit bank with banksmen authorised to make airport-style body searches whenever they wished. Anyone caught with contraband faced instant dismissal.

To ensure no-one could plead ignorance or forgetfulness, many colliery managements erected huge signs at the entrance to the heapsteads reminding miners to search themselves before entering the cage area (see picture in Chapter 6). At some collieries, even packets of crisps were forbidden and pit canteen staff wouldn't sell a miner a meat pie to put in his 'snap' tin unless it was first removed from its foil container.

It almost goes without saying that matches and cigarettes were forbidden (although snuff and chewing tobacco were allowed), but despite the obvious dangers, some miners still tried to smuggle fags and similar suspect items underground, secreted among their clothing. In 1959, a miner at Moorgreen Colliery was sent to prison for smoking underground, so large signs at pitheads were erected reminding men to check their pockets before entering the cage.

It might come as a surprise to some readers, but under certain conditions even dried orange peel could generate a spark. Some colliery managements forbade newspapers too as, if discarded underground in sufficient amounts, they could potentially exacerbate the fire hazard.

Tallies and checks: The official death toll in a coal dust explosion at Blantyre in 1877 was 207 but the actual figure is thought to have been higher because no proper check was taken of who had gone underground that morning. That lax state of affairs was later addressed by the compulsory issuing of numbered metal discs or triangles known as 'tallies' to all workers before they entered a shaft or drift.

The system was based on the 'motty' method of tub identification, by which colliers hewing individual coalface sections in the old days marked their tub(s) with a number or unique symbol enabling officials weighing the tubs at the surface to know who to pay.

Under the new tally system, every miner was issued with a personal pit number, which would be kept for the whole length of his time at that colliery and would be engraved or fitted on to his safety lamp and on to two discs (sometimes known as 'checks'). The miner would hand one tally to the banksman at the top of the shaft and retain the other with its matching number while underground. He would then hand that one to the banksman as he stepped out of the cage at the end of his shift. By counting the tallies and lamps given out each day, the lamphouse staff knew which men were down a mine at any given time.

Similar systems are still in use today (e.g. for construction workers descending into the Crossrail tunnels in central London), but keeping a tally in the modern era means doing so with swipe-cards and in a concession to advancing technology, British Coal began introducing pithead card-reading machines to its remaining collieries in 1993, although the old 'motties' were retained as an emergency back-up.

Today, the mines lie silent, but memorials around the country are a sobering reminder of the many sacrifices made. One of the most thought-provoking places of all is the Welsh National Mining Memorial at Senghenydd, where hundreds of stone plaques pay tribute to the plethora of serious accidents that have rocked the principality over the decades.

Given all the above, it is not surprising that many underground workers are superstitious. The patron saint of miners and tunnellers is St Barbara and a shrine dedicated to her exists in the shaft bottom area of many collieries, especially those in Catholic countries. Christian legend has it that she sought refuge in a cave while fleeing from her wicked father in the 3rd century. St Barbara's Day is celebrated each year on December 4.

In 1993 British Coal began replacing miners' brass identification tallies with a modern computerised swipe-card system. This card was issued to Annesley-Bentinck Colliery miner David Amos by Midlands Mining following privatisation of the pit in 1996.

A deputy checking for firedamp in the roof of a coal seam in the early years of the 20th century. Note the safety lamps, one fixed to the belt of the miner on the left and the other propped against the seam on the right to enable the collier engaged in undercutting to see what he's doing. Notice also the saw on the left for making props and the fact that neither miner is wearing a helmet.

As occupational hazards go, it would be hard to find one as downright dangerous as this. An undercutter at work, circa 1900. D AMOS COLLECTION

A rare view of an underground ambulance car, photographed at Thoresby Colliery in 2015. With a red cross prominent on its side, this eight-wheeled vehicle carried first-aid equipment and was able to accommodate at least one man on a stretcher.

Left: At Scotland's Barony Colliery in 1962, an entire winding tower collapsed into the top of its own shaft. Thankfully such incidents were extremely rare.

Colliery managements took great pride in maintaining high safety levels and often publicised the fact in signage at the entrance gates.

145

The Aberfan disaster

ONE OF the worst and most poignant mining tragedies didn't kill a single miner.

At 9.15am on October 21, 1966, the pupils of Pantglas Junior School in Aberfan, South Wales, were just about to start lessons when the entire building was buried under thousands of tons of waterlogged shale and coal slurry that slid down from an adjacent spoil tip without warning.

A total of 144 people died, 116 of them children aged between seven and ten. The deputy headteacher, Mr Beynon, was found dead clutching five children in his arms as if he had been protecting them.

A nearby farm and row of terraced cottages were also engulfed and several adults perished in those buildings.

Miners from local mines, especially the one that had produced the tip — Merthyr Vale Colliery — left their jobs to help the 2,000-strong rescue team dig for survivors, but largely in vain.

The landslip occurred after a period of heavy rain, but it was later found that the tip had been destabilised by a spring that flowed beneath it and the NCB was blamed by the official inquiry for extreme negligence in allowing it to be built over the spring despite earlier warnings from villagers.

The heap was later removed as a safety precaution and many similar tips — incorrectly referred to almost universally by the national media as 'slag heaps' — began to be landscaped or at least lowered in height, so as not to pose such a threat to surrounding buildings.

Some of those left in the 'middle of nowhere' following demolition of their parent colliery were allowed to remain in situ but were planted with trees or grass to stabilise them and blend them into the countryside.

Today, a memorial garden stands on the site of the Aberfan school and the bodies of the children, their teachers and the other victims lie in the village's cemetery, their graves marked by a long row of special white arches visible right across the valley.

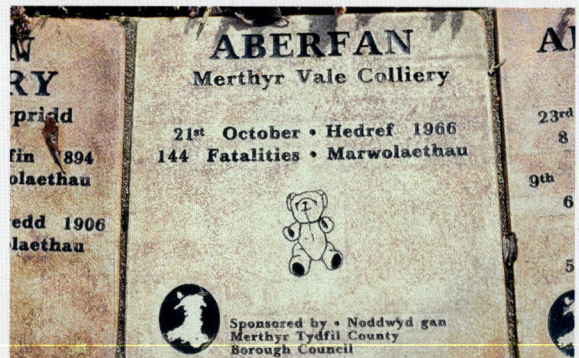

The extent of the devastation is evident in this aerial photograph. Today, the children's short lives are recalled by the emotive sight of this teddy bear at the Welsh National Mining Memorial at Senghenydd and by these lovingly-maintained graves in Aberfan cemetery.

CHAPTER 16

The story of coke

No smoking!

LONG BEFORE it became better known as a popular soft drink, coke was a household name in Britain. In fact, some of the earliest railway locomotives burned it instead of coal following the introduction of a law in 1845 requiring steam engines "to consume their own smoke".

Coke is a hard, grey, porous substance formed by the baking of bituminous coal in an oven in the absence of air to drive off volatile matter, leaving a strong yet lightweight carbon-rich element suitable for using in the blast furnaces of iron and steel plants.

It is also used as a smokeless fuel in homes and factories, which is heavily ironic … for the method by which it is produced is one of the smokiest imaginable and the pyrotechnic display at the discharge stage of the coke-making process is an astonishing visual spectacle never to be forgotten by anyone allowed to witness it at close quarters.

The coke industry in Britain began as far back as the 16th century when coal was heated in earth mounds laid on the ground. When the process was improved in the 1700s by the introduction of dome-shaped brick ovens, the name 'beehive' was coined and at one time there were tens of thousands of such structures dotted across the nation's coalfields. A major breakthrough came in 1709 when industrialist Abraham Darby discovered that coke could be used instead of charcoal in the smelting of ore to produce iron – a major factor in the lead-up to the Industrial Revolution.

By the 1850s, railways were being extended all over Britain and with thousands of trains running every day, it was becoming impractical and expensive for coal to have to be converted into coke in order to keep emissions low, so once

the fireboxes of locomotives began to be fitted with brick arches to burn off excess gases, the 'consumption' law was quietly forgotten.

The developing world was by then fully in the grip of the Industrial Revolution and the demand for iron and steel for construction and engineering was reaching phenomenal proportions, placing enormous strain on the nation's still rather rudimentary beehive ovens. It was, by then, becoming clear that tall vertical ovens made of cast iron and lined with refractory bricks would carbonise the coal more efficiently and plants of this design began to be built during the last two decades of the Victorian era.

The new ovens were arranged side by side in the form of massive 'batteries' baking coal around the clock and lighting up the night sky with an orange glow as their incandescent products were removed from the ovens and quenched with water to cool them down.

Several by-products are produced during the carbonisation process – notably gas, bitumen tar, benzole, coal-oil and ammonia. In earlier centuries, these would have been allowed to escape to the atmosphere or be dumped as waste, but it was then found that the gas could be captured and stored for domestic and street-lighting purposes. The coal-oil was used to produce aviation fuel for the Royal Air Force during the Second World War and since then commercial uses have been developed for all the other by-products too, resulting in a surprisingly varied selection of household products produced either directly or indirectly, such as soap, aspirin, nylon and even perfume.

At one time, by-product coking plants were the most complicated refractory structures built by man and the coalfields and steelworks of Britain possessed almost 200

A panoramic view of Smithywood coking works in March 1982, which at the time was one of the last industrial premises in Britain still using steam locomotives on a regular basis. This huge plant, on the northern outskirts of Sheffield, was opened in 1929 and at its peak it produced 6,000 tons of coke, 68,000 gallons of tar, 29,000 gallons of benzole and 100 tons of ammonium sulphate a week. It was demolished in 1987 and the site is now occupied by a business park. NICK PIGOTT

of them, converting between them a staggering 30m tons of coal a year into coke at the height of the industry's influence midway through the 20th century. When the Bolsover plant opened in Derbyshire just before World War Two, it was the largest of its type in the world.

The last of the old beehive ovens in Britain were closed in 1958 and an indication of just how extensively the country's heavy industry has been destroyed since then is that even their efficient replacements have been almost totally eradicated. There are now only two left – one at Appleby in Scunthorpe and the other at Morfa, near Port Talbot in South Wales.

Until December 2014, there were half a dozen still in operation (including the last independent commercial plant at Monckton, Yorkshire), but that and three steelworks-owned ones were shut down between then and March 2016, primarily as a result of competition from cheap Chinese imports.

The Dawes Lane complex in Scunthorpe was one of the country's biggest with 75 large ovens arranged in three batteries. Each chamber was approximately 50ft long, 18ft high and 3ft wide and at its peak the plant was capable of producing more than a million tons of coke a year for the North Lincolnshire town's blast furnaces.

For the manufacture of high-quality steel, carbon must be as volatile-free and ash-free as possible, so bituminous coal must first be 'coked' to remove such impurities.

There are three main grades of coke, one for blast furnaces, one for foundries and one for factory and domestic use. With regard to the latter, readers of a certain age will recall its widespread use as a smokeless fuel, marketed under trade names such as Coalite, Sunbrite, Phurnacite and Rexco in the days before gas-fired central heating became the rage. Smokeless fuels normally have a sulphur content of less than 2%.

It is somewhat ironic that the plants producing smokeless fuel were some of the smokiest themselves... although that stands to reason as the volatile components had to be removed before reaching the consumer. The awesome moment at which incandescent coke is pushed out of the oven and into the coke wagon is a sight no-one who witnessed it could ever forget, evidenced by this scene at Scunthorpe's Dawes Lane ovens prior to their closure in 2016. NICK PIGOTT

Early coke ovens were shaped like beehives, hence their name.

Coke oven operatives today are required by regulations to wear 'space-man-style' protective clothing and helmets.

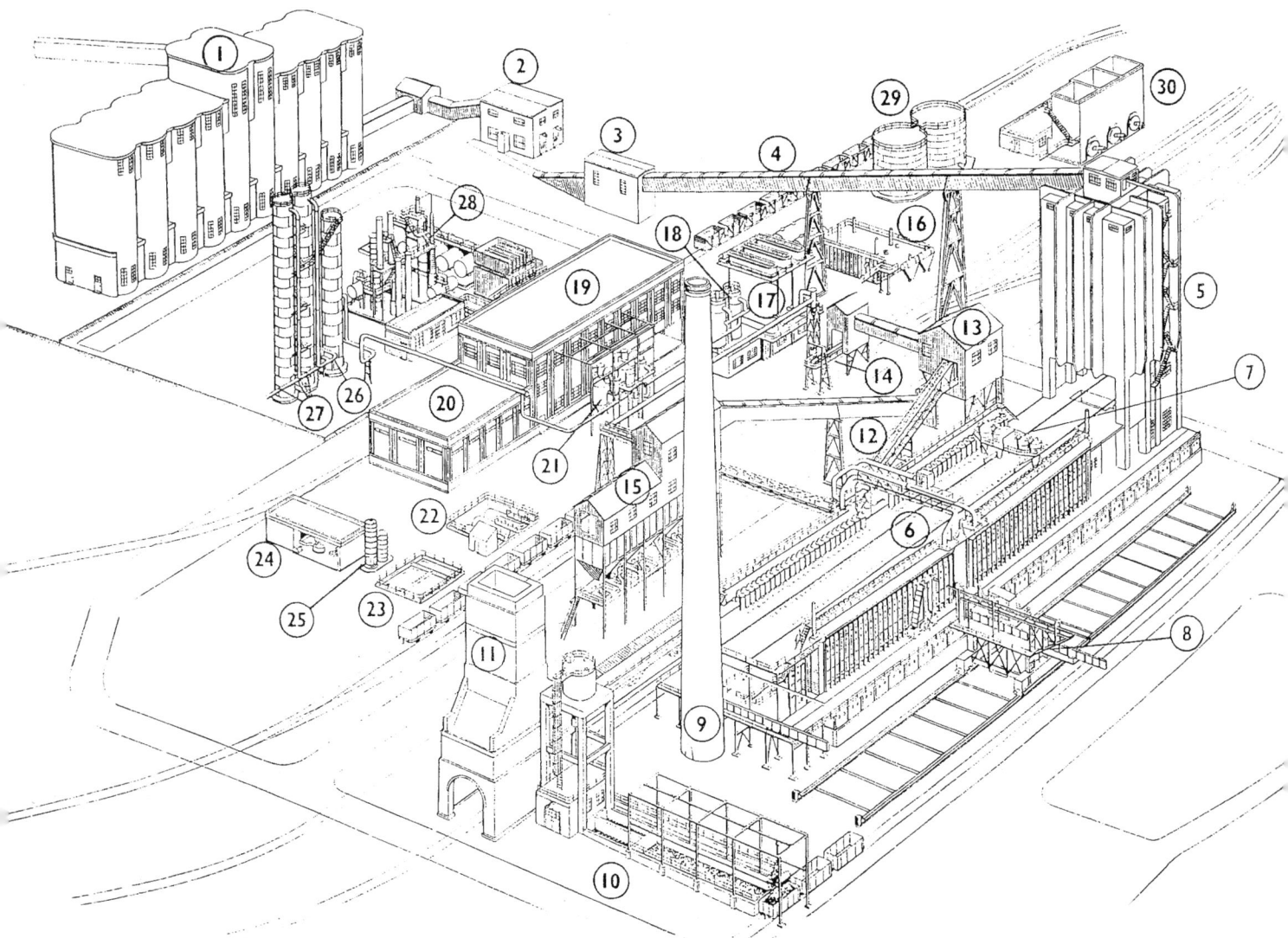

A diagram of a coking plant, showing the principal components. Many of those are highly technical in nature but the relevant ones are: 1) Coal blending bunkers; 2) Coal crusher house; 6) Coke oven batteries; 7) Charging car; 8) Pusher machine; 11) Coke quenching tower; 13) Primary coke screens; 24) Lime-mixing station; 27) Benzole scrubbers; 28) Benzole plant; 30) Water-cooling towers. (The coke car and guide car are not visible, being on the other side of the ovens).

Following the Clean Air Acts of the 1950s and 60s, smokeless zones began to be introduced in Britain and, even in regions where they were not yet compulsory, young housewives hankered after the hot, low flame of modern coke stoves in place of smoky, labour-intensive open coal fires.

That commercial aspect partly explains why many coking plants were attached to collieries, for the coke and the by-products generated profitable sidelines, including export trade markets.

So, how does a coking plant function? Every morning, laboratory technicians at Scunthorpe and Port Talbot analyse the day's blend of metallurgical (coking) coals to ensure they have the high carbon content and other characteristics required to make lumps of coke strong enough to support a 50ft column of ore, limestone and

other substances in a blast furnace without collapsing under the weight. Coke that's not hard enough would be crushed, preventing air from finding its way easily through the furnace. The fact that most metallurgical coal is more brittle than coke is one of the reasons why it is not placed directly into the furnaces, the other being that it can lose much of its calorific value in fume emission before it fully ignites.

Not all types of bituminous coal are suitable for coking and the chemical analysis of the carbon, sulphur, moisture and ash content has become even more important now that Britain has no deep shaft mines and virtually no opencast sources left, for the coal is having to be transported from as far away as Colombia, Australia and Russia ... which is one of the reasons why recent attempts have been made

At the Bolsover smokeless fuel plant in February 1993, freshly-produced coke cools off in railway wagons before leaving the works. On the hill in the middle distance can be seen 400-year-old Bolsover Castle, the buildings forming one of Britain's most peculiar juxtapositions until demolition of the plant. NICK PIGOTT

to open a coking coal mine near Whitehaven, Cumbria (see Appendix H).

In some cases, foreign coals are lower in sulphur content than British types anyway, so they result in better-quality iron and steel. Buying in coking coal from abroad is not as new a phenomenon as might be imagined, for back in 1976, the chairman of the Coke Oven Managers' Association revealed that it was "cheaper to import coal from Australia to Port Talbot than to move it by train from Staffordshire to Port Talbot!" He also pointed out that sea freight charges from the US to Wales were approximately the same as rail freight charges within Wales!

Whatever happens in the roller-coaster nature of the UK steel industry, it will be important for the owners of the Appleby and Morfa ovens to ensure they can retain an element of self-sufficiency in a politically-uncertain world. Indeed, it has even been suggested that the term 'coking coal' be dropped because of today's negative connotations and be replaced by the phrase 'coke raw material'.

Once the lab technicians have established that the day's supply of coal has the required high carbon content, density and other qualities, it is taken from a coal-blending bunker, crushed and then charged by gravity into the top of the ovens (known in the industry as carbonising chambers). Each oven can contain about 30 tonnes of coal, which is

heated by gas flues in a virtually airtight, very low-oxygen environment, allowing the fixed carbon and residual ash to fuse together to form the hard, grey, porous coke. The moisture content and volatile crude vapours leave the chambers by 'ascension pipes' and are condensed and cleaned at the plant's chemical works to form the various by-products.

The old beehive ovens used to take 72 hours or more to carbonise the coal fully, but modern plants can do it in as little as 18 hours as they reach temperatures of well over 1,000ºC (1,832ºF). The plants are in operation day and night, all year round, even on Christmas Day, as the process cannot be slowed down or stopped without risking serious damage to the oven walls. As it is, the chambers have to be fired in a certain order to prevent the walls between them warping as a result of overly rapid cooling.

A typical coke works is served by four separate sets of rail lines. One set on the roof, along which a charge car runs in order to load the crushed coal into the ovens; one broad gauge set at the rear for the enormous pusher machine (which literally pushes the red-hot coke out of the oven); and two at the front – one for a guide car and one for a locomotive-powered coke car. In all four cases, there is a spare vehicle on standby to ensure continuity in the production process.

When it is time for an oven to be discharged, the guide

The enormous pusher vehicle at Dawes Lane. This ran along the back of the batteries and used powerful rams to open the oven doors and push the coke through to the wagon on the other side.

car is brought up alongside and unscrews the oven's front door remotely. The same procedure is carried out at the rear door by the pusher vehicle, which then uses a powerful mechanical ram to drive the red-hot coke through the guide car's cage and into the waiting coke car, resulting in a 'firework' display like no other!

The still-incandescent product is then quickly taken in the coke car to the adjacent quenching tower for cooling. That too creates an awesome spectacle and at Port Talbot in 1981, a new set of ovens had to be built at Morfa to replace those at nearby Margam following residents' complaints about clouds of smoke and plumes of steam. Today, the process is more environmentally friendly, although the white vapour billowing high into the sky as coke at 1,000° hits cold air followed by water at 10° still qualifies as one

of the most dramatic sights in industry.

Not surprisingly, the operators and maintenance staff who work at these ovens have to wear special clothing and 'spacemen'-style helmets to protect them from the intense heat.

To make iron, the coke is mixed with iron ore and limestone and fed into the top of a blast furnace. Air is then blown through the blast pipes at the bottom to raise the temperature. The iron ore reacts with the coke and gives up its oxygen to it, producing molten iron that trickles to the bottom of the furnace and forms a layer of liquid iron which is run off.

Impurities in the ore combine with the limestone to form a liquid 'slag' which, because it is lighter than iron, floats on top and is tapped separately.

A coke push viewed from under the quenching tower at Dawes Lane.

Apart from the last handful of coal-fired power stations and opencast mines, the only places to see massive stockpiles of coal in Britain these days are cement factories and steel plants. At Scunthorpe, coal destined for Appleby coke works is stored in silos and handled by the giant bucket-wheel excavator visible on the right.

A scene at Glasshoughton works showing Robert Stephenson & Hawthorn fireless locomotive No.8082. At the time of the photo (1970), the loco was believed to be the last everyday working example of a lineage of Stephenson motive power dating back to the early-1800s. BRIAN SHARPE

CHAPTER 17

Focus on a colliery

The jewel in the crown

THORESBY COLLIERY was located just outside the village of Edwinstowe, Nottinghamshire, and was established in the mid-1920s, producing its first coal in 1928.

It was said at the time to be one of the most modern coal mines in the world, but local landowner Lord Manvers, of Thoresby Hall, was not well disposed to the idea of his home being associated with a colliery and tried unsuccessfully to get it named Edwinstowe or Cockglode, after a local spinney.

He also objected to having a smoking chimney near his Sherwood Forest estate, which led to Thoresby being the first colliery in the country to be built with electric winders.

Although upgraded in the 1950s, the mine was far more traditional than many of the more modern 'superpits' it outlived. The reasons for its longevity were partly related to the fact that it has benefitted over the years from highly-productive seams and was generating between 1.5m and 2m tons a year — hence its proud reputation as 'the jewel in the crown' of the East Midlands coalfield.

As can be seen opposite and on the front cover, its upcast shaft displayed a large golden crown, which was still proudly on display when the mine closed in July 2015.

The last seam to be worked there was known as the Deep Soft and there were originally three others — the Parkgate, High Hazel and Top Hard (or 'Barnsley'). Production at the final set of Deep Soft faces didn't start until 2010 and in its last month of operation, the colliery was operating around the clock, sending out at least three main line trainloads of power station coal a day and employing 379 men, some 300 of whom worked underground on a four-shift basis.

The mine's owner, UK Coal, wanted to keep it open and

had even transferred locomotives and a more efficient coal-preparation plant from Warwickshire's closed Daw Mill Colliery, but it needed subsidy to open up new faces and with the subsequent collapse of world coal prices, the Government opted instead to provide a £10m grant for a 'managed closure'.

A few weeks before the pit closed, I was granted permission to take my final look at the underground workings of a fully-operational British colliery. After a smooth and rapid cage ride down No.1 shaft — which at 2,267ft deep is equivalent to more than twice the height of London's Shard, Britain's tallest building — I stepped out into the strong breeze that characterises most deep workings. This was caused by the powerful ventilation fans, which circulated air around Thoresby's many roadways and galleries and sent it up the colliery's No.2 shaft, which was used for skip-winding.

The care-worn arched walls of the roadways at pit bottom looked as though time hadn't moved since they were built in the 1920s and there was a maze of 3ft gauge underground railways going off in every direction, serving storage areas, sidings, loco battery-charging stations and maintenance depots, as well as the coal-getting districts.

The routes leading towards the coalfaces of modern mines are usually several miles long, which is one of the reasons why railways were introduced underground — to carry miners to their place of work. For without the so-called 'Paddy' trains, the men could spend as much as half their paid shift time walking to or from the coalface.

At Thoresby, they still had a long journey even after the train had dropped them off, having to walk almost a mile to the end of the coal-loading gate and then riding a conveyor

King Coal's crowning glory. A close-up of Thoresby's upcast headgear in 2015 showing the golden icon that adorned the East Midlands' most productive pit. ROBIN STEWART-SMITH

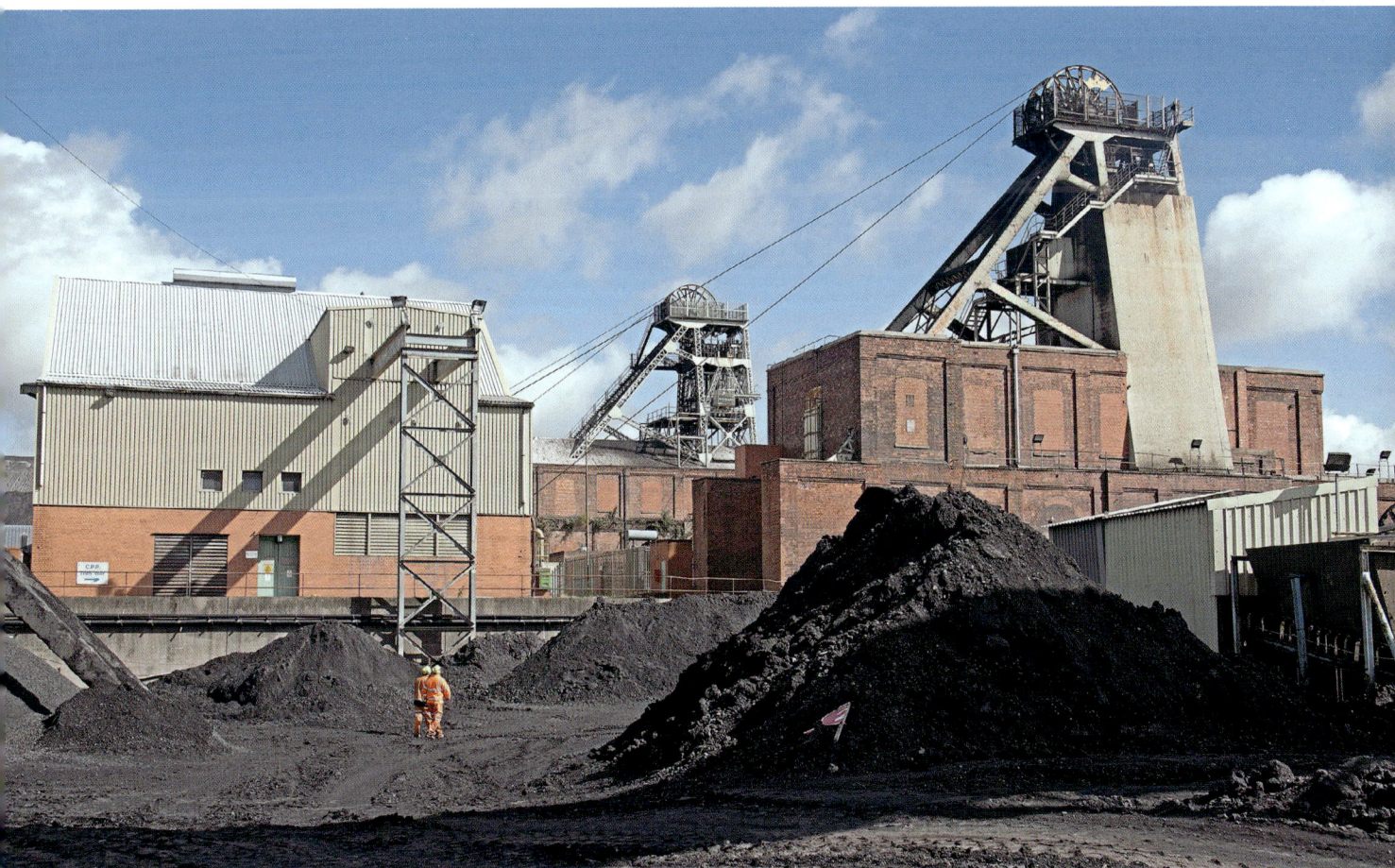

A general view of the colliery. Both sets of headgear at this pit featured substantial brick-built heapstead buildings at their bases. ROBIN STEWART-SMITH

One of two half-sheaves that acted as gate guardians at the entrance.

A rare view inside an onsetter's cabin. These were located at the foot of the
man-riding shafts and this one at Thoresby was 2,200ft below the ground.
BARRY GRAHAM

belt to the face itself.

As faces in modern mines were often at a deeper depth
than the bottom of the shafts, the men at the cutting edge in
some collieries had to toil at depths of 3,000ft or so ... equivalent to England's highest mountain, Scafell Pike. Without

man-riding systems, they would have had to climb back up
the drifts at gradients as steep as 1-in-4 after a tiring shift
in sweltering temperatures that could reach 100°F (38°C).

In its final year of operation, Thoresby still had a workforce of 600 mineworkers, down by more than half on its
1980s level, but nevertheless a healthy figure for the 2010s.
In terms of staff hierarchy, it conformed to the traditional
seniority ranking system that had stood the test of time at
almost every major mine, namely a colliery manager, to
whom the following second-tier officials reported directly:
undermanager, ventilation manager, surveyor, electrical
engineer, mechanical engineer and safety officer.

On the third tier of seniority were the overmen and on
the fourth tier of officialdom were the deputies, who were
responsible for day-to-day operations in the various underground districts. Other specialist operators, such as electricians, reported to their respective second-tier executive.

In pre-nationalisation years, mine owners would often
delegate the running of their collieries to what was known
as an agent, or viewer, to whom the colliery managers
themselves would report, but this system is not thought
to have survived beyond the late-1940s.

Despite its extensive rail system, Thoresby, in common
with other modern mines, sent its coal outbye via conveyors
and skip hoppers. Less than three weeks from closure, 48
skips were being wound every hour and the 20ft diameter

The natural synergy between the coal and rail industries in the days when both were under state ownership resulted in mutually beneficial ventures such as the naming of main line locomotives after collieries. BR Coal Sector Class 58 No.58046 stands under the rapid loader at Thoresby during its naming ceremony on June 29, 1991. ROBIN STEWART-SMITH

Thoresby's stockyard was served by a 3ft gauge railway system for moving wagons and locomotives in and out of the downcast shaft. NICK PIGOTT

winding wheels at the top of No.2 shaft were spinning every couple of minutes, 22 hours a day, seven days a week.

Household coal (in cobble-sized lumps) was collected from the pit by lorries after being washed and processed in the coal preparation plant, but the product intended for power stations was crushed and moved to the top of a large elevated 'rapid loader' bunker for dropping into main line railway wagons.

Even in its final year of operation, Thoresby possessed a fleet of 16 underground locomotives, seven of which remained in daily use until the end. All were battery-electrics built by Midlands-based Clayton Equipment Co, three of which were just five years old.

The mine also had an ambulance car and a limestone spreader vehicle to apply white stonedust powder over the tracks and roadways in order to reduce the risk of coal dust explosions.

After closure, two of the colliery's British-built 'Pony' locomotives were taken to the surface to be donated to nearby mining museums, one at Bilsthorpe and the other at Pleasley. The rest of the fleet was abandoned to its fate underground, along with 15m tonnes of easily-accessible reserves.

It can be seen that Thoresby (along with Kellingley and Hatfield) retained its 'major league' status a remarkable 30 years beyond the end of the 1984/85 miners' strike. Its productivity rate remained high right until the end and the 700,000 tons it produced in the first half of 2015 were on target to give it yet another 1.5m tonne yield for the year.

"We're more productive at the moment than we've ever been ... but the country just doesn't want us," rued colliery manager Derek Main in the mine's final month. "The price of coal has fluctuated over the years and could easily rise again in the future — but by then it will be too late!"

The price did indeed rise, shooting up in 2017 and again in 2021, but it was indeed too late, for the site of Thoresby was by then disappearing beneath yet another large housing estate.

All that's left of Thoresby Colliery in summer 2021. The large workshop is the only building left on the site and has been earmarked for conversion into the centrepiece of an 800-home estate. However, despite being planned as part of the same development (they are even illustrated on the house-builder's promotional sign at the entrance!), the winding house and headgear have been demolished.

CHAPTER 18

Superpits

The brave new world

YOUNGER READERS and those who never saw a coal mine might be surprised to learn that many collieries were located not in grimy industrial towns but in open countryside, surrounded by farmland.

Many modern mines had very few houses next to them, the NCB providing large car parks bordered by neatly-trimmed lawns and laying on shuttle bus services for those miners who still relied on public transport.

Such mines also possessed structures that looked like concrete tower blocks instead of traditional winding gear.

These were the so-called superpits. Some were built from scratch, others came about as a result of mergers between older or smaller mines, but they all had something in common – they were enormous.

One of the new state-of-the-art collieries – Comrie, in Fife – was built before the NCB came into existence. It was established between 1936 and 1939 by the Fife Coal Company, which sent its engineers to the US and the European mainland to study the very latest mining practice and incorporate it into a showpiece colliery on a greenfield site, complete with spacious layout – a complete contrast to the clutter of older pits and mining villages.

Below ground, the roadways were generously proportioned and ventilation air was blown into the pit rather than being drawn through by extractor fans. At the face, each undercutter machine was so easy to operate and adjust that one man could do it. There were pithead showers and even a training school so that miners could improve themselves by learning the history and theory of coal and its strata.

In many ways, Fife Coal's brave new world set the seal for the NCB's own modernisation programme of the 1950s,

although Comrie itself never really lived up to its potential. Another large state-of-the-art Scottish colliery from the early NCB era – Rothes – also under-achieved, due partly to drainage problems, and was closed after just four years.

The political embarrassment surrounding debacles such as those included the controversial abandonment of a would-be superpit at Airth, near Falkirk, while it was still only partly built – but another of the board's flagship superpits, Seafield, on the coast near Kirkcaldy, fared much better. It employed 2,500 men drawn from 13 old worked-out collieries further west, and had a coalface that was 100 yards long. It was described as being "more like an underground factory than a coal mine."

Blocks of flats? The visual differences between the Koepe winding towers of a superpit and those of a traditional mine were striking, as evidenced by this view of Parkside Colliery, near Manchester.

Lea Hall Colliery in Staffordshire was part of a joint venture between the NCB and the Central Electricity Generating Board to supply the adjacent Rugeley power station directly by covered conveyor belt and this aerial photograph was taken in 1961 soon after the complex went into production. The mine was closed 30 years later and the power plant no longer exists either.

Seafield Colliery, just south of Kirkcaldy in Fife, was a modern superpit built by the NCB in the late-1950s alongside the Edinburgh-Dundee main line, along which preserved A4 Pacific No.60009 *Union of South Africa* is passing with a steam special on September 8, 1973. The colliery was closed in 1988 and is now a housing estate. GAVIN MORRISON

A panoramic view of Rothes Colliery, Fife. Although many millions of pounds were spent by the NCB on the construction of this Scottish superpit in the 1950s, it never lived up to expectations and was closed in 1962 after fighting a losing battle with water inundation. Even before the end of main line steam in Scotland, its sidings had become overgrown and J38 No.65901 is passing a rather forlorn scene in 1965. Still extant at that time was the aerial ropeway (far right) leading to the spoil heap, while in the right background can be seen the tip of an older colliery near the aptly-named Coaltown of Balgonie. W J V ANDERSON/RAIL ARCHIVE STEPHENSON

The impressive sight of a superpit at night. The huge covered conveyors that so typified British Coal's modern mines are prominent in this 1990s view of Harworth Colliery's rapid loader section, as diesel-electric No.58045, bearing the black diamonds of British Rail's Coal Sector logo, creeps slowly through. COURTESY DAVE DARWIN

Other state-of-the-art mines in Scotland included Monktonhall and Bilston Glen, but by the time of the 1994/95 sell-off there was only one colliery left to privatise north of the border – the Longannet-Castlebridge complex.

In England, new or rebuilt superpits were opened at Parkside, near Manchester, in 1957, at Lea Hall, Hem Heath and Wolstanton in Staffordshire and, in the Nottinghamshire coalfield, at places like Cotgrave and Bevercotes, the latter being Britain's first fully-automated colliery. In the eastern part of the Yorkshire field, Kellingley was opened in 1965.

In South Wales, all-new showpieces were built at Abernant and Cynheidre, which were opened to exploit deep-lying anthracite seams at the western end of the South Wales coalfield. In the bituminous southern part of the field, Nantgarw was converted into a superpit at great expense for the operation of horizon mining (see Chapter 8), but its steeply-inclined seams, combined with a big staff turnover, militated against its efficiency and although it wasn't finally closed until 1986, it was always considered something of a 'white elephant'.

Most superpits were instantly recognisable by virtue of their large square or rectangular Koepe friction winding towers, but appearances above ground could be deceptive. As seams became exhausted, it was not uncommon for neighbouring collieries to be merged underground to form a superpit, with the surface buildings at the smaller or older pit taken out of use or mothballed.

In such cases, one or more headstocks at the 'closed' site might well remain in operation for several months, or even years, for the winding of men or materials or to facilitate ventilation.

South Yorkshire boasted several superpits, including Maltby Main, near Rotherham. Seen in 2006, it closed seven years later.

Arguably the most 'space-age' headstocks ever erected in Britain were those at the ill-fated Thorne Colliery, near Doncaster. As was sadly the case at several superpits, they lasted a far shorter time than intended, in this case from 1979 to 2004.

CHAPTER 19
Surface railways

Coal and steam: the perfect marriage

Some collieries were relatively tiny, wedged between a river and the side of a valley; others were enormous, sprawling across several acres of open countryside ... but what almost all of them had in common was a railway connection.

Railways primarily came into existence to serve collieries, but as they developed into a nationwide network transporting general commodities and passengers too, they had the effect of opening up new coalfields and the mining industry thus found itself having to grow rapidly to cope with the new discoveries and increased demands.

The natural affinity between coal and trains didn't stop there, for the railway companies became big customers of the coal owners in order to fuel their steam locomotives – and for more than a century until the advent of reliable motor lorries, the coal owners needed the railways to get their product to every factory and to every little town and village in the land.

This was achieved by establishing a small coal yard or siding at virtually every country station, from where the local coal merchant would collect, bag and deliver with a horse and dray.

Today, such yards are a distant memory, although a few traditional merchants do still exist in the 2020s and their storage areas – often separated by half-walls made of old wooden railway sleepers to denote different grades of coal – are a nostalgic reminder of a once-ubiquitous sight.

The first colliery branches were basic plateways and waggonways established in the 1700s to enable coal to be taken in chaldron waggons from pit to coastal or riverside wharfs. They would be allowed to run downhill by gravity, braked by a man riding on the vehicle and hauled back by horse when empty. On some lines, the process was speeded up by coupling a 'dandy cart' to the waggon, enabling the horse to ride in it on the way down.

The first successful railway in the world on which steam locos were regularly operated on a commercial basis was the Middleton Colliery line in Leeds, which opened in 1812 using a rack-and-pinion system.

Until the advent of the Liverpool & Manchester Railway passenger line in the 1830s and subsequent 'railway mania' a decade later, the majority of steam locomotives built in Britain were for colliery or associated use and this led to numerous manufacturers springing up in the industrial cities of the north to meet demand.

By the middle of the 19th century, the railway age was well established and virtually every major colliery was connected. Whenever a new mine was authorised in a hitherto-undeveloped area, the rail link normally had to be laid at an early stage in order to transport all the equipment needed to sink the shafts, erect the surface structures and build the colliery village. Sometimes the risk of constructing a single-track branch from the nearest main line would be borne by the coal company and sometimes by the railway company, although the latter tended to be cautious at that stage as the mine would not yet have proved a commercial success.

In the case of Bilsthorpe Colliery, the independent

163

A silhouette of double-headed Hunslet 0-6-0STs *Whiston* and *Wimblebury* hauling MGR wagons at Littleton Colliery in November 1993. Working steam had finished at the Staffordshire pit some years earlier, but an enthusiasts' photo charter ensured one final fling on the colliery's steeply-inclined branch line. NICK PIGOTT

This 1822 vintage Hetton Colliery 0-4-0 was still working when photographed for *The Railway Magazine* in 1905. In its early years, it had been a contemporary of the famous and now-preserved 'Puffing Billy'. Note how the cab is on the side of the boiler rather than at the firebox end.

Before the invention of locomotives, chaldron waggons were run downhill by gravity.

Mansfield Railway declined to build the necessary extension from the Rufford branch due to a dispute over rates, so the Midland Railway was appointed and when it too dragged its feet, the Great Central Railway was approached. That galvanised the MR, which said it would build a contractor's line at the Stanton Iron Company's expense but that, if the pit proved successful, the permanent line would be built at the MR's expense. The mine was indeed a success, although by the time the permanent way was

required, the MR had become part of the London Midland & Scottish Railway, which duly picked up the bill.

By 1924, British mines were producing 267m tons a year and the railways were transporting 225m tons of that (84%). About 95m tons was exported and the railways' share of that pit-to-port traffic was an impressive 90%.

So keen was the Great Western Railway to guarantee itself a constant supply of good quality Welsh steam coal that it owned its own collieries at one time. The coal companies, on the other hand, owned their own fleets of main line railway wagons, which, once unloaded at their destinations, had to be marshalled again in order to be sent back to their respective collieries. It was a colossal logistical operation, yet the wagons were never officially pooled despite such an arrangement being advocated several times in the 1930s.

At vesting day on January 1, 1947, just under a quarter of a million standard gauge wagons (60,000 of which were internal user vehicles) were handed over to the NCB, which in turn handed them over to the British Transport Commission upon the formation of British Railways exactly a year later.

The private-owner wagons were mostly wooden-bodied and almost invariably carried the name of the colliery or its

Few photographs sum up the heyday of coal mining in Britain as well as this: It is virtually impossible to even count the astonishing number of wagons in this South Wales marshalling yard, let alone comprehend the extraordinary effort that went into filling them. The private owner wagons bear the names of various coal companies, including Davis & Sons of Cardiff, David Bevan & Co and Nixon's Navigation.

company in large capital letters on the bodyside. Complicating the matter was the fact that many coal merchants and municipal utilities possessed their own branded wagons too.

As early as 1920 or so, the GWR was hiring 21-ton steel-bodied wagons to coal-owning companies to help eliminate old wooden wagons of eight to ten tons capacity, and when British Railways came into existence in 1948, it decided to standardise on 21-ton and 16-ton wagons to replace the hotchpotch of private-owner vehicles. Some 300,000 of the new types were built (the vast majority of them 16-tonners, as not all colliery screens could accommodate the larger ones), but as an indication of how rapidly trends change on the railways, even those had become virtually extinct by the early-1990s.

Fortunately, the last few examples were preserved by the Great Central Railway in 1992 following an initiative launched by the author of this book and they can be seen running as 'Windcutter' trains on certain steam gala days and other special occasions.

In 1958, BR still owned 16,000 steam locomotives with a coal consumption rate of 10.7m tons a year ... yet within a single decade that figure would plunge to absolute zero!

'Black diamonds' still accounted for 63% of all the freight carried by BR in the mid-1950s and South Yorkshire's Wath marshalling yard (which wasn't even one of the largest on BR) was taking in 53 full-length coal trains a day — an average of one every 28 minutes round the clock from no fewer than 21 different local collieries.

During the Beeching era of mass locomotive withdrawals and train service closures in the 1960s, the network of small coal yards was replaced by a smaller number of concentration yards, from where lorries could collect and deliver locally. The road transport companies, of course, soon realised that it would be cheaper and less hassle not to have the transhipment stage ... and yet another form of traffic was lost to the railway.

From 1965, the Merry-Go-Round (MGR) system of power station coal transport was introduced using a fleet of 10,960

An almost spotless white overhead electric loco glides incongruously through the grime of a typical colliery scene – NCB No.14 on the Harton Electric Railway in September 1968. TREVOR OWEN/COLOUR-RAIL

Ancient wooden-bodied coal wagons still in existence at Ashington Colliery in June 1987. NICK PIGOTT

specially-built air-braked hopper wagons, each capable of holding 32 tonnes of pulverised coal. Diesel locomotives fitted with slow-speed controls hauled them through the colliery loading and power station discharging terminals without stopping. In more recent years, the four-wheeled MGR wagons have been phased out in favour of 75-tonne capacity high-sided bogie vehicles operated by railfreight companies such as EWS and Freightliner Heavy Haul.

The last trainload of coal to depart from an operational British deep mine left Kellingley Colliery for Drax power station at lunchtime on December 18, 2015. Since then, all rail movements have been of imported, stockpiled or opencast coal.

Transport on the main line network is only part of the story though, for most collieries had their own internal railway systems on the surface (in addition to subterranean systems, which are dealt with in the next chapter).

Standard gauge tracks were normally laid in and around the colliery yard to enable full and empty wagons to be moved in and out of washery screen sidings and be taken to the main line exchange sidings. As the years went by, these internal systems grew larger and more complicated and some even resembled minor marshalling yards with their own engine sheds, wagon repair depots and workshops. Some serving several collieries, such as the Lambton,

A little-known aspect of railway and mining history is the workmen's passenger train. These were run by companies to take workers to remote locations they would have struggled to reach by public transport and utilised old coaching stock that had usually seen better days elsewhere. Officially they were private, but local people 'in the know' frequently hitched a ride on them. In this 1964 scene near Ashington, NCB 0-6-0T No.31 is making good progress with former suburban coaches also lettered NCB. These miners were lucky, though… others, such as those who worked at Blaenserchan Colliery in South Wales, had to travel in converted goods vans! W J V ANDERSON/RAIL ARCHIVE STEPHENSON

A colliery with a passenger platform within its infrastructure… BR Western Region pannier tank No.3647 waits at Glyncorrwg South Pit halt with an unadvertised workmen's service in April 1964. This 'Paddy' service ended later that year. A P GOFF

Hetton & Joicey Railway, in County Durham, were extensive enough to be thought of as networks rather than branches.

The internal systems and their locomotives became part of the NCB in 1947, which partly explains why steam traction consequently clung on at collieries considerably longer than was the case on BR, well into the 1970s and even early 80s in some cases. The fact that the fuel supply for the engines was free and readily available also had a large bearing, of course.

Unlike BR, which implemented a standardised numbering system for the myriad locos it inherited, the NCB left such matters up to its area managements. Some introduced systems revealing the division, area and colliery the machine was allocated to, others merely carried on with vague local arrangements.

Due to the fact that high speeds most certainly weren't necessary or advisable on the switchback nature of most colliery tracks, quite a few former main line locos found a new lease of life on coal work after being pensioned off their primary duties. Among the best-known were former Great Western Railway pannier tanks, but there were also ex-North Staffordshire Railway 0-6-2 tanks that ran in that railway's livery on the Walkden coal system and even an

British Rail Type 1s Nos.20135 and 20071 slowly bring a rake of MGR wagons through the loading bunker at Bickershaw Colliery before setting off for Fiddlers Ferry power station on July 31, 1970. STEVE TURNER/RAIL PHOTOPRINTS

Because they were introduced in the mid-1960s, Merry-Go-Round coal wagons are associated very much with the diesel era, so a photograph of one being hauled by a steam locomotive is an eye-opener. The location is Morpeth, Northumberland, and the newly-built wagons are heading for Blyth staithes with a full load behind J27 0-6-0 No.65842.

ex-London, Brighton & South Coast Railway E1 class 0-6-0T at Cannock Wood, in the West Midlands. This hand-me-down policy continued into the modern traction era, with many of BR's short-lived diesel shunters going on to have longer lives in industrial use than they did in BR service.

By far the most common form of steam loco used in UK collieries were the 0-6-0 and 0-4-0 saddle tank types, thousands of which have been used over the years. When it came to the engine chosen to represent the NCB in the Stockton & Darlington Railway 150th anniversary celebrations at Shildon in 1975, Bagnall No.2779 from County Durham's Vane-Tempest Colliery was given the honour and proudly took its part in the cavalcade of glamorous and famous passenger locomotives.

At the 'Rocket 150' celebrations near Rainhill, Lancs, five years later, the NCB was afforded an even greater honour when nearby Bold Colliery was chosen as the base for an all-star locomotive cavalcade, with some of the thousands of spectators eschewing the trackside grandstands to get an even grander view from atop the pit's spoil heap!

Among the most unusual engines to work in colliery service were two Beyer-Garratt articulated steam locomotives – No.6729 at Sneyd Colliery, Staffordshire, and No.6841 at Warwickshire's Baddesley Colliery, the latter loco now preserved.

Almost certainly the most unusual design of locomotive to work the surface lines of a major British colliery was the Beyer-Garratt 0-4-4-0T type, examples of which were based at Baddesley and Sneyd collieries in the West Midlands. This is maroon-liveried No.3 (6729) operating at the latter pit in June 1961 and passing a delightful glassless signal that probably hadn't worked in years. COLOUR-RAIL

Some of BR Western Region's Class 1500 pannier tanks saw use at Coventry Colliery after their main line days were over and received maroon paint in place of their BR livery. In this June 1969 scene, No.1509 has its smokebox cleared of ash as classmate No.1502 stands adjacent to the pit's winding tower. COLOUR-RAIL

In the non-steam category, contenders for the most unusual were without doubt two mines with overhead catenary on their surface rail systems. Those were the remarkable and extensive Harton Electric Railway — a standard gauge system that linked Harton and Westoe collieries with staithes in South Shields and didn't close until July 1989 — and the Whittonstall line, a 2ft 2in gauge network on the Durham/Northumberland border that served a number of drift mines in the area. The latter was a 500v overhead system and among its locos was a steeple-cab 0-4-4-0 built by Hanomag in Germany in 1910 and scrapped 20 years later.

Not all mines were located close to main lines, necessitating purpose-built branches, along which industrial engines would trundle several times a day with loaded wagons, returning with the empties. The length of the branches varied tremendously, from a quarter of a mile or so to ten miles or more. In steam days and before the advent of the MGR system, main line locomotives rarely worked onto colliery premises — but in the main line diesel era they did so on a permanent basis.

The last standard gauge loco in regular internal use at a British deep coal complex was Barclay 0-6-0 diesel-hydraulic No.615 of 1977, which worked at Gascoigne Wood disposal point in South Milford, Yorkshire, until at least 2004.

In addition to a standard gauge surface system, many mines in pre-skip winding days also possessed narrow gauge tracks whose gauge matched that installed underground. This was to enable full tubs of coal to be moved from the shaft top to the weighhouse and washery and back again when empty. Such tracks were also used for storing wagonloads of spares and supplies before they were taken below for onward movement to the coalface or wherever.

In more recent years, the standard gauge industrial locos and wagons tended to be replaced by a maze of covered conveyors on the surface and the many colliery sidings were consequently replaced by a much simpler layout enabling slow-speed MGR trains to run into a rapid-loading bunker and then out again, either via a run-round headshunt or — where space allowed — a balloon loop.

Each train was capable of hauling 1,000 tonnes-plus and each rapid loader typically held around 5,000 tonnes, so the risk of delays caused by breakdowns in the colliery process was greatly reduced.

Conveyors underground also made the coal-carrying duties of subterranean narrow gauge systems redundant, although many were retained for man-riding purposes.

The unusual sight of a large main line steam tender locomotive on a colliery internal system. Ex-LMS 8F 2-8-0 No.48151 and an unidentified Class 58 diesel give shuttle rides at a Sutton Colliery open day, Notts, on September 10, 1988. ROBIN STEWART-SMITH

Diversion of the East Coast Main Line at Selby

ONE OF the strangest developments concerning the relationship between coal and main line railways involved the newly-discovered coalfield in the district of Selby, North Yorkshire.

In April 1976, the Secretary of State for the Environment, Anthony Crosland, ruled that retention of the East Coast Main Line on its traditional route through Selby could only be achieved "by leaving an unacceptable amount of coal, incompatible with the new coalmining project".

The dramatic decision was thus taken to construct a major diversion several miles to the west in order to let the NCB have unfettered access to the extensive deposits.

The new line was opened in 1983 and although Selby continued to be served by trains, it lost its direct connection to York and its through main line expresses to London.

CHAPTER 20
Underground transport
The 'Paddy trains'

A HUGE RANGE of materials had to be transported underground in a colliery in addition to miners and coal. Firstly, there was the infrastructure required to develop the roadways, such as roof supports, then the machinery required to win the coal, especially cutters and conveyors, then the pipe and cable components to provide electricity, compressed air, fresh air and water. Also needed were vehicles for emergencies – an ambulance car and, in some mines, a fire-fighting wagon.

In fact, it has been estimated that the conveyance of coal, spoil, men and materials could constitute as much as three-quarters of a modern deep mine's operation.

Back in the 1600s, four-wheeled tubs known as 'trams' or 'drams' running on wooden rails began to replace baskets, sleds, corves and barrows for the movement of coal underground and in the 1700s mechanisation began with the increased use of iron rails and the invention of reliable stationary steam engines.

At first, they were placed underground (with their exhaust taken to the surface by flues in the shaft) and they hauled the tubs along roadways using ropes, but so many fires were caused by that method that the boilers were placed on the surface with their steam pipes running down the shaft to underground cylinders. The problem with that was excessive condensation in the long pipes and although steam locomotion became possible in the early-1800s, it was not prudent to send engines through the tunnels for various reasons, the most obvious being pollution and the risk of gas explosions.

That led to a search for more suitable sources of power and in the mid-1800s the first compressed air rope-haulage engines were introduced, but the compressor plants also required the presence of stationary steam engines on the surface, from which the ropes went down the shaft – still a complicated and unsatisfactory process.

At around the turn of the 20th century, electrical equipment began to be used underground, but for mines that couldn't be certified gas-free, the electricity had to be generated by small power stations built at individual colliery pitheads and the need to flame-proof the subterranean equipment made the process slow to develop.

In those days, most coal was being hauled from the face to the pit bottom along narrow gauge tracks in half-ton or one-ton capacity tubs hauled by horses or ponies, of which there were an estimated 70,000 in British mines at that time.

In the 1920s, progressive colliery owners began to introduce small battery-electric locomotives (initially imported from the US) and at the end of that decade, British company Greenwood & Batley Co, of Leeds, also started building battery-electric locos, later joined by English Electric and Huwood.

The technology was in its infancy though – the power was relatively weak and the locos could not work for long between charges. It took the development of reliable diesel traction to mark a big breakthrough, but although a few diesels were tried underground in the late-1930s, they suffered from the same problem as steam engines – the risk of fire and noxious fumes emitted in a confined space.

Pits with low to zero firedamp risk would, at that time, have been officially classified for fire-risk purposes as Naked Light Mines, with the others being known as Safety Lamp Mines, but shortly after coming into existence, the NCB decided that the differentiation created too much of a 'grey area' and did away with the naked light classification

Flame-proofed diesel locomotives were used underground at many mines before the widespread introduction of battery-electric traction. This Huwood/Hudswell Clarke machine is hauling a six-coach man-riding train half a mile below the surface at Thoresby Colliery in March 1959.

for safety reasons. Thereafter, all mines were assumed to be gassy and all underground machinery had to be flame-proofed unless special exemptions had been granted.

To achieve this, electrical plant and traction motors had to be encased within one-inch-thick steel housings with machined faces and seals no greater than 20 thousands of an inch to prevent the possibility of a spark passing to the atmosphere. Part of the equipment's daily examina-tion – which had to be done only by authorised electricians using special tools – ensured that no tolerances had slack-ened off during the previous day's operations.

Even then, locos and other electrical apparatus had to be stopped and switched off by law if the methane content in the air rose higher than the permitted level and, as coal in its natural state constantly emits methane, regular checks of firedamp-detecting equipment had to be made.

In addition to flame traps, diesel locomotives working underground had to have exhaust conditioners to remove noxious gases. These comprised an aluminium box in which there was a small quantity of water to extinguish any red-hot carbon soot before it could be emitted. Even the paint on underground machinery had to be fire-retardant.

Each new design had to be submitted to the Safety in Mines establishment at Buxton, Derbyshire, for thorough testing, followed by the issuing of what became known as a 'Buxton Certificate'. It was to be 1938 before the first such certificates were issued for diesel locomotives, but due to the war, their widespread introduction was delayed until the late-1940s.

As part of the NCB's modernisation programme in the 1950s and 60s, huge loco fleets were introduced and, by 1975, there were more than a thousand running 'unseen by the public' in provincial Britain, almost exclusively flameproof diesel-mechanicals or battery-electrics. With some coalfaces several miles from the pithead, however, their slow speed, especially on steep gradients, meant that miners in some districts were spending almost half their paid shift time travelling to and from work!

Pantograph-fitted electric locomotives drawing power from overhead wires were quicker, but the high risk of a spark between the 'pan' and the overhead wire meant they could only be used in mines with extremely low methane levels. The Mines Inspectorate granted exceptions for about half a dozen pits ... although even in those, the trains were only allowed to run along the intake airway roads, not return airways.

An idea of the rough treatment locomotives received underground can be gained from these views of a Clayton-built Co-Co battery-electric loco when brand new in 2010 and in service at Thoresby in 2015.

The collieries concerned were Chislet (Kent), Gedling (Nottingham), Sandhole (Lancashire), Silverwood (South Yorkshire) and Easington (Co. Durham).

There had also been a system at Barnsley's Wharncliffe Silkstone Colliery as early as 1890 using a Yorkshire Engine Company-built overhead wire loco hauling coal wagons up a 500-yard long drift, but that operation is not thought to have lasted long.

The term used to describe overhead electric traction in the British mining industry was 'trolley locos' although they weren't actually fitted with trolley poles. Main line-style pantographs were preferred, as they gave the overhead conductor wire more surface area over which to slide, thus reducing the sparking potential. The conductor wires also had to be fixed to spring tensioning devices to compensate for the possible movement of the earth strata above them.

The first four electrics, built by Metropolitan-Vickers, were delivered to Sandhole Colliery in 1953. That system was highly successful and remained in use until the closure of the mine in 1962, permitting large tonnages to be moved on a very narrow track gauge of 1ft 9in.

The overhead system installed at Chislet in the early-1960s was the first of its type in Britain to work underground at 550v DC. It was just over 1½ miles long and was used for man-riding trains as well as coal. The average gradient was 1-in-40 against the load but the English Electric-built locos – which replaced battery-electrics – were able to maintain a speed of 10mph.

Gedling Colliery's 500v DC system was opened by NCB chairman Norman Siddall in 1983 to run on rails along a so-called underground 'motorway' (i.e. a high, exceptionally wide, well-lit haulage roadway). The 60-tonne locos could haul trains at 25mph, higher than was possible with battery or diesel traction and, by reducing travelling time by two hours per shift for 140 men who had previously had to walk along a three-mile roadway, they increased productivity at the mine by 65,000 tonnes per year.

Upon the closure of Gedling less than nine years later, the locos were transferred to Harworth Colliery, near Doncaster, but a planned underground electric line there never went ahead and they were returned to their manufacturer, the Clayton Equipment Co, of Hatton, Derbyshire.

One fleet of overhead electric locomotives that did see further use was Silverwood's, which were transferred to Easington Colliery following modifications.

In addition to the collieries mentioned above, at least two locations, Harton and Whittonstall, had overhead catenary on their surface systems (see previous chapter).

To return to the story of subterranean diesel traction, diesel-hydraulic locos capable of hauling miners' trains at speeds of 20mph began to be introduced in the late-1970s and at about the same time, Clayton Equipment Co perfected a battery-electric flameproof loco with flange-cum-rubber tyres, capable of climbing gradients as steep as 1-in-10 at reasonable speeds. Christened the 'Pony', it was small enough to go where the original living ponies had trodden and as the manufacturer continued to improve the design, such locos were adopted on a large scale by the NCB.

Clayton later produced much larger and more powerful eight-wheeled rubber-tyre/flange versions and followed those up in 2010 with a fleet of 150hp, 200v 12-wheeled machines with polyurethane-lined flanges for Thoresby Colliery.

As for rolling stock, the introduction of locomotives into

One of Gedling Colliery's twin-pantograph electric locomotives pictured underground in the 1980s. Built by the Derbyshire-based Clayton company, these powerful machines were able to haul man-riding and equipment trains faster than battery or diesel locos. Gedling, near Nottingham, was one of only a handful of British mines equipped with an overhead electric rail system. DAVID AMOS

the pits in the 1940s had enabled the NCB to modernise the entire underground coal-carrying fleet. Having inherited a mishmash of half-ton and one-ton tubs with numerous different wheel sizes, the new organisation swept virtually the entire fleet away over its first few years and introduced thousands of large mine cars capable of carrying between two and four tons and fitted with brakes, springs and standardised couplings. (Blidworth Colliery was eventually blessed with massive seven-tonne cars).

Many subterranean networks featured ferocious inclines, so several extra safety devices had to be installed to prevent runaway trains in addition to the normal scotches and securing chains. These included retarders, sand or gravel drags, hinged flip-over wheel stops and hydraulically-operated metal gates across the track.

Although the NCB had spared no expense in re-equipping collieries with mine cars, it remained the case that conveyor belts powered by flame-proofed electric stationary motors had many advantages; they didn't need to be filled and emptied, they ran continuously round-the-clock

and they didn't need to be physically transported up and down shafts. They were also far more suited to the automated nature of modern coal-shearing and loading machinery.

Their disadvantage was that they couldn't turn corners well, necessitating right-angled transfer points between sets of belts. Therefore, some pit managements continued to use locomotives to move loaded mine cars all the way to the pit bottom. There, they were pushed into the shaft cages either by hand or by special mechanical rams in the tracks. As each one went in, it pushed an empty car out the other side, the empties having just descended in the cage from the pit top.

The empty tubs would then be 'caught' by a creeper mechanism in the track, which slowly pushed them into a line ready to be taken inbye by a locomotive. Meanwhile, the full cars were wound up the upcast shaft to the surface, pushed out of the cage by empty cars on a similar principle and allowed to run down a slight slope by gravity before being slowed by a retarder for entry into the weighhouse.

So many miles from pit bottom were some coalfaces that special dispensation was given for miners to ride on conveyor belts if the rail tracks didn't extend far enough. Note the miner at the higher level travelling in the opposite direction. BC

They were then moved to rotary tipplers, into which they were either pushed by hand or by another set of rams, the coal being tipped out onto conveyors and taken to the preparation plant for washing and grading.

As a further stage of the NCB's modernisation programme, all winding of loaded wagons up shafts was gradually phased out and the upcast shafts of the country's major collieries were fitted with high-capacity coal-carrying skips in place of cages.

So, during the last quarter of the 20th century, most of the deep-mined coal in Britain was moved to the surface by conveyors and skips – but although miners could (and often did) ride on conveyors, proper trains and carriages were far more suitable and popular for humans.

Passenger-carrying trains at collieries have traditionally been nicknamed 'Paddy Mails' and the stopping-off points (platforms is too grand a word) as 'Paddy Stations'. These terms are throwbacks to the early days of main line railway construction in the mid-1800s when contractors' trains were run for navvies, most of whom were of Irish origin. Once Britain's main line passenger network had been built,

the phrase largely fell out of use and was restricted to a few workmen's specials, but when subterranean man-riding trains began to be introduced in collieries on a widespread scale from the 1940s onwards, the term was resurrected and became a quasi-official part of mining terminology, remaining in use in many (but not all) pits until the very end of the deep-mining industry.

The quality and comfort of man-riding carriages varied from colliery to colliery (some were enclosed by a roof, others not) and speed was usually restricted to about 5mph due to the undulating nature of the track in most mines – a result of subsidence and natural strata movement over the years.

'Paddy trains' were referred to as running either 'inbye' or 'outbye', with 'inbye' being in the direction of the coalface. Each crew consisted of a guard/shunter as well as a driver and some mine railways had internal colour-light signalling systems too.

Each colliery possessed an underground locomotive maintenance depot – known in mining terminology as a garage – and battery-charging stations were positioned at

PIT BOTTOM AREA
Note this is a designated shunting zone

LOCO	ROUTE COLOUR	MAX WEIGHT (TONNES)		
		PONY	Bo-Bo	Co-Co
ALL *1		9.0t	20.0t	20.0t
ALL		4.0t	9.3t	20.0t
PONY ONLY		9.0t		
PONY + Bo-Bo		4.0t	9.3t	
ALL		15.0t	20.0t	20.0t

LOCOMOTIVE ROUTES & WEIGHTS

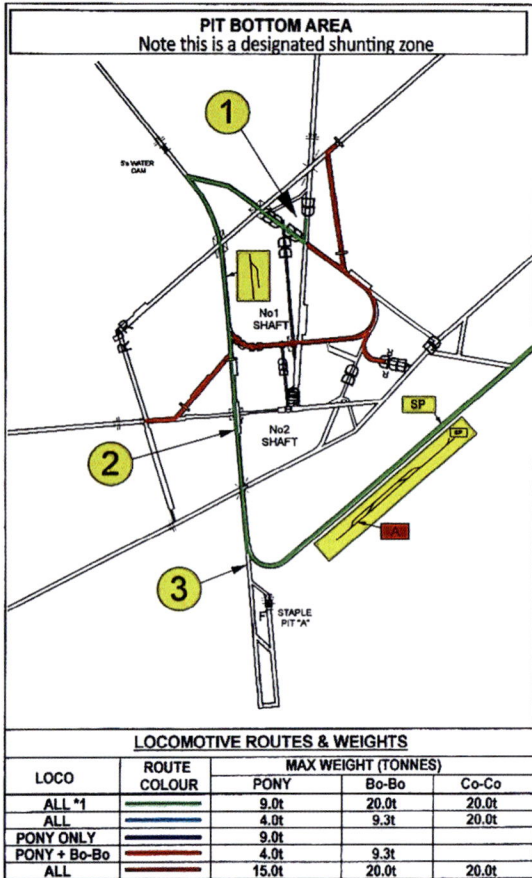

A diagram of the pit bottom area at Thoresby, showing the surprisingly complex layout of the rail system in that central hub of the mine. Nos.1 and 2 on the diagram are battery-charging stations and No.3 indicates the garage (loco depot). Letter A shows the location of the ambulance car and the letters D and R across the tracks indicate ventilation air doors and regulator doors respectively.

Not what it seems

MOST LOCOMOTIVES were too long to fit inside a shaft cage and too complicated to take apart and reassemble underground, so an ingenious way to take them down was devised. This involved 'slinging' them vertically underneath the cage, as seen in this remarkable shot at Silverwood Colliery, and then carefully bringing them round to the horizontal once they had reached shaft bottom. At some pits, a specially-designed sling receptacle was built in which to lower locos and other large items of machinery.

various points around the system to ensure locos could be kept topped up with power.

Some pits, Kiveton Park for instance, didn't need to worry about such matters, as their Paddy train carriages were rope-hauled rather than loco-hauled.

When it came to really steep gradients, neither trains nor conveyors were suitable. Conventional steel-wheeled locos were limited to about 1-in-15 when hauling loads; rubber-tyred locos to about 1-in-10 and traditional conveyor belts couldn't be elevated to much more than 1-in-4, as the coal then began rolling backwards. Scraper-chain conveyors fitted with cross-beam pushers partly solved that problem, but for anything really steep, a rope haulage system was necessary.

There were several different rope systems but they were either of the simple direct type, in which tubs were raised or lowered along an inclined track, or the endless-belt type, which operated continuously with tubs being clipped on and off the rope at each end. Some pits had subterranean rope inclines as steep as 1-in-2, alongside which worker refuges had to be provided every 20 yards in case of runaways.

177

Test tracks

BECAUSE IT was not practical to test locomotives and drivers in underground conditions, test tracks were set up on the surface at selected collieries around the country.

It was the NCB's aim to have a training centre in each of its area zones, not only to teach young apprentices, but also to give refresher training to longer-serving miners to improve their knowledge and keep them up to date with advancing technology.

The centres were necessary to teach drivers how to handle the variety of hazards they might encounter underground, not the least of which was the control of skidding on adhesion gradients of 1-in-15 or steeper. To bring more realism to the tests, grease was often smeared on the rails. Some centres also featured short lengths of arched roadways built on the surface.

Once the coalmining industry began to contract after 1985, central training centres for each area became

A 'streamlined' man-riding train on trial at Bevercotes Colliery in the 1980s.

uneconomic and, in the 1990s, training was devolved back to individual pits ahead of the sell-off of mines to the private sector. Kellingley test centre was one of the last to survive, not closing until the early 1990s.

By 1956, an astonishing 2,000 miles of conveyor belts had been provided for the underground and surface systems of Britain's mines. By 1980, more than 95% of coal moved under the ground was by those means – and in some collieries whose faces were many miles from the pit bottom, men were allowed to ride on conveyors under strict safety conditions, sometimes having to 'launch' themselves face-down from a low bridge onto a moving belt. It could take quite a bit of practice to do this and whenever VIPs, journalists and other guests visited such a mine, the belt would normally be stopped or slowed down to allow them to climb on and off in safety.

Other forms of underground transport included monorails, which are more suited to running up and down steep drifts below the shaft bottom level, but which can only be installed in mines boasting strong roadway roofs. One such system could be found at Babbington/Cinderhill Colliery, near Nottingham, whose miners went to and from work in ski lift-style chairs. Generally speaking, large powered monorail systems were rare in British mines but they are still used for man-riding in other countries, particularly Poland, where special 'freight' traction units enable equipment, tools and stores to be conveyed to coalface gate roads as well as men.

In South Yorkshire, Silverwood Colliery had, in the late-1980s, an unusual rope-hauled high-speed 'Paddy Mail', capable of hauling 124 men at 20mph and, at the other end of the speed scale many years earlier, Worsley,

Monorail man-riders, such as this one in a Polish colliery, were rare in Britain but ideal for reaching coalfaces accessed via steep subterranean drifts descending from shaft bottoms.

near Manchester, initially sent its coal out by a network of underground canals built by the Duke of Bridgewater.

In the heyday of the NCB, redundant locos and rail vehicles from closed collieries were salvaged for spares, re-use elsewhere or for scrap, but as the pit closure programme began to accelerate in more recent years, the cost of bringing them to the surface began to outweigh their value, meaning there are today thousands of vehicles and conveyor systems abandoned deep in the bowels of the earth, many under water or gradually being crushed – a fact few people outside the mining industry are aware of.

CHAPTER 21

Pit communities

Pride and passion

LEISURE TIME was at a premium until the advent of the eight-hour working day in 1870, but the fact that many miners' families lived in close-knit areas in which virtually everyone shared the same occupation made a hobby or other interest vital if men were to be mentally stimulated.

Among the most popular pastimes were brass bands (many collieries had their own), pigeon-keeping, whippet-racing, bowls, darts, dominoes and, of course, football and rugby. Many mineworkers also kept allotments and specialised in growing prize vegetables despite the propensity for coal dust to get everywhere, even between the leaves of cabbages.

In the mid-1800s, some mining communities were more akin to Wild West frontier towns with rough navvies from outside areas spending most of their wages in ale houses. Nevertheless, most Britons in Victorian society were God-fearing, even if many mineworkers themselves weren't always so, and there was hardly a mining community in the country that didn't possess a church, chapel or other place of worship. This was particularly so in Wales, which in the 1860s had more than 3,000 nonconformist chapels, the most popular ones in the south being Baptist and Methodist, which enabled miners to follow a religion other than the mainly Anglican creed of the coal owners.

Church, chapel and clergy were towers of strength to miners and their families, especially in times of worry, hardship or tragedy. Many colliery workers consequently became lay readers or Sunday School teachers in their spare time.

In the narrow valleys of South Wales, the mountains could mean mines such as Maerdy existing in bleak isolated surroundings and although other pits in the valleys could be less than a mile apart in some cases, each was the self-contained centre of its own community with its own atmosphere, idiosyncrasies and methods of working, its own loyalties and even sometimes its own vocabulary.

Nicknames were particularly common among miners and it was often the case in some of the smaller pits that every underground worker would be referred to by their mates with a jocular moniker such as 'Knocker' or 'Lofty' rather than by their real name. Not all endearments were particularly complimentary ('Squirt' or 'Nutter' for instance), but all were taken in good heart and were part of the unshakable camaraderie that characterised the profession.

In such tight-knit communities, miners and their families almost invariably turned out en masse for the funeral of a colleague or village resident who'd perished in a pit accident, even if they'd not been particularly close to him personally. It was a sort of unwritten law and helped cement the bonds of loyalty.

Nobody needed to lock their doors in such places in the monochrome days before mass car ownership. Monday was always wash day in the coalfields and wives would pray that the wind wasn't blowing from the smokestacks or washery screens. When a colliery closed, the wives and mothers living nearby would joke sarcastically: "Well, at least we can now buy white sheets for the beds!"

A woman's lot was made tougher if the men in her household were on different shifts, for that meant different sleep times, different meal times and (in the days before pithead showers) different bath times.

A widow with sons was something of a 'catch' due to the ability of males to bring more income into a household than girls and it was not uncommon for a newly-widowed

Although the popular perception of coal mines is related to a heavily-industrialised urban environment, hundreds of collieries were established in open countryside, surrounded either by fields or bleak mountain terrain. The 1940s harvest scene above was captured at Auchincruive, Ayrshire, and the scene below was taken in 1985 at Maerdy Colliery, in South Wales.

Cheers! There was nothing more satisfying after a long, hard shift on the coalface than slaking the thirst with a pint on the way home.

woman to be showered with proposals of marriage even before she'd had time to bury her husband. It is reported that one woman with four sons accepted a proposal on her way to the funeral!

Although some pits were located in urban areas, the railways and factories of the Industrial Revolution created more jobs in formerly rural areas than agriculture ever could. This helps explain the enormous and rapid increases in population that took place in Britain during that era – some hamlets of 50 or so souls mushrooming into towns of perhaps 10,000 inhabitants in just a few years. For instance, the 1870s saw no fewer than 14 collieries and their attendant housing established within a two-mile radius of Hamilton West station in Lanarkshire, while the South Wales valleys experienced a particularly astonishing transformation with the narrowness of the terrain resulting in long rows of terraced houses along the valley sides.

In the early years of the 20th century particularly, a large number of pits were established among open fields away from traditional mining areas and some of the more

enlightened coal owners, inspired by the 'garden city' movement, provided pleasant tree-lined villages for workers and their families to live in. The Dukeries coalfield in Nottinghamshire was one that particularly benefitted from this when it was established in the 1920s.

As these 'model villages' developed in virgin countryside with few, if any, existing amenities, it was necessary for the coal owners to provide housing on a similar basis to the tied cottages of the agricultural industry. Although trying to appear paternalistic, some companies would impose strict conditions on their workers in return for cheap rent. If a miner or his wife owed money at the company-owned shop, for example, the debt would be deducted from his wages. Many felt they were living in a sort of commune and that they might as well have been paid in coupons instead of money. If their 'face didn't fit' or their work was considered sub-standard, they could be thrown out of their home as well as their job, with little comeback.

Such a village was Bilsthorpe, Notts, built on moorland several miles from the nearest town of any size and owned by the Stanton Ironworks Company. In just ten years

Kicking a football around in the streets of mining villages was how a lot of kids developed the skills that made them stars later in life.

between 1921 and 1931, its population went from 134 to 1,972 and then rose to 3,000 during the 1930s.

Rents were on a weekly lease and that kept mineworkers' minds concentrated on obeying the company's rules, which included keeping gardens tidy, keeping noise down and not engaging in 'immoral behaviour'. There was even a company-employed 'pit bobby' to keep law and order and those who stepped out of line persistently could find themselves jobless and homeless. Even dogs were banned for a while, especially whippets, as their presence was thought by the owners to encourage betting. Militancy and membership of 'unapproved' trade unions was not tolerated.

On the plus side, residents of mining villages tended to benefit from electric street lighting several years earlier than those of neighbouring communities (the 1890s in the case of Newstead, Notts) because generators began to be installed at collieries in order to power newly-acquired machinery. Several communities also benefitted from comparative luxuries too; the cinema built by the owners of Bullcroft Colliery for its miners had 1,000 seats and was even bigger than the cinemas in nearby Doncaster town itself.

A national Miners' Welfare Fund was set up in 1920, funded by a penny levied on every ton of coal plus contributions from miners. This helped build institutes, with games rooms, libraries, brass band facilities and colliery football

teams. Until then, most kids in pit villages had to hone their skills kicking a can around in the streets.

The strength and physique of miners made them good sportsmen, though, and it was said that if a football or cricket boss needed a new centre-forward or fast bowler, he had only to whistle down the nearest mine shaft!

Among famous footballers and cricketers who either worked in the pits or hailed from mining families were the Charlton brothers Bobby and Jackie, Nat Lofthouse, England fast bowlers Harold Larwood and Fred Trueman and the legendary football managers Sir Matt Busby (Manchester United), Bill Shankly (Liverpool) and Jock Stein (Glasgow Celtic). Annesley Colliery alone produced four England cricket internationals!

World War Two effectively broke the power of the coal owners as the Government's Essential Work Order of 1941 meant the men had greater job security and therefore more ability to organise themselves industrially, politically and socially. The arrival of the NCB saw a widespread extension of canteens and social clubs from the 1950s onwards and "the Welfare" fast became the centre of community life in almost all mining districts, frequently proving more popular than the local pubs. There was often a bowling green or tennis court attached and some pits, such as Rossington, even had their own gym.

Not the sort of image one expects in the shadow of a coal mine... Yorkshire Main Colliery at New Edlington was one of the few that provided its employees and their families with a swimming pool.

Perhaps the best perks of all, though, were those enjoyed by workers and families at collieries boasting their own swimming pools!

Once a year or so, the miners' welfare organisers would run a trip to the seaside for members and their families, with the main line excursion trains often undertaking rare passenger mileage along freight-only branches serving the collieries. Among permanent seaside facilities provided were a mineworkers' holiday resort at Rhyl, North Wales, and two convalescent homes on the Lincolnshire coast near Skegness, one for Nottinghamshire miners at Chapel St Leonards and another for Derbyshire men at Winthorpe.

For the younger ones in the mining villages, majorette-style juvenile marching bands were formed and competed against bands of neighbouring collieries, the girls and boys resplendent in beautiful brightly-coloured uniforms.

The other glamorous aspect of life in the coalfields concerned the annual galas, the most famous of which is the Durham Miners Gala, which dates from 1871 and is still held to this day, having evolved into 'the Big Meeting', a major gathering for the Labour and trades union movement generally. For years, many of the regional galas featured a 'Coal Queen' beauty pageant (see Appendix C).

In 1947, the NCB took over ownership of all colliery houses and, 39 years later, began selling them to tenants who wanted to buy. After only five years, 32,000 homes had been sold.

The relatively massive pay rises that followed the 1972 and 1974 strikes meant that miners' wages better reflected the risks and nature of their work and, as a result, most were able to afford cars and foreign holidays... yet the spirit and solidarity of the pit villages remained strong, even after the devastating 1984/85 strike.

Sadly, there is today no longer a single British mining village that has at its heart the original reason for its existence – an operational deep shaft coal mine.

The names of several pits do, however, live on in their football clubs. The most successful of these is arguably Frickley Colliery FC, long-term members of the Midland League in the years when that competition sat just below the Football League and who (as Frickley Athletic) finished runners-up in the National Football Conference in 1986. If that feat had been achieved today, the club would have been in the National League play-offs for promotion to the Football League.

A colliery side that once played at Britain's largest and most glamorous venue was Rainworth Miners' Welfare

One of the most common sights in Britain until the end of the 1960s was the coalman and his lorry. These labourers – often as coal-begrimed as the miners themselves – would heave hundredweight sacks off the back of their truck and run (or stagger) along the side-passages of people's homes before emptying the contents into the coal cellar or shed. RAIL ARCHIVE STEPHENSON

FC which, in 1982 reached the final of the FA Vase at the old Wembley Stadium – but the most extraordinary feat of all concerns West Auckland FC, a North-Eastern team composed largely of miners who won the first World Cup!

That was the Sir Thomas Lipton Trophy, which was competed for in the Italian city of Turin in 1909 by clubs representing nations. West Auckland were invited to represent Britain after the English FA declined to nominate a larger club and the miners – all amateur players – had to pawn their belongings to afford the journey to Italy. Against all the odds, they won the cup by beating Swiss side FC Winterthur in the final. But even greater glory lay ahead, for two years later West Auckland went back to defend their title – and won it again by defeating none other than the mighty Italian professional club Juventus!

For this, the plucky pitmen were allowed to keep the trophy and the modern-day road sign outside the village tells drivers they are entering the 'home of the first World Cup'.

Other North-Eastern miners' teams included Chilton Colliery, champions of the powerful Northern League in 1928, and Horden Colliery, winners of the North-Eastern League in 1938. Non-league clubs in the modern game bearing names reminiscent of their glorious past include Atherton Collieries, Pontefract Collieries, Ashington Colliers, Maltby Main, Rossington Main and Gedling Miners' Welfare.

"Our pits might be lost but at least our teams are still winners," said one old timer – and another added poignantly: "They might have taken away our jobs ... but they can't take away our memories."

Reading all about it

UNLIKE RAILWAYS, collieries have never attracted a mass enthusiast following. Consequently there have been no glossy monthly magazines available through high street shops.

The main periodicals have been business titles targeted at mining professionals, such as the *Colliery Guardian*, staff newspapers for the benefit of NCB employees such as *Coal News*, or the NUM's own newspaper, *The Miner*.

Coal News began life as a magazine called *Coal* in May 1947, only a few months after nationalisation, and provided a link between management and mineworkers. Its title changed when it moved to a newspaper format in 1960. An earlier publication was the *Iron & Coal Trades Review*, which ran from 1866 to circa 1963 when its name was changed to *Steel & Coal*.

CHAPTER 22
Strikes and stoppages
Coal not dole

CLASHES WITH authority seem to have been a tradition in the coal industry. As early as 1619, coal masters in Newcastle asked for injunctions against strikers and, in 1740, 'flying pickets' – a tactic that was to be used by Yorkshire miners in the long 1984/85 strike – first appeared when a withdrawal of labour closed most of the Tyne collieries and a big group from Newcastle travelled to a pit that had continued working in order to 'persuade' its men to join the dispute.

A United Association of Colliers was formed in 1825, followed by the first national organisation, the Miners' Association of Great Britain and Ireland, 16 years later. It soon attracted more than 100,000 members despite the fact that Ireland was better known for peat and lignite deposits rather than black coal, but the association was to prove short-lived. Several regional associations followed and eventually coagulated into the Miners' Federation of Great Britain (MFGB) in 1888, led, from 1924, by Arthur Cook, who famously declared during the dispute that was to lead to the 1926 General Strike: "Not a penny off the pay, not a minute on the day."

A miners' strike in 1893 was triggered by a drop in the price of coal that caused colliery owners to propose a 25% wage reduction in an attempt to maintain profits. In not unnaturally rejecting that, the MFGB called for a national minimum wage and the result was a lock-out that went on for much of the summer.

The confrontation involved riots, violence and intimidation by gangs of strikers and it ended in tragedy when troops were called in to quell a disturbance at Ackton Hall Colliery, near Featherstone. Faced with an angry crowd of 2,000 throwing stones and refusing to disperse despite

being read the Riot Act, the soldiers were ordered to shoot and two miners were killed.

The dispute was finally settled by Government intervention and although the miners returned to work, they did not gain a national wage to replace the complicated structure of locally-agreed rates paid by the various mine-owning companies.

In 1910, an unrelated local dispute concerning a new seam in Penygraig, South Wales, led to miners there being locked out by the owners, Cambrian Combine. That escalated into a strike by all the workers employed by Cambrian, exacerbated by the company's plan to use strike-breakers. Police were called in and violent clashes ensued, culminating in rioting and shop window smashing in the Rhondda valley town of Tonypandy on the night of November 8 that year. Home Secretary Winston Churchill decided to authorise the deployment of troops to reinforce the police contingent and although there are no records of shots being fired by the soldiers, the events made him unpopular in the South Wales mining communities even after he had become Britain's wartime leader 30 years later.

Meanwhile, pressure for a minimum wage continued and, in 1912, Britain was gripped by its first national miners' strike involving every coalfield. Almost a million men took part and after a bitter dispute lasting more than a month (in which many had to scavenge for coal on spoil tips to keep their families warm), they finally managed to secure from the owners a Government-approved minimum wage and an agreement that colliers working in difficult seams wouldn't be disadvantaged.

Two years later, the First World War broke out and the mines were temporarily taken under State control. During the hostilities, the Government approved several pay rises to ensure the collieries remained in full production. Many miners hoped State ownership would become permanent after the war, but in 1919 the industry was handed back to its previous owners.

It wasn't long before another major dispute broke out, again resulting in a lock-out. This time it was caused by the Government's scrapping of wartime price controls in 1921, leaving the coal owners with lower profits, so once again they attempted to cut miners' wages to compensate. That led to another national strike and lock-out, which lasted three months and severely damaged other coal-dependent industries and, with it, the country's economy. After three months of hardship in which many miners and their families were forced to scavenge for coal on spoil heaps, those who still had a job were forced to accept terms that were substantially the same as those on offer when the strike started.

Such internecine struggles between different sections of the British community were proving almost ruinous in many respects, not only for the population as a whole, which had to stoically carry on as best it could, but for the miners themselves. During the 1921 confrontation, for example, some were so desperate that they risked their lives by lowering themselves down abandoned bellpit shafts to salvage what pieces of coal they could find for their families.

Even when the lock-outs ended, there were so many men looking for work (as many as 200 at each colliery in some cases) that the companies had to employ police to keep them away as they were hindering work at the pitheads. Many were still behind with their rent and other bills as a result of the 1921 stoppage when the even bigger dispute of 1926 started.

By then, Churchill had become Chancellor of the Exchequer and had put the country on the Gold Standard, increasing the cost of exports by 10%. Britain's pits, already at a disadvantage against foreign producers following the Great War, could not compete with overseas mines and coal began to stockpile at the pitheads. At first, the Government provided a subsidy to maintain wages at their present level, but when the subsidy ran out in April 1926 there was yet another lock-out.

The Trades Union Congress called the infamous General Strike in support and the major industries of the entire country ground to a standstill in May of that year, but after nine days in which members of the public volunteered to keep the railways and other essential services running, the resolve of the TUC and the other unions collapsed and the miners were left to continue the fight on their own for six months.

It all ended in ignominious defeat, for at the end of the

dispute those fortunate enough to still have a job were forced to go back on longer hours and lower wages, making a mockery of Cook's rallying call. Many remained unemployed for several years.

At the height of the 1926 dispute, a large number of miners affiliated to the MFGB in Nottinghamshire grew unhappy at the way the federation was handling matters and this led to the formation of a moderate breakaway body, the Nottinghamshire Miners' Industrial Union, under the leadership of George Spencer. Although the so-called 'Spencerites' reluctantly decided in 1937 to return to the federation, the difference in attitude between the Nottinghamshire men and the more militant trade unionists in other parts of the industry (especially in neighbouring Yorkshire) was to cause long-lasting animosity that would have serious repercussions half a century later.

The wounded MFGB remained in existence until being reorganised with other federations into the NUM on January 1, 1945 – just two years before the formation of the NCB with which it was to cross swords so many times in later years.

Although it is a sweeping generalisation, it is worth noting that NCB executives tended, on the whole, to view East Midlands miners as moderates and those from the North, Wales and Scotland as traditionally more militant. The Kentish miners fell into the latter category, partly because of a large influx of northern Britons displaced by pit closures in their own areas. The initial workforce at Betteshanger was a case in point; hardly any were local men, they descended en masse onto the little seaside resort of Deal with their families in the 1920s and reportedly caused a deal of resentment in the town. Along with other Kentish pits, it seemed to attract a higher than average number of union hard-liners from other parts of the country.

Compared with what had gone before and what was to come, the 1950s and 60s were relatively peaceful times in the coalfields. Although the natural reduction in collieries through closure of old and uneconomic mines had resulted in the huge but gradual loss of 400,000 jobs, the NUM had offered little resistance due to high investment in the industry generally and its leaders were in any case reluctant to make demands on a Labour Government during the mid-to-late Sixties. But the old order was changing and a tranche of younger activists with strong left-wing views were taking over positions on the NUM area councils.

Signs of what lay ahead came in October 1969 when calls for a better deal for surface workers escalated into a major unofficial strike affecting 140 of the nation's 307 collieries (including all those in Yorkshire). It was settled after two weeks but during that time, the NCB lost £15m and 2½m tons in lost production.

In the long strikes of the late 19th and early 20th centuries, workless miners and their families often had no option but to scavenge spoil heaps for the small lumps of coal that had slipped through the screens. This Lancashire scene was photographed during the long strike of 1893.

That 1969 strike was the first major dispute since the 1920s and the first since then to feature widespread picketing of mines by strikers.

Less than three years later, the 'flying pickets' were in action again, this time as part of an official dispute. The 1972 strike was staged over a pay claim and lasted for almost the whole of January and February, during which time the country briefly entered an official state of emergency with the imposition of power cuts and a three-day week by the Conservative Government of Edward Heath to conserve electricity.

The dispute was characterised by violence at numerous pits and a picket was killed in an accident at Hatfield Colliery, near Doncaster, when a coal lorry mounted a pavement during clashes. In Birmingham, more than 2,000 pickets descended on Saltley coking plant in a bid to prevent supplies from entering and leaving.

The strike ended when the Government acceded to the majority of the NUM's wage demands, but as the decade progressed, runaway inflation began to force up prices and erode the effect of pay rises. When the Government attempted to tackle the inflationary pressures by capping public sector pay, the NUM invoked an overtime ban.

That caused shortages in coal supplies and in December 1973, Heath announced that the country was to be put back on a three-day week. Widespread power cuts were enforced on a regular basis and for the next few weeks the nation had to live by candle-light for much of the time, with all but essential factories and services prevented from working full-time.

The NUM's response was to call a ballot leading to a full-blown strike, which began on February 5, 1974. Two days later, an angry and frustrated Heath called a snap general election on the issue of 'who governs the country?'

The adversaries: NUM leader Arthur Scargill and NCB chief Ian MacGregor, who went head-to-head in the 1984-85 strike.

A rare photograph of Prime Minister Margaret Thatcher wearing a miner's helmet during an underground visit to Yorkshire's Wistow Colliery in 1980.

He confidently expected the electorate to back him with a mandate to tackle the militants full-on, but instead – seemingly tired of the constant strife and the Government's inability to deal with it – many floating voters switched sides and Heath failed to win an overall majority. After being unable to gain Parliamentary support from minority parties, he conceded to the socialist Harold Wilson administration, which then acceded to the miners' demands. A second general election in October 1974 gave Wilson an overall majority.

In a short time, the miners had been elevated, in the words of CEGB chairman Arthur Hawkins, "from rags to riches" and the 1970s had become a challenging time for British industry generally, characterised by constant walk-outs and 'down-tools' incidents over numerous grievances, many of a local or trivial nature. Senior men found it extremely difficult to run businesses efficiently and there was huge anger and frustration in management and government circles at union activities. At one time, the NCB was described as "unmanageable" and it was clear that even Labour Government ministers were tearing their hair out with exasperation over the apparent hopelessness of the situation.

After the infamous 'Winter of Discontent', the electorate was so fed up that the Conservatives were restored to power in 1979 with a mandate to 'sort the unions out'. The party's leader by then was the uncompromising Margaret Thatcher, a staunch right-winger who came to power pledging to curb inflation and reduce union power.

Rumours of a 'hit list' of 50 pits began circulating in 1980/81, prompting a further wave of militancy in the coalfields and resulting in the Government being forced into a climb-down to avoid another damaging miners' strike. On that occasion, Prime Minister Margaret Thatcher shelved the pit closure programme but her memoirs later revealed that she vowed to herself that no union would ever be allowed to wield such immense political power again.

In 1982, the long-serving and relatively moderate NCB chairman Sir Derek Ezra retired to be succeeded by Norman Siddall and the following year Mrs Thatcher was re-elected with a huge majority. She asked Siddall to stay on but he declined due to ill health so she turned instead to the uncompromising ex-head of the British Steel Corporation, Ian MacGregor.

A few months previously, the NUM had elected as its president a firebrand left-winger who had been actively involved in organising the 1970s strikes. His name was Arthur Scargill, an ex-Yorkshire miner and former member of the Young Communist League. The stage was set for a classic confrontation between the right and left wings of British politics...

The 1984/85 strike: In March 1984, the Government announced that the billion-pound annual subsidy to the coal industry would be withdrawn, that the energy market would be opened up to cheap imports and that loss-making collieries would be closed.

The reasons were threefold: Firstly, the Prime Minister was an advocate of free market policies; secondly, the coal industry was losing £1.5m a day and was once again in decline following the temporary boost of the mid-1970s and thirdly, the Conservatives had a long-term plan to privatise the industry and needed to streamline it in readiness by closing scores of allegedly loss-making collieries.

The NUM, on the other hand, was convinced there was also a fourth reason – 'payback' for the ignominious defeat the miners had effectively inflicted on the Heath administration ten years earlier.

The miners faced a stark dilemma: accept a slow and painful death or man the barricades once more to try to save their jobs. The majority decided to back their new leader and opt for the latter.

Given the outcome of their successful 1970s campaigns, they were confident they could force the Thatcher Government to capitulate again as it had in 1981, but this time

The longest and most bitter miners' strike took place in 1984/85 and was characterised by numerous physical clashes between police and pitmen. PA

there were three chinks in their armour. Firstly, the 1984 strike was called in the spring, secondly the Government had ensured that coal stockpiles at power stations were at maximum levels, and thirdly, the miners were no longer a united force, for the East Midlands men decided to carry on working in protest at the strike being called without a ballot of individual members, which made it undemocratic and illegal. They were joined by others, particularly from Lancashire and North Wales, who, in local area ballots earlier in the year, had actually voted to reject a strike.

The traditional solidarity of those who did down tools – backed by loyal wives and families – ensured that the 'Coal not Dole' dispute dragged on for almost exactly a year and the coalfields became battlefields as miners and police (many of whom were mounted on horses) clashed in what almost degenerated into a class war.

The strike was described by the BBC as "the most bitter industrial dispute in British history". Much of the bad feeling resulted from the Government's decision to draft in officers of the London-based Metropolitan Police – another case of history repeating itself, for members of the same force had been sent to help quell the South Wales riots in 1910.

A surprising amount of the violence was, however, internecine in nature ... directed by strikers against strike-breakers (or 'scabs' as they were referred to). In some cases, it

extended to attacks on property and death threats to the families of working miners. Over the year, tens of thousands of stones and half-bricks were hurled at the buses and other vehicles – some of them armoured – taking strike-breakers into and out of collieries.

There were pitched battles in the streets and gardens of pit villages as police charged the miners, hitting them with batons and riot shields. The miners fought back with stones, fists, boots and anything else they could lay their hands on.

At its height, 142,000 mineworkers were involved, making it the biggest dispute since the 1926 General Strike. Many police and pitmen were seriously injured in the clashes, but remarkably, fatalities were restricted to three – two pickets plus a taxi driver who had been driving a non-striker to work. Two miners were sentenced to jail for his manslaughter.

The strike broke families financially as well as morally. For the first few weeks, the households managed to get by. After a couple of months they had eaten into their life savings and before long they were having to borrow from relatives or sell belongings just to put food on the table. Disillusioned, desperate and broken, many were forced to return to work and, by February, there were more at work than on strike.

Tragically, many families are still split to this day; there are brothers who haven't spoken to each other for 30 years because one went back to work and the other didn't. Some

189

marriages even broke up because of the strain everyone had been under.

The dispute finally ended in early March 1985 — a defining moment in British history, for it significantly weakened not only the NUM but also the entire trade union movement in the UK. The men who had held out to the bitter end marched back to work with their heads held high, but the atmosphere in the collieries was never the same again and the strike remains a touchy and highly controversial subject.

Within weeks of it ending, the first of the new tranche of pit closures were implemented. The NUM leadership had been right; the Government was quite clearly determined to cut the industry and the union down to size.

MacGregor later wrote in his memoirs: "Now we had succeeded, we were going to exert our right to manage the enterprise without the need to genuflect to the NUM every time we wanted to do anything. If they thought they were marching back to where they had left off, they had a very rude shock coming!"

Cortonwood Colliery, in Scargill's 'back yard', was one of

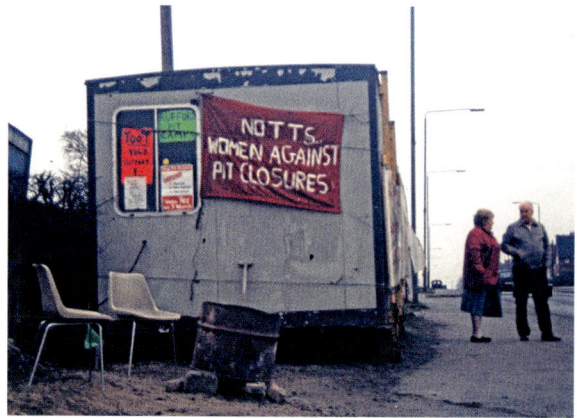

'Women against pit closures!' Doing their best to stave off the inevitable, the wives, mothers and daughters of Rufford men established a camp outside the colliery in 1993.

the first to go in 1985, followed by almost all of the 70-odd mines MacGregor had always had on his hit list (despite his denials to the contrary the previous year). By the end of 1985, almost half the pits in the traditionally militant South Wales coalfield had been condemned.

Most miners, however, seemed resigned to taking the enhanced severance deals they were being offered; there

Orgreave coking works, near Sheffield, which in June 1984 became infamous as the site of a violent confrontation between police and miners known as the 'Battle of Orgreave'. ROBIN STEWART-SMITH

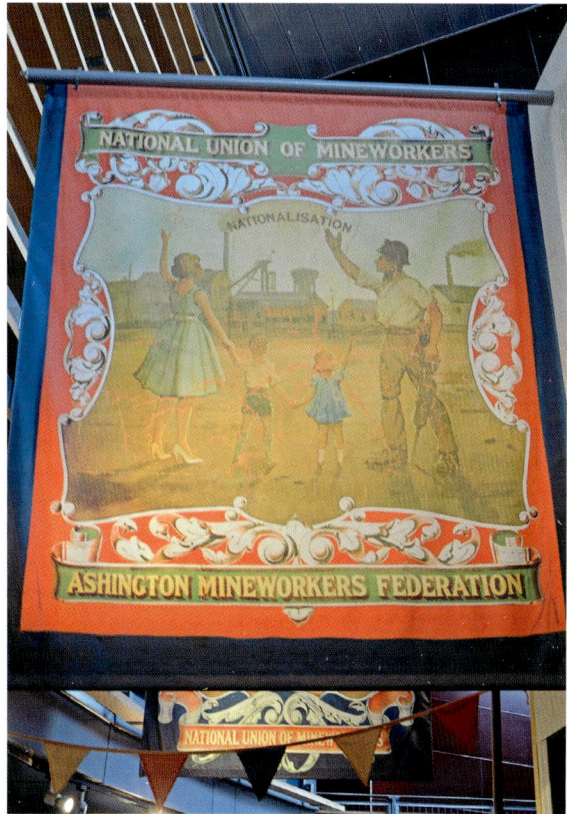

Among the most powerful symbols of miners' solidarity over the years have been the banners of the individual union lodges and federations. Similar in style to those produced by the Soviet Union to inspire industrial and agricultural workers during the years of the revolution, they were produced by the coal board as well as the unions and often portrayed an idealised world in which happy families would benefit from lifelong security.

was no more fight left in them, only bitterness.

Unsurprisingly, Prime Minister Thatcher's name remains mud in most former mining communities to this day, although she did insist to MacGregor that the NCB give all mineworkers the maximum redundancy and pension packages.

There is a school of thought that the Government might have orchestrated the strike in order to trigger a confrontation for which it had prepared well, but some reports claim that Scargill was preparing to call a strike in the early-1980s anyway and that the miners had unwittingly become foot soldiers in a left versus right battle. Their losses on that 'battlefield' were indeed those of an annihilation; at the start of the strike there had been an army of 140,000; by the turn of the century their ranks were down to just 4,000 and by 2015, they'd all gone ... along with tens of thousands of other NCB staff and contractors, many of whom hadn't even belonged to a union.

After all these years, the real truth of what was going on in the camps of the adversaries at the time will probably never be known. What we do know, courtesy of 1978-dated documents released under the 30-Year Rule, is that plans had indeed started to be drawn up that year to curb the strength of the NUM.

Where the 1984/85 strike will stand when history comes to judge the coal industry is a moot point. Was it the end of an era and the start of an error? It all depends which side of the political fence it's viewed from. Those of an intractable right-wing persuasion will see it as an ill-advised, hot-headed, politically-motivated campaign that ultimately and ironically destroyed everything it had set out to save, while those on the political left will take the view that the miners bravely did what anyone else would have done in their position ... and that was to stoutly defend their jobs and their livelihoods. It is quite obvious that if they had stood by and done nothing, the pits would eventually have been closed anyway, so their view was that they had at least to make a fight of it.

The biggest loser was the United Kingdom itself. In terms of wasting a valuable national asset — not just the coal but the vast network of mines so painstakingly built up by previous generations — the successive governments of the 1970-2015 era can be said to have cut off their noses to spite their faces, but neutral observers will doubtless point to the 30 years of relatively strike-free harmony that followed the mid-Eighties in British industry generally.

It's just a tragedy that so much irreplaceable infrastructure and so many lives had to be wrecked to achieve it.

The turreted headquarters of the NUM in Barnsley.

Other unions

IT IS widely believed in the non-mining areas of Britain that the coal industry generally was a traditional hotbed of discontent, but that was not the case in all regions. In fact, the East Midlands areas of Nottinghamshire, Leicestershire and South Derbyshire had a moderate reputation that resulted in them falling out with their more militant brethren and forming the Union of Democratic Mineworkers (UDM) in 1985.

The East Midlands men felt that the NUM had tried to railroad them into industrial action for political reasons. They also objected to the picket line intimidation of non-strikers and to the illegal calling of the 1984/85 strike without a ballot.

Other trades unions in NCB days were the National Association of Colliery Overmen, Deputies & Shotfirers (NACODS), which represented middle managers, and the Colliery Office Staff Association (COSA) for surface-based white-collar workers. Senior managers belonged to the independent British Association of Colliery Management.

The NUM is still in existence and its headquarters is still in Barnsley, but its membership is reported to have plummeted from 170,000 in the early-1980s to a mere 300 or so. Today it mainly concentrates on providing help and advice to former miners struggling with injuries and industrial diseases.

CHAPTER 23
Drift mines

Going down at an angle

THE PRINCIPAL difference between a deep mine and a large drift mine is the means of entry and exit. Once underground, the infrastructure and hazards are very similar.

The earliest drift mines were contemporaries of vertical bellpits and followed the seam, either on the level or at a slightly ascending inclination to make them self-draining.

Until the Second World War, drifts were basically used to exploit areas of shallow coal and most used rope haulage for transport, although conveyors began to be used later.

In the early NCB era, it was realised that many shallow shaft mines could be made more efficient if the coal-raising shaft was replaced or supplemented by a surface drift and conveyor, thus allowing continuous production from face to surface rather than intermittent shaft winding. Many reconstructions were carried out; South Derbyshire's Cadley Hill Colliery, for example, was provided with two parallel drifts, one containing a high-capacity cable belt for the coal, the other a high-speed man-rider, but at most modified mines the drift would almost invariably be used for coal-raising and at least one headstock and shaft would be retained for handling men and materials.

The small mines in the Forest of Dean are all accessed via drifts. This is the entrance to the operational side of Hopewell mine, the other entry being used to take members of the public into a worked-out part of the gale.

The modern loading point at Gascoigne Wood, to which the coal from all five Selby mines was sent via underground drifts.

Some smallish collieries that had been struggling to get 30 tons of coal an hour to the surface by pushing tubs in and out of cages increased their production rate tenfold and the introduction of zigzag drifts later made it possible to access seams almost as deep as those of vertical shafts.

West Yorkshire's Prince of Wales Colliery, originally sunk in 1872, had large new drifts inserted in the 1970s that were designed to more than double its production and extend its life expectancy to beyond 2000 (it closed in 2002). Daw Mill had two shafts and one drift, as did the modernised Snibston, while the now-preserved Big Pit at Blaenafon had one of each type, the consequent lower headstock maintenance costs said to be one of the reasons why it was selected for preservation.

Working in a drift mine might not, at first glance, seem as bad as working in a deep mine, yet before the advent of proper health & safety regulations, men were so desperate for money that they would follow coal seams further into

the sides of mountains than was good for them. By advancing the face further and further from the mine entrance, they would reach areas that had barely enough air to keep a candle burning and they would have to keep coming out of the mine to allow their lungs to recover.

The traditional name for a small drift mine is footrill (sometimes spelt footrail) and most operated on traditional means with dram tubs, rope haulage and wooden pit props.

There were once numerous drift mines in South Wales, but in 2021 there is just major one left in operation — Aberpergwm, in the Vale of Neath, whose operator, Energybuild, describes it as the only source of high-grade anthracite in the whole of Western Europe.

This large drift complex (occasionally described as a deep mine) had closed in 2015 but was able to re-open in 2018 due to anthracite (which is virtually smokeless) being classified as a strategic resource and thus exempt from UK bans. Its estimated reserves are 40m tonnes and it was still

The last two anthracite drift mines in South Wales are located within sight of each other on either side of the A465 dual-carriageway in the Vale of Neath. In the distance is part of Aberpergwm mine, which reopened in 2018, and in the foreground is the former Unity colliery at Cwmgwrach, which was placed into care and maintenance in 2013 and was still mothballed in 2021.

in full operation in 2021.

Close by, at Cwmgwrach, is another anthracite drift mine, Glyncastle (formerly known as the Unity mine). It has even greater reserves of almost 90m tonnes but it has been mothballed for some time under a programme of care and maintenance. A planning application was refused in 2019 and two years later the mine remains closed. Its previous owners had gone into administration in 2013 while attempting to secure funding for a changeover to longwall mining. Following closure, plans were put forward to turn it into an opencast operation but changes in Welsh environmental policy now make it extremely difficult for such schemes to receive planning permission, even when not intended for energy-generation purposes.

Over the border in Gloucestershire's Forest of Dean, a handful of tiny drift sites survive, operated by Forest Free Miners (see Appendix E).

Northern England's last operational drift mine, Ayle Colliery, on the border of Cumbria and Northumberland, was still in operation in 2021 as the low-sulphur Alston anthracite it extracts is also exempt from the new thermal coal ban, but plans for an all-new co-operative drift mine at New Crofton in West Yorkshire have yet to germinate.

To finish on a light-hearted note, it is said that some of the young colliers working in Welsh drift mines in years gone by would deliberately let their lamps go out at about midday on a Saturday. This would mean having to walk back to the entrance to get them relit, but once there, they would have less than an hour to the end of their shift, so they would sign off early ... and hurry off to play or watch rugby! In a shaft mine, they wouldn't have been able to do that as the onsetter, banksman and cage winder would all have to have been involved.

CHAPTER 24

Opencast mining

Taking the roof off

Although sourcing of coal from outcrops in ancient times could loosely be classed as 'opencast' and there were small quarry-style pits in Staffordshire in the 1840s, the concept of surface mining as we know it today didn't really get under way until the early-1940s when the Second World War caused a sudden demand for extra coal with insufficient time to sink new shafts.

Before then, excavators and mechanical shovels hadn't grown large and powerful enough to strip off huge tonnages of overburden, but the advent of giant dragline machines enabled opencast mining — effectively quarrying — to become more viable. The NCB's Opencast Executive came into being in April 1952, its sites having previously been operated by contractors on behalf of the Ministry of Fuel & Power.

Many opencast operations lay on the sites of old collieries that closed before their reserves had been fully exploited and, in some cases, such as the former Minorca Colliery, near Measham, Leicestershire, so much coal was extracted between 2013 and 2016 (1.9m tonnes) that it is a wonder the original mine was ever shut down in the first place!

It is, of course, much easier to identify and access coal seams once they're all exposed to the open air, but the big drawback with opencast mining is the sheer amount of land it requires.

Although the operations are classed as 'shallow', this is a relative term for even the seams nearest the top can be well over 100 metres deep, which means that so-called 'surface' mines can extend as far into the earth as some of the deepest British stone quarries. To achieve such depths naturally requires a massive tract of land to be stripped and

In the 2010s, a thick seam – more than 12ft in places – was opened up on the site of Leicestershire's Minorca Colliery, which closed in 1980 before its reserves could be fully exploited. This photo reveals the remarkably well-defined dividing line between the coal and the shale mudstone above it. NICK PIGOTT

A general view of the Minorca site in 2016. Such operations are able to reach depths of several hundred feet but cannot access the higher-quality 2,000 and 3,000ft seams Britain has now abandoned with its decision to end deep mining. Left: This cast iron-wheeled rail veteran had been abandoned underground in the Measham district of Leicestershire and was discovered during opencast mining in 2015.

one pit, near Margam, South Wales, created a canyon about a mile and a quarter across, while another in Leicestershire engulfed an entire farm ... not just the fields but the house and barns too.

In theory, there is no limit to how deep an opencast mine could be excavated, but reaching the very deepest seams would require voids the size of a small town and it thus becomes uneconomic beyond pre-determined weight ratios of overburden versus coal.

The rocks above and between most coal seams are

predominantly shale, mudstone and sandstone and as those layers are removed, they are typically used to backfill previously-excavated areas. Then, when the coal has been removed, the topsoil and subsoil are placed back on top. Because rock naturally swells and expands during the excavation processes – a phenomenon known as bulkage – it is usually possible to restore the land to about the same level it was before the mining started.

Apart from their method of extraction, surface mines are similar to traditional collieries insofar as they ideally need a means of washing and grading the coal before it is sold to power suppliers and other customers. For this, there is normally a preparation and washing plant located at a nearby 'disposal point' and distribution centre, to which the coal is taken by truck from outlying pits. Two such installations still open in the early 2020s were Onllwyn and Cwmbargoed, the latter producing dry steam cobbles, which are softer than anthracite but cleaner-burning than house coal. With the closure of these washeries and their associated opencast sites, Britain's steam lines need to find other coal sources (see chapter 27).

The fact that some opencast mines expose the subterranean galleries of demolished collieries has given rise over the years to a number of remarkable 'finds'. These include the discovery of old room & pillar workings, which give historians and industrial archaeologists a bird's eye view (literally!) of just how underground mining was undertaken in previous centuries. One such 'honeycomb', uncovered during strip mining at Coleorton, Leics, in the early-1990s, was reliably dated back to the late-1400s, making it one of the oldest in the world. The height of those medieval pillars was an average 4ft 6in.

The Wellington/Coalbrookdale area of Shropshire was once riddled with more than 200 ancient and relatively shallow bellpit cavities. Opencast mining not only extracted one and a quarter million tons of coal that would otherwise have been left in the ground but made the land stable enough for developments connected with Telford New Town in the 1970s.

Also unearthed in various parts of the country in recent years have been items of mining equipment abandoned underground when collieries closed, such as coal-cutters, conveyor belts, locomotives and mine cars. The remains of an iron-wheeled wagon recently uncovered when old workings in the Measham area were exposed is thought to date back to late-Victorian times.

Today, opencast accounts for 80% of coal production in Australia and almost 70% in the US (which has the largest site in the world, at Powder River Basin). China too has numerous vast open pits, yet the British opencast scene

Right: Opencast coal mining Chinese-style! Three Class SY steam locomotives, all moving, come into line with each other momentarily as they make their way along different levels of the giant 'crater' at Jalainur, northern China, on March 9, 2009. (This remarkable three-way coincidence occurred by chance and is not a result of digital manipulation.) NICK PIGOTT

has been systematically eradicated in the half-decade since the last deep mine closed.

The principal surface sites have been in Northumberland, County Durham, South Wales and Central Scotland, with Hargreaves Services, Banks Group and Celtic Energy having been among the leading players, but in the 2019-21 period alone, Hartington, Bradley, Shotton, Brenkley Lane, Fieldhouse and House of Water mines were closed and planning applications for new sites at Druridge Bay and Dewley Hill were refused. Nant Helen and Ffos-y-Fran were expected to cease operation by 2022, bringing the curtain down on British coalmining, apart from a handful of tiny hand-worked pits, mainly in Gloucestershire (see Appendix E).

With the 2023/24 coal exit deadline looming, it is doubtful if any companies will continue to submit bids, especially as protests by 'green' campaigners accompany every planning application.

This is despite strict regulations protecting watercourses and restricting the number of heavy lorries. Noise and dust suppression measures are also enforced, overburden is used to build bunds around pits to screen them from public view, and the majority of sites are restored to farmland or woodland afterwards. Yet controversy has continued to rage.

Often mistaken for a colliery by passing motorists on the M1 motorway was Oxcroft, in Derbyshire, which was one of several disposal points in the UK. Usually containing a preparation plant, these complexes gathered coal from surrounding opencast mines or from collieries with no modern washeries of their own, and processed it for loading into trains for onward distribution.

CHAPTER 25

End of an era

The last one — Kellingley

T HE HONOUR of being the last of Britain's many deep mines to survive in operation fell to Kellingley Colliery, in North Yorkshire.

Known as the 'Big K', it just managed to reach its golden jubilee before the axe fell on December 18, 2015.

When the last miners came up from the final shift, they posed for the national media's cameras laughing and joking – but the bravado was skin-deep only; a few minutes later, some of the men were in tears.

Kellingley had been Britain's first two-million tonne colliery, which was one of the reasons for its longevity, the other being its strategic position close to three major power stations – Ferrybridge, Eggborough and Drax. Its five-year deal with the latter ran out at the end of 2015 and was not renewed due to cheaper coal prices abroad.

For some years after the closure of the mine, Drax continued to burn four million tonnes a year in three of its six boilers (the others were fired on biomass), but the supplies came from Colombia and the US.

"How can it be right that it's cheaper to transport coal half-way round the world – in trains running right past the gates of this very pit – to a power station we can see across the fields?" asked one of the miners as he came to the surface for the last time. "It's crazy, it's a disgrace ... the country has thrown away its birthright."

Kellingley was one of Britain's newer collieries, being opened in 1965 after seven years of development. A modern, fully-mechanised superpit with shafts sunk down to 2,500ft, its skilled workers were considered by the NCB to be 'technicians' rather than miners and its output was twice that of the old collieries on the other side of nearby Pontefract. In fact, so prodigious was it that in 1977 a single face (B49s)

was able to claim a European record of almost a million tonnes a year ... more than most mines, at that time, were able to produce from all their faces combined.

The triple-decker cage at Kellingley could hold 120 men and hurtled them more than half a mile into the bowels of the earth. They then caught a train for a six-mile, 45-minute journey before spending the last ten minutes lying on a mile-long conveyor belt travelling at 9ft a second. On that, they would be spaced out at 23ft intervals for safety reasons. Once at the face, they worked for up to eight hours in 94°F heat and 98% humidity.

As more and more pits were shut down, the 'Big K' attracted displaced colliers from all over the country and employed so many Scotsmen that it had a pipe band in the Yorkshire heartland of the traditional brass band. The success of Kellingley helped inspire the opening of the adjacent Selby coalfield in the 1970s.

Although its faces had extended seven miles from the shafts by the end, the mine still had 30m tonnes of reserves – enough to keep it open for 15 more years – but the Government refused financial aid to its owners UK Coal and instead arranged to subsidise a 'managed closure', throwing the 450-strong workforce onto the scrapheap.

The very last piece of coal was symbolically brought to the surface on December 18 by miner Kevin McDonagh and the last tonne of coal was due to be put on display at the National Museum of Mining at Caphouse Colliery, near Wakefield, along with a memorial that had stood outside the office for many years, bearing the names of 17 men who lost their lives at Kellingley in its half-century of operation.

Because Kellingley's winding gear was enclosed in metal cladding, nobody from outside the industry passing its

Kellingley's headgear viewed from the top of the adjacent coal preparation plant a month before closure. NICK PIGOTT

It's all smiles for the camera, but the faces masked a deep sadness and, in many cases, resentment at the loss of jobs and the death of an industry: This was the very last shift at the very last deep shaft mine, December 18, 2015. PA

Although the last train of freshly-mined coal left Kellingley behind Type 5 No.66152 on December 18, 2015, services continued for a further six days to remove the stockpile. The curtain finally came down on Christmas Eve when No.66118, carrying a 'last train' headboard to mark the occasion, departed for Drax power station. GORDON EDGAR

gates on the Knottingley-Goole road on December 19 would have noticed that its sheave wheels had stopped spinning (as they would have done at the penultimate deep mine, Thoresby), but in the streets of nearby Knottingley that day, thousands of miners and their families turned out for a huge march, poignantly described by NUM branch officer Keith Poulson as "a celebration of the working lives we have shared together".

As had happened at Daw Mill and other locations, the demolition men moved in with almost indecent haste.

Millions of pounds worth of cutters, conveyors, power supports, trains and ventilators were abandoned underground, there being no other British deep mine to transfer them to, and all the surface structures, including the massive coal preparation plant seen in the above photograph, were unceremoniously razed to the ground. While they were coming down, a solar farm was going up in a field just 30 yards away.

A more striking symbol of the changing times would be hard to imagine.

What a difference six years makes: Kellingley Colliery in 2015 and, below, the same scene in 2021. All traces of the mine have been swept away (the surviving steel tower was not part of the main coalmining operation) and a solar farm has been established in the foreground. NICK PIGOTT

CHAPTER 26

Closures and demolitions

Destruction of an industry

IT IS difficult to comprehend how quickly and extensively almost all signs of the vast colliery complexes have been swept away in Britain through demolition and redevelopment. Daw Mill, for instance, was closed in 2013 and unceremoniously wiped off the face of the earth within a matter of months.

That mine's abandonment was brought about by an underground fire, but there have been numerous other reasons for closures over the years. These include geological faults, exhaustion of coal reserves, decline in demand, roof falls and floods, as well as mergers of neighbouring mines, in which haulage roads are linked underground and one set of surface buildings are taken out of use.

Closures weren't simply a case of infrastructure removal; they also had a debilitating social and mental effect on the people they affected. For no matter how dangerous, dirty or

Although some people who worked in the pits were glad to see them go, the great majority of mineworkers feel tremendous sadness at the way their industry was systematically destroyed. This symbolic photograph was taken at Calverton Colliery, Nottinghamshire, in January 2000 but could just as easily have been at any one of the hundreds of deep mines demolished since the 1960s. ROBIN STEWART-SMITH

204

A steel girder headstock comes crashing down in a mass of twisted metal at Victoria Colliery, Biddulph.

unhealthy some of the jobs were, the men whose livelihoods they had been often lost their sense of purpose following redundancy and experienced feelings of worthlessness as a result of enforced idleness and loss of camaraderie.

Some of the older men sadly lost the will to live and it was not uncommon in pit villages for there to be two or three funerals a week in the months following closure and demolition of a community's raison d'etre.

A mine's own 'funeral' was not a straightforward affair, for decommissioning involved far more than demolishing the headstocks and surface buildings; the shafts had to be filled and capped and the subterranean aquifers had to be protected from pollution that might occur once the roadways and workings begin to flood.

The usual way of sealing off a mine is to remove all the ropes and pipes from inside the shaft, drill large holes through the wall into the strata at the bottom and then pipe in concrete to form an anchored seal. Thousands of tons of roadstone or rubble are then poured on top of that and finally the shaft is capped at the top with more concrete.

Deterioration starts quickly once the fans, pumps and power are turned off. Depending on the type of geology, a mine can quickly fill with water and its roadway roofs and sides can begin to converge as the forces of nature take their course. Millions of pounds' worth of mining machinery and railway equipment is abandoned underground and left to its fate, as there is no use for it elsewhere.

Even relatively small mines involve substantial work to decommission. Derbyshire's Eckington Colliery, the last operational mine in the Midlands, closed in January 2019 and its drift had to be filled with concrete, strengthened specially to prevent subsidence where it passed under Network Rail's main Rotherham-Chesterfield freight line. The mine entrances also had to be capped, the conveyor, screen and workshop dismantled and the explosives store made safe. Finally, the whole site had to be landscaped.

'Space-age' they might well have been when erected in the 1970s, but that didn't save the unique headstocks of Yorkshire's Thorne Colliery from a crash landing when the fateful decision came in 2004.

It's all highly contentious when it's considered how much work and money goes into sinking and establishing a mine in the first place and when it's realised that the capping is as good as permanent – for even if a future generation decided it wanted to reopen collieries in the event of a global energy shortage, lack of maintenance coupled with geological pressures will by then have made it totally impractical.

Unlike in 1939 (war) and 1973 (Middle East oil crisis), Britain would have nothing to fall back on in terms of high-quality deep-mined coal – and to rub salt into the wound, it was reported in late-2015 that the developers of a new potash mine in North Yorkshire had been forced to turn to foreign experts to sink their shafts because British engineers had lost the knowledge!

Long-term mothballing of the nation's last three deep collieries might have been an option, but even that would have required Government aid, as it would have meant not only maintaining the integrity of the infrastructure but keeping the underground ventilators and pumps in continuous operation. Harworth Colliery in Nottinghamshire was

mothballed for eight years between 2006 and 2014 and reportedly required a team of 100 men simply to keep it ticking over. Former employees are of the opinion that it wouldn't have been possible to re-open it anyway as the very deep workings were being crushed, one of the reasons production was suspended in the first place.

Even if it was ever decided to sink a new shaft into the workings of an old mine, the replacement headgear and surface structures wouldn't be anywhere near their predecessors anyway, for the new colliery would be sunk closer to the extremities the headings and faces had reached when the old one closed, which could be several miles away. According to UK Coal figures in 2009, the cost of sinking shafts and opening a new deep mine would be a billion pounds and it could take anything up to seven years before it was able to produce any coal. In that time, a war could have been fought and lost.

Far more likely to occur in the event of a serious energy emergency or foreign trade embargo would be a political and environmental U-turn resulting in a rash of new opencast mines.

Short-lived: Britain's last all-new deep mine

IN THE 1970s, the research teams of the NCB were looking at several areas in which to expand once the older pits west of the Pennines and in Scotland had become exhausted. The new regions included a famous East Midlands beauty spot — the Vale of Belvoir, south-west of Grantham, beneath which lies at least half a billion tonnes of coal.

Three new superpits were planned on the outer edges of the vale — in the villages of Saltby, Hose and Asfordby — and would be served by railways operating on the Merry-Go-Round system, taking coal to Trent valley power stations. Production was predicted to last about 75 years and provide employment for well over a thousand miners.

Fierce local opposition — not least from the Duke of Rutland, whose stately home, Belvoir Castle, towered over the vale — forced the longest and most expensive coal planning inquiry ever held in Britain. In the end, British Coal was allowed to go ahead with only one of the collieries, Asfordby, west of Melton Mowbray.

One of the reasons for that decision was that Asfordby lay in a locality already used for heavy industry (Holwell ironworks), whereas the other two would have been built in unspoilt rural areas. Being adjacent to British Rail's Old Dalby test track, Asfordby also required the shortest rail connection of the three and was only nine miles from the existing Cotgrave Colliery.

Asfordby's shafts were sunk in 1986 but it was to be the mid-1990s before coal came fully on stream due to the area being bedevilled by more serious geological faults than British Coal had bargained for. Apart from this, the coal turned out to be the wrong quality and had to be taken to Rufford, near Mansfield, for blending with other grades before it could be marketed — a process known as 'sweeting'.

Britain's newest colliery thus turned out to be a 'white elephant' and was closed in 1997. The virtually new Koepe winding towers were demolished by explosives a year later and some of the larger ancillary buildings became part of the rail test centre.

These photographs by the author show the demolition of the two modern headstocks in March 1998. A warning siren, a series of explosions, a sickening thud, a cloud of dust … then silence.

Then and now

THE VAST majority of disused collieries in Britain have been demolished, especially those closed during the last two or three decades as a result of the modern emphasis on redevelopment. A few closed 40 or more years ago have had their surface buildings adapted for new uses but most sites have been redeveloped for a wide variety of purposes.

A stark but all-too familiar illustration of how the country has changed can be seen in these two images at Hucknall, a few miles north of Nottingham. Below, on May 4, 1979, the colliery there is in full production and a Class 56 locomotive is bringing Merry-Go-Round hoppers through the rapid loader as two Class 20s pass on what, at that time, was a freight-only route serving Hucknall, Linby, Newstead and Annesley pits. The photograph above right, taken from the same location, reveals three of what are now the most commonplace sights in Britain ... supermarket, car park and housing estate. In two positive moves for railways, the ex-BR line in the foreground has been reopened to passengers as the Robin Hood Line and trams from Nottingham now also serve Hucknall.

Some of the other uses to which sites have been put:

The site of Wearmouth Colliery is now occupied by Sunderland FC's 48,000-capacity Stadium of Light, plus an Olympic-sized swimming pool.

Ashington, which still had rows and rows of Victorian-style wooden-bodied wagons in its sidings as recently as the late-1980s, is an upmarket business park complete with fountains and flower beds. Attractive, but rather sterile compared with its former use.

Shirebrook's site hosts the headquarters of a major sportswear company.

Cotgrave is one of many sites that have been turned into housing estates.

Cortonwood, one of the flashpoints of the 1984/85 strike, is now one of numerous sites that have been turned into retail parks or supermarkets.

Other uses for old colliery locations include golf courses, country parks, warehouses, distribution centres, logistics parks, fast-food outlets and leisure centres as well as the ubiquitous housing estates — in fact anything, it seems, but wealth-producing manufacturing industry.

Even people with a trained eye would be hard pressed these days to know they were passing a former colliery if they weren't familiar with the area.

PICTURES: A KAYE AND R STEWART-SMITH

CHAPTER 27

Preservation and heritage

Where to see collieries today

ALTHOUGH BRITAIN lost its last operational deep shaft mines in the 2010s, half a dozen or so collieries survive as museums fulfilling the important role of educating future generations of children about one of their country's greatest-ever industries.

The largest and best-stocked visitor centres housed in original colliery buildings are those at Caphouse, Blaenafon, Lady Victoria, Lewis Merthyr, Pleasley and Woodhorn.

The first three are the national mining museums of England, Wales and Scotland respectively and possess extensive infrastructure, informative displays and academic research facilities.

Caphouse Colliery opened as the Yorkshire Mining Museum in 1988 and was promoted to national status seven years later. Compared with some of the giant complexes that sprang up in the NCB era, it was modestly sized but its historic 19th and 20th century buildings have been complemented by a modern extension and it now commands a large site embracing the adjacent Hope pit, which has a winding tower of its own.

The very rare tandem headstock at Snibston mine, which can trace its ancestry back to the days of railway pioneer George Stephenson. The colliery's yard and external areas were re-opened to the public in 2020 following a period of closure.

The National Coal Mining Museum for England is based in the former Caphouse Colliery near Wakefield, Yorkshire. The historic original buildings are complemented by a large modern extension... and hour-long underground tours further enhance the experience for visitors.

Among the many features on its site at Overton, near Wakefield, are pithead baths, washery screens, winding engine house, compressor house, fan house, blacksmith's workshop, elevated conveyor, water treatment lagoons, boiler house and smokestack chimney. A 'Paddy train' service connects the Caphouse and Hope sites on certain days.

The museum's biggest attraction, however, is its ability to offer members of the public the chance to descend 459ft beneath ground level and be guided by former miners through some of the roadways and coalfaces they formerly worked in. The tour takes over an hour and participants walk for half a mile in total, passing through several narrow and low-roofed sections. For safety reasons, they have to be kitted out with hard hat, lamp and battery pack and – as it is still classified as a working mine – they have to surrender in the lamproom any contraband items they might be carrying (including cigarettes, digital watches, keys, cameras and mobile phones) due to the possible presence of methane in the mine.

Remarkably, Caphouse also possesses an original furnace shaft, down which visitors can peer before starting

their underground tour. The winding engine is still operational and can turn the pulley wheels for demonstration purposes, but it runs on compressed air rather than steam and the cage is now lowered and raised by a separate electric winder. The shaft is original and is believed to be the deepest brick-lined one still in use in Europe. The whole complex is completed by a half-mile long drift, which provides ventilation to the workings and can be used as an emergency egress if necessary. The drift enabled a shearer/loader from Kellingley to be taken underground in pieces for re-assembly at the Caphouse coalface.

The National Coal Museum of Wales is based at Blaenafon's 'Big Pit', which opened to the public in 1983 and was made a UNESCO World Heritage Site in 2000. Like Caphouse, it offers genuine underground tours, which go 295ft down using the original headgear, shaft and cages.

Despite its name, Big Pit is relatively small but it punches well above its weight and makes for a fascinating and informative day-out. Surface buildings include winding engine house, saw mill, pithead baths and a rare water-balanced headstock. It also has a drift and fan house helping to ventilate the workings and there is the station of a standard

Above: How children learn about the past: Excited youngsters prepare to go underground at the Welsh National Mining Museum in Blaenafon. **Right:** A new experience… three-year-old George Reeves, of Leicester, sees coal for the first time in his life during a visit to the Great Central Railway in 2015. (Back in 1992, the GCR rescued Britain's last few surviving 16-ton coal wagons following an initiative launched by the author of this book and now runs them at galas and other special events.)

gauge heritage railway close by. As at Caphouse, safety gear and contraband regulations apply underground.

In keeping with their museum status, both sites feature comprehensive libraries and research study facilities.

Those two collieries thus provide visitors with an experience as close to real mining as it's possible to get in Britain today (although to completely replicate the astonishing underground atmosphere, with its extraordinary sounds, sights, smells, sensations and temperature variations is, of course, impossible in a non-operational mine).

A small number of other locations in the UK offer underground access to genuine mines, but via drifts rather than vertical shafts. These include Apedale, Beamish, Dudley and Hopewell (see panel at end of this chapter for contact details).

The grandest of the three national museums in terms of impressive surface infrastructure is Lady Victoria Colliery at Newtongrange, south of Edinburgh. Although only able to offer a simulated underground experience, its extensive tall engineering buildings provide a nostalgic reminder of the heavy industrial era and contain superb displays,

research facilities and mining machinery exhibits. It also houses Scotland's largest winding engine.

Lady Victoria dates back to the 1890s and was opened as a museum in 1984, three years after its closure as a working pit. Virtually everything of historical architectural value has survived and it thus forms an almost complete example of a major Victorian colliery, so much so that it is listed Category 'A' by Historic Scotland and in 2008 it was voted Scotland's Most Treasured Place in an online poll.

Unlike the other two national museums, it can be reached easily by main line train, Newtongrange station on the recently-reopened Waverley route being just a short walk away.

Another well-preserved mine is Lewis Merthyr Colliery, located at Rhondda Heritage Park west of Pontypridd,

In their heyday, colliery yards could be as busy as many of those of similar size on the main line network and that at Lady Victoria Colliery, south of Edinburgh, was no exception. Today, the tracks and wagons seen in this 1966 NCB scene have gone, but most of the buildings have survived and house the excellent National Mining Museum of Scotland. NATIONAL ARCHIVE

South Wales. It contains several surface buildings as well as two fine headstocks and, like Lady Victoria, offers a simulated subterranean experience.

Bilsthorpe Heritage Museum in Nottinghamshire is a little gem, a modest-sized but well-stocked visitor centre based most unusually in an old squash court and tucked away off the beaten track in a former pit village. It was opened in 2014 and is run by a passionate volunteer team including helpful and knowledgeable ex-miners.

Apedale drift mine, on the once-extensive North Staffordshire coalfield, has an excellent visitor centre boasting underground tours and a large and very well-stocked museum display building. It is also served by a nearby heritage railway, as are Blaenafon and Beamish.

The winding towers and other surviving buildings at another Staffordshire site, the former Foxfield Colliery, are not normally open but can be seen from Foxfield Railway steam trains on certain dates. Most of the other

museums listed at the end of this chapter offer some form of rail-related exhibit or short demonstration ride.

Snibston Colliery, in Leicestershire, formerly had a standard gauge preserved steam railway too, but it was closed down in 2015 along with the award-winning and relatively new 'Discovery' science museum alongside it. Although the museum has been demolished, the mine's yard reopened to the public in 2020 as part of a £3m Snibston Colliery Park leisure facility, complete with café and children's adventure playground.

Regular guided tours inside the surface buildings under the leadership of ex-miners are no longer available, but the public can get close to the headstocks, winding houses, lamp room, fan house, gunpowder store and medical centre. Well-illustrated information boards have been erected alongside each structure and there are also several items of machinery on display, including undercutters and a roadheader.

212

Creative thinking has turned a former squash court into a fine coal museum at Bilsthorpe Heritage Centre in Nottinghamshire.

Snibston is located in the aptly-named town of Coalville and is unique in possessing both a tandem headstock and a conventional winding tower. The tandem structure, in which there is a separate shaft for each cage, stands on the site of the original colliery founded in 1832 by railway pioneer George Stephenson and one of the shafts is old enough to have originally been used for furnace ventilation (see chapter 14). In 1999, the buildings were identified by the Government as of national importance and the mine was classified as a Scheduled Ancient Monument, joining those of Lady Victoria, Caphouse, Blaenafon and Chatterley Whitfield on the list as the five most substantially-complete coal mines left in Great Britain.

Chatterley Whitfield is the daddy of them all ... bigger even than Lady Victoria and the only one to have retained virtually all its many original buildings, but sadly, it's also one of the most neglected despite the valiant efforts of an active Friends group. Already on Historic England's Heritage at Risk register, it was named by the Victorian Society in 2019 as one of the ten most endangered buildings in England and Wales.

The site is extraordinary in possessing no fewer than four headstocks, all with their winding wheels in place, along with washery screens, winding houses, office blocks, bath house and numerous ancillary structures. After closure in 1977, it became a museum with 70,000 visitors a year (many taking underground tours) but those trips had to stop in the early 80s after a dangerous build-up of floodwater and methane underground led to the shafts having to be filled and capped. The preservation scheme struggled on as a surface attraction until closing down in 1993 and since then the Friends group has only been allowed to open to the public on a few days a year, by prior booking. It would be an architectural tragedy if this fenced-off and overgrown site was allowed to deteriorate beyond the point of no return.

As can be seen in the 'then and now' photographs

overleaf, the main difference is the sprouting of trees and bushes and the lifting of the railway tracks and loading plant. This Staffordshire gem is, however, a national treasure and should be given the restoration funds and tender loving care it deserves.

The nearest Welsh equivalent of Chatterley Whitfield in terms of surviving buildings is Navigation Colliery in the town of Crumlin, west of Pontypool. This remarkable site still features two winding engine houses, fan house, pumping house, bath house, heapstead, stores, workshops, powder store and a 300ft high chimney. The big difference is that Navigation no longer possesses its headstocks. The site has been derelict for several years but there is local pressure to renovate the buildings for public use.

At the former Haig Colliery in Cumbria, the engine house, steam winding engines and one remaining headstock are no longer open to the public following closure of the museum there in 2015, but those structures are protected as scheduled ancient monuments and the offices there have, rather ironically, been used recently by West Cumbria Mining, the firm controversially bidding to sink an all-new deep coal mine at nearby Woodhouse. (See Appendix H).

The extremely tall headstocks at Clipstone Colliery in Nottinghamshire are also listed as structures of national importance and it is hoped they will be incorporated into a mining museum-cum-visitor centre following their purchase by a Mansfield-based tourism company in 2020.

The final addition to the ranks of preserved headstocks (making more than 40 in all) are the two at Hatfield Colliery, near Doncaster, which Historic England saved from demolition in November 2015 with 48 hours to spare. The winding house was rescued too and the rapid loader still stands (thought to be the only one left in the country), but the office block and several other surrounding buildings there have since been demolished.

Sadly, almost all other surviving colliery sites in Britain have suffered at least partial demolition of miscellaneous surface structures, with washeries and rapid loaders having been the biggest victims.

There were a few anxious moments at the Cefn Coed Colliery Museum in 2016 when the Welsh Government drastically reduced the height of the two winding towers at the former anthracite mine on safety grounds, but in 2021 work was underway to return the listed structures to their full size, after which the site will reopen to the public. A steam winding engine and compressor have also survived there.

The North Wales coalfield is represented in preservation by Bersham Colliery near Wrexham, which still boast its winding engine as well as engine house and headgear, the

The well-maintained Lewis Merthyr Colliery, in the Rhondda Valley, offers a simulated underground experience and can be reached reasonably easily from Trehafod station on the Cardiff-Treherbert line.

latter having once been located at the nearby Gatewen pit.

Beamish museum, in the North-East, is the only place where the traditional design of washery screens can be seen in use by trains (albeit preserved ones) and it also has the only example of a working vertical-cylinder winding engine. This was moved from the nearby Beamish Second Colliery, the adjacent 'Mahogany' drift mine being in its original location.

Pleasley and Astley Green are among museums containing beautifully-restored winding engines, some steam, some electric, and open days occasionally allow members of the public to see such veteran machines in action. The winding engines at Washington 'F' pit and Elliot mine are also among those restored to working order.

Astley Green – better known now as the Lancashire Mining Museum – has the added attraction of a magnificent lattice-steel headstock and recently took delivery of an ancient horse gin transferred from the Nottingham Industrial Museum.

Pleasley, Caphouse, Lewis Merthyr, Crumlin Navigation, Cefn Coed, Chatterley Whitfield and Lady Victoria still possess examples of the once-ubiquitous tall brick 'smokestack' chimneys attached to engine houses, while the latter colliery also retains a long covered footbridge that took miners over a main road to the pithead baths.

Close to Lewis Merthyr at Trehafod is the Hetty winding house, pithead gear and fan house of the old Great Western Colliery. These structures owe their survival to retention of the shaft after that mine's closure in order to provide ventilation for neighbouring Tymawr Colliery. The 1875 steam winding engine has been restored and slightly modified to work on compressed air.

One of the largest engine house buildings to survive is at Penallta Colliery, between Caerphilly and Ystrad Mynach, where there are plans to turn its derelict shell and that of the adjacent bath house into apartments alongside the two headstocks that proudly stand on the site. Llwynypia Colliery's winding house in Tonypandy is also preserved and a few miles west of there is the South Wales Miners' Museum at Cynonville, which although not housed within a former colliery building, has won a Prince of Wales Award for its interpretative exhibits, including a traditional miner's cottage scene and a short tunnel for children to climb through. Established in 1976, it has been attracting as many as 100,000 visitors a year.

The derelict winding house, bath house and loco shed of Firbeck Main Colliery, Nottinghamshire, survived until demolition in 2020/21, while across the county at Thoresby, the former engineering workshop (once one of the biggest in the Midlands) has been retained and is hopefully to be

The most complete coal mine still standing in Britain in terms of surviving buildings and headstocks is the disused Chatterley Whitfield Colliery in Staffordshire – now unique as the only one possessing four winding towers. As can be seen in these 'then and now' photographs, the main difference is the sprouting of trees and bushes! In the 1990s, it was open to the public and operated underground tours but the workings flooded and the public visits were heavily restricted, since when the site has become increasingly run-down and overgrown. It is, however, a national treasure and should be given the restoration funds and tender loving care it deserves.

refurbished as a community facility for a housing estate being built on the remainder of the site.

The earlier a mine closed, the more likely its ancillary surface buildings will have survived reasonably intact due to their re-use by commercial businesses. New Haden Colliery near Cheadle, Staffordshire, which shut in 1943, is a good example and even possesses a concrete Baum clarifier tower, but such remnants are usually on private land.

Staffordshire is also home to the Museum of Cannock Chase in Hednesford, which is located on the site of the former Valley Colliery (once a training pit for young miners) and includes a mining gallery.

But by far the most innovative re-purposing of a disused coal mine has to be the opening in 2021 at Tower Colliery of the 'Phoenix', the fastest seated zip-wire in the world! This 70mph cable has been erected in two sections on Rhigos mountain at the top of the Rhondda valley and allows participants to ride more than a mile from the summit

down to a visitor centre established next to the headstock of what used to be Wales's last deep mine. One can't help being reminded of the aerial ropeways that once carried spoil between collieries and waste tips. Now the payloads are human!

Although not exactly 'preserved', there are still a great many Miners' Welfare social clubs plying a healthy trade in former colliery villages and giving ex-colliers and their families the opportunity to maintain old friendships.

Finally, there are a number of surviving headstocks belonging to mines or former mines producing tin, lead, gold, haematite, fluorspar, potash and other minerals, and some, such as Geevor (Cornwall), Florence (Cumbria) and Magpie (Derbyshire), have winding towers resembling those of collieries, but those are not part of this survey.

(Please note that at the time of publication, Covid-19 restrictions were still in effect at some of the public venues mentioned in this chapter.)

The effect on steam railways

ONE OF the sectors most affected by the rush to reduce greenhouse gases in Britain is the heritage steam railway movement.

The UK's 100 or so preserved lines currently account for a minuscule fraction of the nation's carbon emissions – a mere 0.02% (even less than half the amount created by barbeque charcoal!) – and their volunteers are confident of making further reductions by adopting carbon-neutral offsetting measures.

In the years following closure of Britain's collieries, opencast coal has been available to heritage lines, but those supplies will dry up shortly when Ffos-y-Fran, near Merthyr Tydfil, closes.

So, following a decision by the Department for the Environment to ban the use of domestic coal, trials of so-called 'biocoal' were undertaken in the summer of 2021 in a bid to find an alternative fuel for steam locomotives.

The trials featured three types of smokeless fuel – Ecoal50, Homefire Ovals and Briteflame – pitched against the traditional Ffos-y-Fran variety.

The Ecoal50 nuggets – comprising 50% biomass in the form of crushed olive husks and 50% crushed anthracite – were the best performing of the smokeless

trio and were said to have been as good as the Welsh product but with 40% fewer emissions and a much smaller ash residue.

Until the results of the trial can be fully evaluated, particularly with regard to 75mph main line steam operations, the heritage railway movement is having to rely on ever-dwindling sources of traditional coal, including imports from Russia. These are low in sulphur and volatility (so are much cleaner-burning), but would nevertheless be outlawed under the terms of a new UK Environment Bill aimed at reducing emissions from fossil fuels.

The Bill is expected to be passed in late 2021 and although heritage coal-users were being assured by Government ministers that locomotives, traction engines, winding engines, vintage steamships and blacksmiths' forges would be exempt, Heritage Railway Association president Lord Faulkner was working to insert an amendment that would turn the assurances into guarantees.

"A complete ban would be a totally disproportionate response to the climate change agenda and damage the great cultural and economic value of the steam sector to the British economy," he said.

The preserved headstock at Astley Green Colliery in Lancashire is undoubtedly one of the most striking lattice steel examples left in Britain. Standing at just under 100ft tall, it is the last survivor in a coalfield once chock-full of collieries and is now a protected monument. The winding house and its unique tandem compound steam engine have also survived and are part of the Lancashire Mining Museum.

The surviving locations
Collieries open to the public:

(Note that some of the museums are open only on limited occasions and it is advisable to check before travelling. This is particularly so since the advent of the Covid-19 pandemic restrictions in 2020/21.)

CAPHOUSE
National Coal Mining Museum for England,
New Road, Overton, West Yorkshire WF4 4RH.
(ncm.org.uk) tel: 01924 848806.
Number of headstocks: 1 (plus 1 at Hope Pit on the same site).

BLAENAFON ('BIG PIT')
Welsh National Coal Museum, Blaenafon World Heritage Site, Torfaen NP4 9XP.
(museum.wales/bigpit) tel: 0300 111 2333 or 029 2057 3650.
Number of headstocks: 1

LADY VICTORIA
National Mining Museum of Scotland, Newtongrange,
Midlothian EH22 4QN.
(nationalminingmuseum.com) tel: 0131 663 7519.
Number of headstocks: 1

WOODHORN
QEII Country Park, near Ashington, Northumberland
NE63 9YF.
(museumsnorthumberland.org.uk/woodhorn-museum)
tel: 01670 624455.
Number of headstocks: 2

LEWIS MERTHYR
Rhondda Heritage Park, Coedcae Road, Trehafod, South
Wales CF37 2NP.
(rctcbc.gov.uk) tel: 01443 682036
Number of headstocks: 2

PLEASLEY
Pit Lane, Pleasley, Nottinghamshire NG19 7PH.
(pleasleypittrust.org.uk).
Number of headstocks: 2

APEDALE
Apedale Heritage Centre, Loomer Road, Chesterton,
Staffordshire ST5 7LB.
(apedale.co.uk) tel: 01782 565050.
No headstocks as underground access is via a drift.

ASTLEY GREEN
Higher Green Lane, Astley, Manchester M29 7JB.
(lancashireminingmuseum.org) tel: 01924 895841.
Number of headstocks: 1

SNIBSTON
Ashby Road, Coalville, Leicestershire LE67 3LN.
(leicscountryparks.org.uk) tel: 0116 305 5000.
Number of headstocks: 2
Note: It is not normally possible to enter the buildings,
but the colliery premises are accessible.

BESTWOOD
Park Road, Bestwood, Nottinghamshire NG6 8ZA.
(visit-nottinghamshire.co.uk) tel: 0115 927 3674.
Number of headstocks: 1

CHATTERLEY WHITFIELD
Chell, near Stoke-on-Trent, Staffordshire ST6 8UW.
Open to the public only rarely, by prior appointment:
(chatterleywhitfieldfriends.org.uk).
Number of headstocks: 4

BEAMISH
Living Museum of the North, Beamish, County Durham
DH9 0RG.
(beamish.org.uk) tel: 0191 370 4000.
Number of headstocks: 1
NB. The winding tower was relocated from nearby Beamish Second Colliery but the Mahogany drift mine (which
is open to the public) is in its original position.

BERSHAM
Rhostyllen, near Wrexham, North Wales.
(old.wrexham.gov.uk) tel: 01978 297460.
Number of headstocks: 1
(Open on limited Sundays).

CEFN COED
Neath Road, Crynant, South Wales SA10 8SN.
(npt.gov.uk) tel: 01639 750556
Number of headstocks: 2
Note: In 2021, this site was temporarily closed for restoration, so check before travelling.

TOWER
Rhigos Road, Hirwaun, near Aberdare, South Wales
CF44 9UF.
(zipworld.co.uk) tel: 01685 706666.
Number of headstocks: 1
Note: Although the mine itself is closed, the yard can
be accessed by the public in connection with a zip-wire
attraction opened on the site in 2021.

HOPEWELL
Cannop Hill, Speech House Rd, Coleford, Gloucestershire
GL16 7EL.
(hopewellcolliery.com) tel: 01594 810706.
Note: This is a drift mine; the large half-winding wheel
and wooden replica headstock on the surface are for
display purposes only.

WASHINGTON 'F' PIT
Albany Park, Washington, County Durham NE37 1BN.
(sunderlandculture.org.uk) tel: 0191 5612323.
Number of headstocks: 1

FOXFIELD
Whitehurst Lane, Dilhorne, Staffordshire.
(foxfieldrailway.co.uk) tel: 01782 396210.
Number of headstocks: 2
Note: This site is not normally open but can sometimes
be accessed during special events

The headstocks of Clipstone Colliery – the tallest lattice steel winding towers in Britain – have happily survived and are earmarked as the centrepiece of a proposed mining museum in the East Midlands village of Clipstone.

Collieries not normally open to the public:

(Due to demolition of surrounding buildings, most of the following tend to comprise winding houses and headgear only. The exception is Navigation, which has numerous buildings but no headgear.)

CLIPSTONE
Clipstone, Nottinghamshire.
Number of headstocks: 2

HATFIELD
Stainforth, South Yorkshire.
Number of headstocks: 2

PENALLTA
Near Ystrad Mynach, South Wales.
Number of headstocks: 2

HAIG
Kells, Whitehaven, Cumbria.
Number of headstocks: 1

BARNSLEY MAIN
Stairfoot, near Barnsley, South Yorkshire.
Number of headstocks: 1

HETTY
Hopkinstown, near Pontypridd, South Wales.
Number of headstocks: 1

CRUMLIN NAVIGATION
Crumlin, west of Pontypool, South Wales.
Number of headstocks: 0

HIGHHOUSE
Auchinleck, Ayrshire.
Number of headstocks: 1

Other preserved winding towers, standing as isolated structures without engine houses, originally belonged to the collieries of Barony (Ayrshire), Frances (Fife), Mary (Fife), Grange (Shropshire), Morlais (Carmarthenshire, now moved to Kidwelly) and Brinsley (Nottinghamshire), the latter being particularly interesting as it's an early wooden tandem headstock (see picture in Chapter 7). There is also a three-deck pit cage preserved on the site of County Durham's Easington Colliery.

DRIFT MINES: In addition to the preserved colliery sites above, a small number of privately-operated drift mines survive in commercial use and are not open to the public. These include two anthracite mines in South Wales sometimes referred to as deep pits – Aberpergwm and Cwmgwrach (the latter currently shut and under care-and-maintenance), along with Ayle Colliery, in Cumbria, and a handful of small gales in the Forest of Dean, some of the latter tending to open and close on an 'as-required' basis.

Also in South Wales is Onllwyn washery, a large rail-served complex at the head of the Dulais valley, which has spent many years as a preparation plant for opencast coal but which is due for closure and conversion into a maintenance depot for a high-speed train testing centre planned for the area by 2025.

A large 'A'-frame winding tower survives in splendid isolation on the site of Scotland's Barony Colliery, near Auchinleck, in East Ayrshire. The bodies of four miners killed in a pit accident in 1962 lie beneath the tower. JOHN CULLEN

Other coal-related museum and heritage sites include:

Bilsthorpe Heritage Museum, Cross Street, Bilsthorpe, Nottinghamshire NG22 8QY. (bilsthorpemuseum.co.uk) tel: 01623 871533.

Durham Mining Museum, Spennymoor Town Hall, County Durham DL16 6DG. (dmm.org.uk) tel: 07577 012882.

South Wales Miners' Museum, Afan Forest Park, Cynonville, near Neath SA13 3HG. (swminers.co.uk) tel: 01639 851833.

Nottinghamshire Mining Museum, Station Road, Mansfield NG18 1LP. (nottsminingmuseum.org.uk) tel: 01623 239750.

North of England Institute of Mining and Mechanical Engineers, Neville Hall, Westgate Road, Newcastle NE1 1SE. (mininginstitute.org.uk) tel: 0191 250 9717.

Museum of Cannock Chase, Valley Road, Hednesford, Staffs WS12 1TD. (museumofcannockchase.org) tel: 01543 8776660.

Blists Hill Victorian Town Museum, Legges Way, Telford, Shropshire TF7 5UD. (ironbridge.org.uk) tel: 01952 433424.

Black Country Living Museum, Tipton Road, Dudley, West Midlands DY1 4SQ. (bclm.co.uk) tel: 0121 557 9643.

Elsecar Heritage Centre, Wath Road, Elsecar, South Yorkshire S74 8HJ. (elsecar-heritage.com) tel: 01226 740203.

The only headstock in Wales still used for its original purpose of lowering people underground in an authentic shaft and cage on an everyday basis is at Big Pit Colliery in Blaenafon – home of the Welsh National Coal Museum. A few pulley wheels at other mines are still operational but are either not linked to a shaft or not in regular use. In this view can be seen two ex-NCB locos, a Hudswell Clarke 0-6-0ST and a Barclay 0-4-0ST.

Derelict but still standing... the buildings of Crumlin Navigation Colliery in 2021. The mine closed in 1967 and although the headstocks and screens are missing, it provides a classic reminder of a once-commonplace Welsh valley scene. NICK PIGOTT

National Forest Centre ('Conkers'), Rawdon Road, Moira, Derbyshire DE12 6GA. This award-winning visitor attraction centred on a former mining area contains a mining display room containing some of the items saved by the **South Derbyshire Mining Preservation Group**. The group's other collection is based at Gresley Old Hall, near Swadlincote.

Prestongrange Museum, Morrison's Haven, Prestonpans, Scotland EH32 9RX. (eastlothian.gov.uk) tel: 0131 653 2904.

Kidwelly Industrial Museum, Carmarthenshire SA17 4LW. tel: 01554 891078. (NB. This site, which contains the former Morlais headgear, was closed for long-term maintenance circa 2021, so check before travelling).

Elliot Engine House, White Rose Way, New Tredegar, Wales NP24 6DF. (erih.net/elliot) tel: 01443 822666.

Aber Valley Heritage Museum, Gwern Avenue, Senghenydd, Caerphilly CF83 4HA. This site is largely devoted to commemoration of the dreadful disaster at Senghenydd in 1913.

Smaller exhibits of coal interest can be seen at the National Gas Museum, 195 Aylestone Rd, Leicester, (nationalgasmuseum.org.uk) and the Nottingham Industrial Museum, Wollaton Hall (nottinghamindustrialmuseum.org.uk). There are also a number of small restoration locations open to the public, such as the site of Califat Colliery, near Swannington, Leics, but surviving surface buildings at the nearby Calcutta and Moira collieries are among several

A sight few, if any, South Welsh miners could have predicted when their last deep shaft pit closed in 2008... members of the public being kitted out with safety harnesses and helmets for a ride on the world's fastest seated zip-wire! The headquarters of the 70mph mountainside attraction have been established in 2021 on the site of Tower Colliery, the surviving headstock of which can be seen through the window.
NICK PIGOTT

Snibston Colliery is unusual in possessing its former engine shed. This is the oldest building on the site and is believed to date from the mid-19th century. The extension was added in the 1920s.

now in private hands as commercial premises or dwelling houses. Also in private hands is part of the former Flourmill Colliery in Gloucestershire (which has been repurposed as a locomotive restoration base), and an 1879 wooden headstock formerly located at the closed Dibnah heritage centre in Bolton, Lancashire.

SOCIETIES AND FORUMS

Finally, there are a number of organisations, websites and internet forums specialising in coal-mining history and ones that can be recommended for more detailed information than can be contained in a general publication such as this, are the **Northern Mine Research Society** (nmrs.org.uk), whose website hosts a superb map of all known colliery sites; **Healey Hero** (healeyhero.co.uk), on which Robert Bradley, a former mining surveyor, helps to ensure it is quite literally a mine of fascinating information; the **Industrial Railway Society** (irsociety.co.uk), **Mine2Minds Education** (miningheritage.co.uk); the

At the National Coal Mining Museum for England, visitors can ride in an authentic ex-underground 'paddy train' linking Caphouse Colliery with Hope Pit.

Rolling stock of a very different kind on view at the South Wales Miners' Museum!

These days, a tell-tale street name can sometimes provide the only clue to a former colliery's existence...

National Association of Mining History Organisations (namho.org); **Subterranea Britannica** (subbrit.org.uk), **AditNow** (aditnow.co.uk) and ukminingremains.co.uk

SAFETY FIRST...

Disused mine sites can be dangerous places. Never enter them without permission – and never throw anything down a hole or remove a ladder or rope. There could be someone underground!

CHAPTER 28

Energy policy and the future

Sunshine replaces 'buried sunshine'

WHEN BRITAIN'S last deep coal mine, Kellingley, closed at the end of 2015, a march through the streets was held to mark not just its demise but the death of an entire industry. Prominent among the crowds were hundreds of banners bearing the words: 'If the lights go out, don't blame us!'

They referred to the British Government's energy policy, which many people claimed was no longer secure or self-sufficient.

The workforces at Kellingley and other former collieries had an understandable right to feel bitter and angry at being thrown on the scrapheap because the UK's energy policy for the next few years still required 20% of the nation's needs to be met by the burning of coal—and to achieve that, much of it had to be shipped thousands of miles from the other side of the world.

To make matters even more bizarre, the Colombian, Russian and Australian imports that were putting British money into other nations' economies were being transported long distances after arriving at UK ports ... to power stations that were themselves sitting on or near coalfields containing millions of tonnes of British coal!

For Kellingley in particular, it was a case of rubbing salt into the redundant miners' wounds, for trainloads of foreign biomass and coal were being moved right past its gates on their way to nearby Drax power station.

The term 'economics of the madhouse' was used by critics and NUM general secretary Chris Kitchen warned: "If the gas supply is ever turned off, we've had it. People say mining was a dirty and dangerous job and good riddance ... but has the nation made a mistake in closing it all down? We've left ourselves no options if we ever need to change our mind."

One would expect an NUM stalwart to feel that way, of course, but anxieties were also felt by senior Conservative politician Lord Howell who, speaking after one of Britain's foreign-owned power stations had come within a whisker of having to ration electricity, warned that energy policy in Britain was not sufficiently long-term or robust and left perilously little margin for error.

Both men were right at the time, but what Kellingley's workforce perhaps weren't able to foresee in 2015 was that the rate of change would be so startling and that by the end of the decade, a huge solar farm containing thousands of photo-voltaic panels would have been established in a field just 30 yards from the perimeter of their demolished colliery!

The irony couldn't have been starker if the panels had been erected slap bang on the pit site itself ... 'buried sunshine' has almost literally been replaced by actual sunshine!

A similar large complex has been built across the road from the former Thoresby Colliery—and some 800 such 'solar farms' and 'solar parks' now exist on other agricultural and brownfield sites up and down the country.

Add the 11,000 or so colossal wind turbines that have sprouted all over the nation's hillsides and coastlines during the last few years (Britain is now said to have the biggest offshore wind industry in the world) and it's easy

Five forms of energy captured in a single photograph: A diesel-powered locomotive hauling a train of biomass passes solar panels and electricity pylons as it runs past the site of Kellingley coal mine en route to Drax power station. In the background of this 2021 picture are the cooling towers of the closed Ferrybridge power station.

to see why the Government was able to announce on April 21, 2017 that, for the very first time, the National Grid had produced all its energy for 24 hours without burning a single ounce of coal.

That was followed by several more coal-free days and culminated in May 2019 with an entire coal-free week. The nation's energy during that period came primarily from natural gas (46%) followed by nuclear (21%), then wind, solar, imported energy, biomass, waste and hydro in that order.

Then, in June 2021, it was revealed that England, Wales and Scotland had completed two successive full months without burning any coal to generate electricity. The coronavirus-driven 'lockdown' of the economy and the consequent plunge in demand for power was the main reason for that, of course, but when it's considered that only nine years earlier, a mere 3% of electricity came from wind and solar and almost half came from coal, it was nevertheless a seminal moment.

Prime Minister Boris Johnson has pledged to make Britain "the Saudi Arabia of wind power" and despite his government's embarrassment over the proposed Whitehaven mine (see Appendix H) it's clear that renewable energy is becoming the norm as the UK — a founder member of the Powering Past Coal Alliance and host of the 2021 United Nations Climate Change Conference — aims for net-zero greenhouse gas emissions by the 2040s.

'Decarbonisation' and 'carbon neutrality' are certainly the buzz words at present. World scientists are warning that fossil fuel burning and rampant deforestation of the type occurring in the Amazon rainforest at the moment must be drastically reduced if humanity is to stave off a cataclysmic collapse of the biodiversity and eco-system on which life depends.

Britain is doing its bit to contribute to the effort; coal-fired power stations have been decommissioned at a rapid rate over the last few years and by 2021 only three were operational as the 2024 elimination deadline grows nearer. Coal consumption in the UK fell from 61m tonnes in 2013 to eight million tonnes in 2020, but the country remains heavily dependent on other fossil fuels such as natural gas, which still provides most home heating and about 40% of electricity. An additional problem with gas is that much of Western Europe, including Britain, is dependent upon Russia for much of its supplies.

Use of the 30 or so gas-fired plants in the UK is declining, however, and the relatively new practice of 'fracking' (the controversial method of releasing shale gas from underground rocks by fracturing them with high-pressure water) might not have a very long life either, as that too is a fossil

Coal-fired power stations such as
Didcot have closed at a rapid rate
in recent years. During the station's
heyday in 1987, Class 56 No.56020 leaves
the since-demolished cooling towers
of the Oxfordshire complex to collect
another trainload of coal from the then
extensive colliery network.
RAIL PHOTOPRINTS

fuel. Even biomass is only partially 'renewable' as it can take years to regrow and it's also unsuitable for stockpiling for more than a few days due to the risk of damp and rot.

Dependency on petroleum and other oil-based fossil fuels is being reduced by the move to battery-powered vehicles, although batteries are still not suitable as a source of large-scale power storage on the National Grid.

Nuclear power has an assured future, with the £23bn Hinkley Point 'C' power station in Somerset due to open in 2026 to supplement the other half-dozen operational plants in providing around 20% of the National Grid supply.

Hydrogen technology as a power source for trains and buses has improved enormously in the last few years and offers a potentially-cheaper alternative to battery-electric vehicles. It is also being touted as a replacement for gas.

And in 2021, the UK's first large commercial tidal turbine came on stream in the Orkney Islands. The advantage of this form of hydro-electric power is that it is entirely predictable and not subject to the mercy of unreliable weather conditions, as are wind turbines and solar panels.

Just how unreliable the latter two energy sources are was starkly illustrated in September 2021 when unseasonably calm weather, coupled with a huge rise in the price of imported gas, forced the National Grid to fire up the mothballed West Burton coal power station in Nottinghamshire to compensate for a serious shortfall.

Re-starting West Burton's boilers just a few weeks before the United Nations Climate Change Conference in Britain (see page 240) was embarrassing enough for the Government, but if similar price hikes and weather conditions were to reoccur a year later, West Burton would be unavailable. It is due to close in September 2022, with Ratcliffe scheduled to follow it into oblivion by 2025.

Nuclear power might be able to fill the temporary gaps left thereafter, but that form of power is plagued by its own controversies, so the dual warning from Mother Nature and the foreign gas owners in 2021 shows how dangerously naïve and short-sighted it is for governments to completely abolish (and demolish!) all their older forms of power and how Britain, in its desire to be virtuous, could be at risk of making itself a hostage to fortune.

If, despite all the technological advances, a major global energy crisis does arise in the future, it will have to be opencast coal that provides the ultimate back-stop, for new deep mines can take years to sink and fully commission. Indeed, it has been said that if Britain ever did need its own coal again in a hurry, it would simply 'slice into the side of a mountain'.

As a result of a recent decision by the Department for the Environment, the purchase and burning of traditional bituminous household coal in Britain is now being outlawed, so with the exception of anthracite – which is not included in the restrictions due partly to its smokeless low-sulphur content – and the specialist types used for strategic steel and cement production, coal consumption in the land that gave birth to the Industrial Revolution will all but disappear ... an unthinkable state of affairs only a few years earlier.

What is especially galling for many in the industry is the fact that lean-burn and carbon-capture systems exist and have done for several years.

'Clean coal' isn't simply an oxymoron; it exists in several ways, one being the use of 'scrubbing' (desulphurisation) units that filter out up to 95% of sulphur dioxide and other flue pollutants from power stations before they reach the atmosphere to cause 'acid rain'. Carbon dioxide can be captured either before or after combustion of coal, depending on the method used.

Precipitators can also remove 90% of fly ash residue, while gasification plants can convert coal into gas to make another form of 'clean fuel'. Gasification, as the name suggests, is a way of producing clean synthetic gas from coal rather than burning the solid and is an updated version of the traditional process that used to produce coal gas (sometimes known as town gas), used for heating and street lighting in the days before natural gas came on stream.

Back in the days when British Coal was in existence, the company spent millions of pounds researching clean-burn technology at its laboratories near Cheltenham and Burton-upon-Trent. The project was abandoned when British Coal was split up for privatisation, but work to reduce greenhouse gases has continued in other parts of the world and has reached such a stage of advancement that there is no real need for coal to be considered 'dirty' in environmental terms any longer.

Clashes of opinion continue to rage, however. In a statement issued after the rejection of planning permission for new opencast mines in the UK's Great Northern Coalfield in 2020, the Green Party said: "Northumberland was the cradle of coalmining in the Industrial Revolution but it can now be at the forefront of the next revolution and lead the way into a post-carbon future." But a spokesman for Banks Mining said: "British industry still needs essential minerals like coal, fireclay and brickshale and they should be mined in the UK in the most environmentally responsible way. At a time of economic crisis, it makes no sense to hand much-needed jobs and supply chain investment to Russia, which will be delighted to meet British industry's continuing need

A symbol of changing times: A wind turbine within sight of Kellingley coal mine (right) and Eggborough coal-fired power station (left distance) in 2015. Prime Minister Boris Johnson has since pledged to make Britain "the Saudi Arabia of wind power" and more than 11,000 on-shore and off-shore turbines are already in operation.

for these essential minerals whilst increasing global greenhouse gas emissions."

The UK Government's Business Secretary told Parliament in July 2021 that it is "essential we have a steel industry as it is a strategic asset for national defence reasons as well as for employment". Coincidentally, in the same month, Japanese industrial giant Mitsubishi opened in Austria a steel plant capable of attaining net zero carbon dioxide emissions by using hydrogen instead of coal. Although only at the trial stage, it does have enormous implications for the planet if it proves a success.

If it doesn't, then the proposed Woodhouse coking coal mine or something similar (see Appendix H) might yet be required if post-EU Britain is to be self-sufficient in steel-making, and that would cause enormous opposition from environmentalists.

A world based entirely on renewable energy is a laudable and essential aim and the Climate Change Conference in Glasgow was expected to move the planet much closer to

that target — but irony and hypocrisy are rife, for as the UK prepares to shut down its last coal-fired power stations, new ones continue to be built elsewhere in the world, despite pressure from other governments.

The UK has in fact decarbonised faster than any other major nation, but the chief executive of Yorkshire's Drax power station (which has switched largely from coal to biomass and is aiming to become the world's first carbon-negative power station) warned in 2021 that the growing problem of coal-fired plant construction in parts of Asia is only likely to become more acute as nations there move from agricultural to industrial economies and demand for energy grows accordingly.

So whatever actions relative minnows such as Britain take, it remains a stark reality that coal will still be by far the largest source of power supply worldwide after 2025 and possibly after 2050 too.

Enormous quantities of 'black diamonds' still lie beneath our feet. Just how many was revealed in the 1980s when

The final irony... back in the 1970s, the NCB ran a national poster campaign proclaiming "People will always need coal". Will that prediction ultimately be proved right?

British Coal sank 950 boreholes to establish the size of easily-retrievable reserves. The results were remarkable – no less than 1.2bn tons in the UK alone – and since then the figure has been dramatically revised upwards in some estimates to as much as three billion, about a third of which is said to be economically recoverable.

As things stand in Britain at the start of the 2020s, it seems highly unlikely that any of it will ever be dug up, but if the situation was to change dramatically in the future, modern technology means coal in clean form might one day enjoy a renaissance.

In the meantime, the industry that put the 'Great' into Britain lies in ruins.

Why did so many mines have the word 'Main' in the title?

MOST COLLIERIES took their name from the town or village in which they were located, but quite a few bore strange or exotic titles over the years. Some of the more unusual included Minorca, Gibraltar, Calcutta, Palace, Diamond, Dean & Chapter, Hole-in-the-Wall, True Blue, Clock Face, Cross Hands, Shuttle Eye, Gentlemen Colliers, Ledston Luck, Fanny and Welch Whittle.

But cast your eye down any list of mines and it will immediately become obvious that a significant proportion, especially in South Yorkshire, incorporated the word 'Main' in their title.

Among the better-known ones were Yorkshire Main, Barnsley Main and Markham Main and it would be natural to assume that the suffix simply indicated a major colliery or one that tapped into the main (i.e. thickest or highest-quality) seam in the area.

That was indeed the case in most situations – yet mines without the word Main in their name often worked the exact same seams and as there were also numerous small and fairly insignificant pits bearing this grand title, the reason is clearly not so straightforward.

The terminology does in fact date back to the early years of mining when private companies were struggling to establish themselves in a ferociously-competitive market. The main pit would be the one that was considered by each firm to be the most important within its own organisation. It might not even have been the biggest the company owned, but it would be the one that either produced the largest output, the most profit or the best-quality coal – the latter being a reason for the firm to market its wares to the public as coming from the 'main' mine.

Even in those days, marketing was an important tool in the battle to establish a foothold and each rival organisation would have aspirations to be the leading coal producer in the area … whether it was or wasn't!

A fair number of coal owners stressed the point by incorporating the word not merely into the names of individual mines, but into their official company titles – Manvers Main Collieries Ltd, Llay Main Collieries Ltd or Houghton Main Colliery Co, for example – and it would thus be natural for the word to be incorporated into the names of the

pits they owned in order to perpetuate that association.

However, with so many coal-owners competing with each other in relatively compact areas, it is debatable how much commercial advantage they'd actually have gained by all using the same word. If anything, customers and the public are more likely to have found the situation rather confusing.

The situation is made yet more complicated by the fact that several large seams of coal bore the word Main in their title too … yet there wasn't even always a correlation between such seams and the names of the collieries working them!

One of the first mentions of the term was as early as 1750 when Montagu Main Colliery opened at Scotswood, near Newcastle. Wynell's Main in North Wales dates back to 1753 and there are numerous examples of relatively small-scale mines bearing the suffix at some time or other in their lives, Measham Main in Leicestershire, for instance. To emphasise the confusing nature of the subject, that pit was referred to as Main in some reference sources but not in others and is thought to have been so called to distinguish it from its neighbour in the Measham district, Minorca, a smaller colliery with which it shared a ventilation system and was under the same management in NCB days.

The smallest example of all was probably Wagon Main, at Lowgates, near Staveley, which is thought to have been little more than a minor drift mine.

Ancient use of the word as the formal place name of a village – Percy Main and Pelaw Main for example – could be related to extremely early coal workings in those areas, but is thought more likely to have emanated from the word Demesne (sometimes pronounced do-main), which means "all the land, not necessarily contiguous to the manor house, which was retained by a lord of the manor".

One of the principal causes of confusion over the decades has been the large number of company takeovers that have taken place since the dawn of commercial mining. Some incoming owners would change the name of a newly-acquired colliery to prevent it clashing with their own 'main' pit, while others from less productive mines would retain the title, especially if its products were well-known and

Barnburgh Main was one of numerous collieries in the Yorkshire area bearing this suffix at one time or another. Others included Aldewarke, Allerton, Brodsworth, Bullcroft, Cadeby, Darfield, Denaby, Dinnington, Elsecar, Hatfield, Hickleton, Maltby, Mitchell, Monckton, Rossington, Rotherham, Thurcroft, Waterloo, Wath and Wombwell. Over the border in Nottinghamshire were Harworth, Firbeck and Warsop.

highly regarded in the locality. This resulted in some companies owning more than one 'main' mine.

The policy was not dissimilar to a promotional ploy used in the crowded South Welsh market when some companies added the popular words 'Rhondda' or 'Merthyr' to the end of their colliery title, even though they weren't located in the Rhondda or Merthyr! Examples were Lewis Merthyr, in Trehafod, and Duffryn Rhondda in the Afan Valley.

Somewhat ironically, one of three collieries in Rhondda itself bore a 'Main' suffix! Another in Glamorgan was Skewen Main. Several other South Wales collieries included the word 'Navigation' in their title — a reference to the supply of coal to steam ships in the Victorian and Edwardian eras — while in the North-East and other parts of England, the word 'Winning' was sometimes added to a colliery name. Winning was a widely-used term meaning coal-getting but it's easy to see that its association with sporting success would be attractive to a mine owner.

Although there were two 'Main' mines in County Durham, there are not thought to have been any at all in the coalfields of Scotland, Lancashire, Derbyshire, Cumbria, Warwickshire, Somerset or Kent.

Following nationalisation in 1947, the need for one-upmanship between competing companies disappeared, but the NCB took the view that it was not worth the effort and expense of changing all the registration documents, nameboards, road signs, stationery and suchlike and so decided to retain most of the original titles. It wasn't until the 1980s that the 'Main' suffixes began to be dropped, an exception being Yorkshire's Markham Main, which was retained to avoid confusion with Markham Colliery in neighbouring Derbyshire. There had also been a Markham Colliery in South Wales.

By far the majority of 'Mains' were in the NCB's South Yorkshire area and at one stage the town of Doncaster was virtually ringed by them.

Appendix B

Pithead baths

Very few miners' cottages had bathrooms, so before the installation of pithead showers, colliers had to walk home dirty and use a tin bath in front of the living room fire. The rest of the family treated this as normal, even diligently concentrating on their school homework in the case of these two daughters.

IN 1951, an NCB official stated: "It is our aim that every miner in every pit should be able to go home clean!" and from then onwards, a massive programme of pithead bath installations was implemented.

One of the reasons for the improvement was a feeling among younger miners that an increasingly-sophisticated public was viewing them as somehow 'unclean', as a breed apart almost. In the days before bathrooms became the norm in houses, colliers had no choice but to walk home in their begrimed clothing and sit in a tin bath in their living room, for which their womenfolk would have boiled several pans and kettles beforehand on an open coal fire. The physical strain associated with the daily lifting of the heavy tubs, pans and boiling devices necessary for such work is reported to have contributed to the majority of miscarriages and other female ailments in the coalfields.

In households in which there were several working miners, a strict seniority pecking order would be in effect with the father or grandfather getting the clean water and the youngest son having to sit in a lukewarm scummy slop vacated by perhaps three or four others.

Surprisingly, not every collier welcomed the pithead improvements at first ... some were naturally embarrassed at having to strip naked and shower in front of their work-mates, but the main reason was a long-standing superstition among the older men that washing one's back and leg muscles every day permanently weakened them.

Hard though it might be to comprehend now, such men believed it was better simply to ask their wife to 'polish' their coaldust-covered back and only wash it properly once a week, or even once a month. Old-timers who had started work in the 19th century had an even greater

The pithead baths at Kellingley Colliery were some of the largest in the country, enabling almost 100 miners to shower simultaneously.

superstition … that washing their backs would cause a roof fall. No doubt plenty of pyjamas had to be used in such households to keep the bed linen clean!

Pithead baths (more usually showers) had been in use in France, Belgium and Germany since the 1880s and one or two English collieries had such facilities — Gibfield in Lancashire thought to have been the first, in 1913. In that same year, the Ocean Coal Company of Wales sent a delegation to Europe to study the baths there and report back. This led to the opening of an architecturally-imposing bath house at Deep Navigation Colliery, Treharris, in 1916.

Other British coal companies were not so progressive and although a 'pithead baths movement' had been formed in the 1890s to campaign for such facilities, it was 1919 before the British Government set up a commission to investigate living conditions in the coalfields. As a result, a miners' welfare fund was established to build libraries, institutes, playing fields, canteens and other facilities for mining communities, funded by a levy of a halfpenny on every ton of coal mined. In 1926, an additional levy was raised specifically for colliery-based showers and nearly 400 mines benefitted between then and the advent of the NCB 21 years later.

The showers themselves weren't the only improvements brought about by the bath construction programme, for they were accompanied by changing rooms in which two lockers were provided for every member of staff — one for dirty, wet clothes and the other (on the other side of the shower block) for clean, dry attire. Warm air from the boilerhouse was also blown through the dirty lockers to ensure overalls were dry the next day.

When Chatterley Whitfield Colliery's baths were opened in 1938, miners had to pay sixpence a week to use them and still had to take their own soap and towel. It wasn't until the NCB took over in 1947 that they were made free.

That bath house, along with those at Caphouse, Blaenafon, Penallta, Crumlin and the previously-mentioned Gibfield, are among the handful that have survived and the latter is in use today as a garage workshop. In its heyday, it featured pulleys and ropes on which men hung their clothes and hoisted them up to the ceiling for safe keeping while they were underground. At the end of their shift, they would hoist their wet clothes aloft for drying. Remarkably, this system is still in daily use at some Polish collieries in the 2020s.

CANTEENS: Progressive coal owners from the 1920s and 30s onwards, and the NCB after 1947, ensured that proper pithead canteens were provided at most large and medium-sized collieries. In addition to breakfast and hot meals, these cafeterias sold snacks, soft drinks, soap, towels and other essentials. They also sold snuff and chewing tobacco (known as a 'twist') … but not pipe tobacco or cigarettes, which were classed as contraband (see Chapter 15).

Appendix C

By Royal Appointment

COAL MINES have had their fair share of royal visits over the years. Kings George V and George VI helped keep the nation's morale up with visits during the war years to places such as Elsecar and Hickleton Main in 1944, and the current Elizabethan era has also seen a number of high-profile VIP tours.

Her Majesty the Queen has made several visits to mines during her long reign and in 1958 she was provided with spotless white overalls for the official opening of Rothes Colliery and again at Silverwood in 1975. It is not recorded whether they were still white when she came back up to the surface!

The official opening of Calverton Colliery by her sister, Princess Margaret, in 1952 led to an unintended consequence. Going underground for the first time, she was shown two of the mine's three faces. When the men working at the third face asked afterwards why she had not visited them, they were told it was "too hazardous"... so they promptly demanded danger money!

Another unusual happening occurred at Bevercotes Colliery on the night before the Duke of Edinburgh was due to make a formal visit. Although the event had been pre-arranged, it coincided with an unexpected lull in production – so an anxious Bevercotes manager arranged for a load of freshly-dug coal to be brought over from Ollerton pit, a few miles away in the same Nottinghamshire coalfield.

He then arranged for it to be deposited at the coalface and, after the royal visit was over, had it returned whence it came. The duke never suspected.

Nearby Newstead Colliery was one of those that had the honour at one time of supplying coal to Buckingham Palace, but it reportedly had to be hand-picked – and whitewashed!

Numerous VIPs, church leaders and politicians have also been afforded the privilege of an underground visit, even Prime Minister Margaret Thatcher, who toured Yorkshire's Wistow Colliery in 1980, four years before the start of the devastating miners' strike.

Mining areas weren't normally renowned for beauty or for bright colours, so the communities positively encouraged their young ladies to enter 'Coal Queen' pageants, often staged in conjunction with local miners' galas or picnics.

The contests began to take off on an organised level in the 1950s under the auspices of the NCB, which co-operated enthusiastically with the NUM in a pyramid of heats that ended with the coronation of the British National Coal Queen at either Blackpool or Skegness.

The prize for winning even a regional heat could amount to more than a week's wages, so there were plenty of entrants and the winner enjoyed an interesting year performing opening ceremonies and suchlike at various

Left: The regional winners line up at Skegness station after arriving by special train for the Coal Queen of Britain national finals in 1972.

Admiring glances from miners as Her Majesty the Queen pays a visit to Silverwood Colliery on July 31, 1975, one of several underground trips the monarch made in her near-70 years on the throne.

pits in the area. She would also have the chance of a crack at the national finals.

Most Coal Queens were the wives and daughters of pitmen and even got to go down the mine now and again for promotional photos and suchlike. "I was petrified," said one winner. "I don't know how the men do it day after day." Another commented: "There's none of the bitchiness you get at contests like Miss England. Everyone is friendly because we all come from mining families."

The national winner became an ambassador for the coal industry, promoting safety campaigns, opening home-warming centres and suchlike and meeting other celebrities. "It was almost like being royalty," said one.

The contests were at their peak in the 1970s but died out with the 1984/85 strike, the last national Coal Queen being Nottinghamshire girl Lyn Tomlinson in 1983.

Tending to his flock thousands of feet below the soil ... the Archbishop of Canterbury, the Rt Rev Donald Coggan, during a visit to the Kentish coalfield in the 1970s. J DAVIES

235

Appendix D

Pit ponies underground

CUDDLINESS AND affection are not words that spring readily to mind when one thinks of collieries, but whenever mining museums stage family gala days, the most popular events with mums and kids are the pit pony rides.

Horses have been associated with mining since the earliest days, powering the revolving 'gin' wheels above the shafts in the years before headstocks, and hauling chaldron waggons back and forth between collieries and wharfs.

After the 1842 Commission banning women and young children from working underground, mine proprietors significantly increased the use of horses and ponies and by the end of that century it is estimated there were at least 100,000 in use and possibly many more. They were found to be not only stronger but cheaper to run because, after the initial purchase, they required no pay other than food and stabling. This led regrettably to some mine owners taking the view that a human life was less valuable than a pony's.

Some mine companies with low roof clearances had to go to the extra expense of ripping rock from the top to give the animals room to walk, but that outlay often paid off, for higher roof clearances meant use of larger tubs and therefore greater productivity.

Even so, there were places in some roadways where the

Passing in an unusually wide roadway are two horses and their minders, the white steed hauling three long pit props towards the coalface. As in most collieries, there was insufficient headroom for the horses to be ridden and most mine managements forbade such practice anyway.

roof had converged, leaving jagged stones sticking downwards and although leather skull hoods, spine pads, metal girdles and other protections were used, many poor horses still had their hide torn as a result. Most miners had a soft spot for the ponies and hated the pain the creatures sometimes had to endure but were too afraid to make a fuss. It was a case of putting the welfare of their wife and children before that of the pony.

A collier's productivity depended on his load being taken to the shaft as quickly as possible, yet in the bad old days no allowance was made as to whether the horse hauling his particular tub was a fresh one... or one that had just returned from another shift and was close to collapse from heat and exhaustion.

The animals were also uncannily sensitive and it has been told by more than one miner that a pony he was leading suddenly stopped and refused to move, no matter how hard he tried to pull or push it. A few seconds later, the roof in front of them collapsed.

The underground stable blocks necessary to house so many beasts of burden were extremely extensive and it is still possible to get an idea of what they were like by visiting the preserved colliery at Blaenafon, in South Wales, which has 45 stalls housed in two separate blocks. Built in 1890, they are surprisingly like farmyard versions to look at, with whitewashed brick walls and the name of each horse or pony painted on a little nameboard on each stable door.

At first, the animals could spend their entire lives underground, but in 1940, the Government passed a law requiring all horses to be brought to the surface once a year, usually at July/August time. Although commonly referred to as pit ponies, only 10% of those used in Wales were technically ponies. Some of the largest horses were up to 15 hands (5ft) high.

A survey in 1913 found the total number engaged in underground work nationally had dropped since Victorian times to 73,000. By nationalisation in 1947, there were still 23,000 and as recently as 1984 there were more than 50 in use at Ellington Colliery, County Durham, a few of which lasted until the 1990s.

If all mines, rather than just NCB ones, are taken into account, the last working pit ponies in Britain were two deployed at a small mine in Pant-y-Gasseg, near Pontypool, which stayed active until 1999.

Appendix E

Forest Free Miners

THERE IS one type of coalmining in Britain that has been a law unto itself for centuries – Forest Free Mining.

The exact origins have been lost in the mists of time, but back in the 13th century, men who worked the tiny hillside pits and adits of Gloucestershire's Forest of Dean were asked by King Edward I to use their skills to tunnel through the fortified walls of Berwick-upon-Tweed during sieges to recapture the border town from the Scots. In return, they were granted privileges, one of which was the right for any male born within 'the Hundred of St Briavel's' to mine coal and iron ore for ever without paying dues or royalties.

In granting this right, the monarch stated that the custom had already existed informally "since tyme out of mynde" and research in more recent years has established that the coalfield was indeed worked before the Roman era.

The rights, which also require each man to be over 21 and to have worked in a Royal Forest of Dean mine for at least a year and a day, were ratified in the Dean Forest (Reforestation) Act of 1668 and reconfirmed by Parliament in 1838.

The tradition has since been handed down from generation to generation and been enshrined in law, so much so that when the British mining industry was nationalised in 1947, the men from the Royal Forest were exempted and allowed to continue owning their own areas of coal-bearing land (known locally as 'gales') along with the small drift mines (footrails) they had established.

By that time, a number of proper deep-mine collieries had also been established in the forest, but those came under the licence of the NCB upon nationalisation. The last of those to survive — Northern United Colliery at Cinderford — closed in 1965.

The gales remained exempted following the handing of Britain's coal reserves to the newly-formed Coal Authority in the 1990s and the drift mines have continued to be worked by their tiny teams of perhaps just one or two men each, using timber roof props, picks and shovels in the traditional manner and supplemented by a few hand-held pneumatic

One of the thin seams underground at Hopewell drift mine.

The historic logo of the Forest Free Miners, signifying a medieval collier atop a royal crown.

tools. The miners work seams (known locally as delfs) of about 2ft 6in thickness and to do so, they often have to lie on their side or stomach.

In the 21st century, half a dozen or so gales, including Hopewell, Phoenix, Wallsend, Cannop, Monument and Foresters Folly at Little Drybrook, were understood to be still operable either full-time or part-time, their owners mining small amounts of bituminous coal for local domestic sale on an occasional or as-required basis. The entire output of all the free pits lumped together amounts to only 2,500 tonnes a year, so Hopewell supplements its income by allowing public visits to a worked-out part of its mine for an admission fee.

Although a gale can, in certain circumstances, be sold to a non-freeminer, it is feared that the true tradition might eventually die out due to the closure a few years ago of the maternity unit at Dilke Memorial Hospital in Cinderford. Changes in UK equality laws in 2010 did extend full rights to females, but the closure has reduced the number of people born within the qualifying area of the Hundred and means that only a baby born at home in the area will in future qualify.

Coal mining outside Britain

LTHOUGH THE mining of deep coal has ceased in most western European countries, there are still many nations in the world possessing large numbers of working collieries.

The 'big six', which between them possess more than three-quarters of the world's coal, are China, United States, India, Australia, Indonesia and Russia.

New deposits are constantly being found and proven reserves now stand at around 1.1 trillion tonnes worldwide. Other significant coal producers in the 21st century include Ukraine, Kazakhstan, South Africa and Columbia.

Poland is the largest producer within the European Union and its 25 or so deep mines – which in appearance closely resemble the superpits Britain once possessed – will continue for the foreseeable future, as 70% of the country's energy generation is still based on coal-fired power stations.

Poland also possesses a vibrant coking coal industry and one of the most important companies in that vital sector is JSW, which operates around half a dozen deep mines and employs about a quarter of the nation's 70,000 miners. In 2021, JSW took the decision to transition out of thermal coal and concentrate on metallurgical coal for the steel-making industry.

In the face of pressure from other EU members, the Polish government has agreed to a gradual winding-down of its mining industry over the next two decades, part of the reason for the long timescale being that it currently has no nuclear-powered energy. It has already closed one of its largest lignite opencast mines and is replacing it with a vast solar farm. Germany also possesses large lignite reserves but, like Britain, is investing heavily in offshore wind-turbines.

In the US, more than half the nation's coal output now comes from opencast mining with the North Antelope Rochelle complex in the Powder River region of Wyoming claimed as the largest surface coal mine on the planet. In the latter part of the 2010s, the Trump administration championed coalmining, but the election of a Democratic government under President Biden is likely to see many of the Republican decisions reversed, as the US bids to achieve carbon-free energy generation by 2035.

It is, however, a stark reality that without the co-operation of the Chinese – the world's biggest users of coal – the global targets aren't going to be met.

"Mother Nature does not differentiate between emissions from specific countries; we're all in this together," stressed US envoy John Kerry in 2021 as he called on the Beijing government to bring forward a decarbonisation programme.

For the time being, with mining continuing in China and Russia on a large scale and with three-quarters of India's electricity still being generated by the burning of bituminous fuel, it's abundantly clear that coal is going to remain high on the political and environmental agenda for many more years as the world struggles to cope with climate change.

Poland retains a vibrant coalmining industry and the Upper Silesian area is notable for numerous headstocks, including the large 'A'-frame types once prevalent in the North Staffordshire and other British coalfields.
NICK PIGOTT

Appendix G

The Coal Authority

THE COAL Authority owns, on behalf of the nation, the majority of the vast unworked coal reserves in Britain and licenses what little is left in terms of current mining operations – mainly opencast.

Formed as an independent body at the time of the industry's privatisation in 1994, it supervised the decommissioning and shaft-capping of closed collieries and now manages the effects of past mining, including any subsidence-damage legal claims that are not the responsibility of licensed operators. Surface hazards such as abandoned mine entries and polluted water discharges come within its brief too.

Most of its 170 staff are based at its headquarters in Mansfield, Nottinghamshire, but the authority has regional engineers based in other coalfield areas to enable it to respond quickly to safety issues wherever they occur.

Communicating with members of the public is one of its priorities and, in this respect, it has a heritage centre containing historic underground plans for the thousands of pits Britain once possessed. In some cases, a single colliery might have had several hundred plans over the course of its 100-years-plus lifetime, so the archive collection is extensive and pinpoints the exact locations of subterranean roadways, shafts and drift entries.

Also based in Mansfield is the modern-day version of the Mines Rescue Service (see Chapter 15).

Appendix H

The proposed Woodhouse Mine

IN 2020 and early 2021, the British Government was accused of "hypocrisy" by environmentalists for approving a new coal mine near Whitehaven, Cumbria, at the same time as preparing to host the United Nations Climate Change Conference (COP26).

Faced with the prospect of international ridicule, ministers back-tracked on the plan to build Woodhouse Colliery as a result of the criticism and as this book went to press, the project was effectively mothballed.

Advocates of the £165m scheme did, however, point out that many of the 'green' activists opposing the scheme were doing so in the mistaken belief that it would be a thermal coal mine contributing to global warming through electricity generation, when in fact it would only produce the metallurgical (coking) version used in steel-making – an industry the UK needs to retain if it is to remain self-sufficient outside the EU.

It does show, however, just how sensitive an issue fossil fuels generally have become in recent years.

As coking coal is officially classified in many nations as a strategic resource exempt from the clampdowns on thermal coal, there are suggestions that its name should be changed to 'coke raw material' or similar to help avoid the bad press and confusion currently surrounding coal generally.

Woodhouse wouldn't even look like a traditional colliery on the surface, with artists' impressions showing low-level canopy-style domes more reminiscent of a large horticultural centre. All noise, dust, processing and storage would be contained within the domes and the product would be moved to railway sidings south of the town by underground conveyor, say the promoters, West Cumbria Mining.

With carbon-free steel technology in its infancy and electric-arc furnaces restricted largely to the recycling of scrap metal, the steel required for Britain's burgeoning construction industry has to be made in blast furnaces somewhere and it therefore makes no difference to the planet's atmosphere whether those furnaces are located in the UK, the US or anywhere else.

In fact, say the mine's promoters, 52m tonnes of metallurgical coal are imported to Britain and Europe by ships every year from the US, Russia, Australia and Colombia ... and that by preventing those tens of thousands of miles of oil-burning transport, a colliery in Cumbria could actually help **reduce** global CO2 emissions.

The company also makes the valid point that coking coal is needed in the manufacture of wind turbines!

Late update: The UN climate summit

The end of coal 'is in sight'

*T*HE UNITED *Nations Climate Change Conference (COP26) was staged just before this book went to press, enabling inclusion of a late summary of the decisions that are relevant to the future of coal.*

"The end of coal is in sight." With that dramatic statement at the start of the United Nations climate change summit in November 2021, the British government urged the leaders of the world's nations to save the planet from catastrophic overheating.

But after two weeks of intense and often heated negotiations, the reality proved somewhat different and after a dramatic last-minute intervention by India and China, it became clear that the mining and burning of both thermal and coking coal is likely to continue in some countries way beyond the deadlines set by UN scientists.

The once heavily industrialised city of Glasgow was the venue for the 26th annual meeting of the Conference of Partners (COP26), hosted for the first time in its history by Great Britain. Described as the biggest political summit ever held in the UK, it was attended by 25,000 delegates from almost 200 nations and the total number of participants amounted to 40,000, including the President of the United States.

Tellingly, however, the leaders of China and Russia - two of the world's biggest coal-producing nations - were conspicuous by their absence. Also missing was the President of Brazil, Jair Bolsonaro, whose administration is allowing mass deforestation in the Amazon rainforest. Narendra Modi, the Prime Minister of India, another major carbon-dependent nation, turned up but was prepared only to promise net zero emissions by 2070... two decades later than the summit's target date.

The UN's aim is to restrict global temperature rises to a maximum of 1.5°C above pre-industrial levels by 2030 and to eliminate coal and other fossil fuels in a bid to prevent droughts, forest fires, crop failures, floods and catastrophic rises in sea levels that could see many low-lying island nations disappear before the end of the century.

British Prime Minister Boris Johnson told the conference it was "a minute to midnight" in the race to save the planet and that if action is not taken now, it will be too late, while the Queen urged delegates in a video address to act "for the sake of our children and our children's children". Britain's internationally respected naturalist Sir David Attenborough also stressed the gravity of the situation.

As the summit neared its conclusion on November 13, it did indeed look as though the final pact document agreed by the delegations would include, for the first time ever, an explicit commitment to "phase out" unabated coal, but at the 11th hour, India and China - the world's two largest users of coal - insisted on changing the wording to "phase down".

Although that might at first glance seem a trivial alteration, it does in fact make a huge difference to the future of the coal industry, possibly ensuring its survival for several more decades before replacement by alternative forms of energy production.

'Unabated' refers to coal burnt in plants with no CO_2 mitigation facilities such as carbon-capture & storage, which at the moment is most of them.

The original pledge had survived four drafts of the pact's text, but the Chinese decided they couldn't support it because it wasn't compatible with the Beijing government's latest five-year plan, which authorises the construction of dozens of new collieries, blast furnaces and coal-fired power stations during that period. In fact, China is currently building more coal power plants than the rest of the world combined and says such development will continue to rise until reaching a peak in 2030, after which it is expected to take several more years to gradually decline.

Visibly upset by the dramatic late intervention, the president of COP26, British cabinet member Alok Sharma, apologised for the unexpected way the summit had ended, saying: "We have managed to keep the 1.5°C target alive, but its pulse is weak."

Another watering-down of the text saw some of the references to "2030" changed to a vague "2030 or as soon as possible thereafter" and a commitment to phase out payment of "subsidies" altered to "inefficient subsidies", effectively enabling coal producers to carry on making financial inducements to customers. But China did join other coal-producing nations in agreeing to stop financing new coal plants in foreign countries – a move welcomed by climate activists as a step in the right direction.

Although the leaders of more than 100 nations indicated a wish to phase out fossil fuel usage within the next 20 years, only 40 signed up specifically to the non-coal pledge, 23 of whom undertook to stop building power plants. These included Europe's biggest user, Poland, along with Spain, Ukraine, Indonesia, South Korea and Vietnam, but not the US, Australia, China, Russia or India, and it would thus remain the case for at least another year that well over a third of the world's electricity would be produced by coal.

The size of the challenge can be appreciated by the fact that there are currently 8,500 coal-fired power stations on the planet and that 40% of them would need to close by 2030 (with no new ones being built) if the 1.5°C target is to be met. Realistically, that is unlikely to happen in such a short timescale.

Most of the delegates were, however, encouraged by the surprise decision of China and the US, the world's two biggest carbon-dioxide emitters, to put aside many of their political differences in order to co-operate on global warming-reduction issues in future.

Agreements on a 30% reduction in methane emissions worldwide by 2030 were also seen as a major success, although Russia, China and India refused to sign. Among the many sources of methane are leaks from certain demolished coal mines, but these account for only a minute fraction of global emissions.

Attempts to end deforestation by 2030, although backed by more than 100 countries, were hindered by a request to insert the word "illegal". The vast majority of Brazil's highly controversial rainforest clearance operations, for example, are authorised by its government and therefore legal. Saudi Arabia, whose economy depends heavily on fossil fuels, objected to attempts to clamp down too strictly on oil production.

Opinions differed on whether the summit had proved a success overall. Environmental activist Greta Thunberg, who demonstrated with other 'green' campaigners at the event, dismissed the talks as "blah, blah, blah" from politicians who for years have been promising much but delivering little – and her view appeared to be backed up by Boris Johnson when he admitted at an early stage of the 15-day conference that pledges made at the Paris summit six years previously were "starting to sound frankly hollow".

Former US President Barack Obama also drew attention to broken promises and urged young generations to "stay angry" in their attempts to inherit a habitable planet.

Obama also criticised his presidential successor, Donald Trump, for calling climate change "an expensive hoax" and for pulling the US out of the Paris accord for four years. Trump, a big supporter of the coal industry, had scrapped many of his predecessor's plans to limit carbon emissions, a policy the new White House administration is attempting to reinstate.

In contrast to his government's bullish November 3 press release, Johnson gave a more realistic appraisal of the situation the following week when he said the Glasgow Climate Pact marked "the beginning of the end" for coal. Pointing out that most of Western Europe and North America had agreed to end financial support for foreign fossil fuel projects by the end of 2022 but regretting that the key target of limiting global warming wasn't met, he commented: "We can lobby, cajole and encourage, but we cannot force sovereign nations to do what they do not wish to do."

The important thing is that plans to specifically reduce coal usage have been explicitly mentioned in a summit final agreement for the first time, he added.

The many 'doomsday' warnings made at Glasgow are not, of course, blamed solely on coal but on all fossil fuels, particularly oil and gas. In fact, a spokesman for CharityAid predicted that failure to include the latter two fuels in the final pact would "give a free pass to rich countries who have been extracting and polluting for over a century to carry on doing so".

Another group, Climate Action Tracker, said its experts had calculated that even when all the pledges made at the summit are totted up, they would only limit temperature rises to between 1.8°C and 2.4°C – far higher than the UN target.

Yet there are other scientists who believe the entire COP programme is basically futile because the Earth is heating up as part of a natural cycle that sees the planet pass in and out of ice ages every so many million years. Efforts to limit warming are, they say, akin to throwing deckchairs off the *Titanic* in a bid to stop it sinking.

Everyone is entitled to their view, of course, but the UN naturally wants to do what it can to prevent the effects of the rise, whatever is causing it. For, as the Maldives delegates told the conference, rising sea levels caused by melting ice caps are a "death sentence on island states such as ours".

Britain has pledged to reduce its own greenhouse gas emissions to net zero by 2050. Net zero doesn't require nations or companies to cease emissions, simply that they must take as much CO_2 out of the atmosphere as they put in. Several corporations have been accused by climate change activists of 'greenwashing' – a practice in which false or exaggerated claims of carbon-neutrality are made in order to continue polluting or receiving subsidies – but the UK has backed much of its commitment with action. It has closed all its deep-shaft bituminous coal mines, shut almost all its coal-fired power plants (the last will go in 2024) and intends to replace the biomass and gas-fired ones with wind or solar technology by 2030. Any still in operation by then will be fitted with carbon-capture & storage facilities.

These moves have helped cut the UK's carbon output by 44% since 1990 and with only 1.8% of its energy having come from coal in 2020, it now accounts for less than 1% of global emissions. Britain retains presidency of COP until the 27th summit in Egypt in 2022 and planned to use that time trying to persuade more nations to sign up to stricter targets, but one of the biggest problems is the sheer inability of poorer nations to modernise their energy systems while struggling to urbanise, industrialise and overcome chronic poverty among their people – a point made forcibly by the Indian delegation.

A balancing act is required as it's an inescapable irony that coal has enabled, and is still enabling, developing nations to grow their economies and help their people not only to emerge from poverty but to stay alive. Indeed, delegates were reminded in no uncertain terms that in India, South Africa and numerous other parts of the world, coal "is still king" and that fossil fuel plants will continue to be built for some time yet. Even Britain, despite its role as host, had not at the time of the summit definitely ruled out the establishment of a colliery in Cumbria (albeit for coking coal; see page 239) or licenses for a new oilfield off the Shetland Islands.

Prime Minister Johnson told journalists during the conference that the mine was "a matter for local planning authorities in Cumbria", and advocates of the Cambo oilfield justify it by saying it would only be for an interim period of a few years to give time for the UK's gas and biomass-fired power stations to be replaced by wind, solar and other forms of renewable energy. Although classed as 'green', certain types of biomass are now claimed by some scientists to produce more CO_2 than coal!

Despite the controversy a new British mine would cause, self-sufficiency in metallurgical coal is seen by many as desirable following Brexit and it would be cheaper and environmentally preferential to extract at home rather than import it halfway round the world. A similar argument was put forward in support of another British mine while the summit was in progress after a Welsh Assembly climate change minister urged the UK government to scrap the mining licence at Aberpergwm colliery.

Aberpergwm, which reopened in 2018, is the only producer of high-grade anthracite in Western Europe and a main supplier to Wales's Port Talbot steelworks, prompting a National Union of Mineworkers spokesman to describe the idea as environmentally "ludicrous" because shutting it would simply force the steel plant to import the near-smokeless product thousands of miles from Indonesia or Australia! It was also pointed out that an additional principal use for anthracite is the vitally important filtration and purification of drinking water around the world.

In another UK development during the talks, it was announced that the technology used in nuclear-powered submarines could be adapted to create small modular reactor power stations, thus providing 500 megawatts of 'green' energy at less than £2bn per plant – a mere tenth of the cost of traditional nuclear power plants. London-based Rolls-Royce is involved in the technology and says it is ready to harness "decades of British engineering, design and manufacturing knowhow" to produce the mini-plants, each of which could power up to 1.3m homes.

On a global level, more than 400 banks and financial institutions, which between them control 130trillion dollars, agreed in Glasgow to support renewable energy forms and to direct funding away from old technology industries, but it remains the case that big profits can still be made from fossil fuels. Vested interests and short-termism are thus contributing to a reluctance in some quarters to make the changes the UN requires.

Another problem facing governments of the more affluent economies is in persuading their electorates to accept massive heating, lighting, car fuel and tax increases to pay for the changes. Many people are keen to pay lip service to carbon reduction until they find out what it will cost them personally.

Before the summit began, optimists were hoping 'COP' would lead to 'coup' and cynics were predicting it would lead to 'cop-out'. In the end, neither party was proved totally correct and although the Prime Minister is justified in claiming the end of coal "is in sight", he might find he needs a pair of binoculars to support that view.

What is abundantly clear is that full decarbonisation won't occur within the desired timeframe, but attitudes are changing and the next 10 to 15 years are going to form a fascinating and important transition period.

Will such a sight ever be seen in Britain again? This remarkable photograph of a deep shaft and colliery headstock in the process of construction was taken at Kellingley, Yorkshire, in the early-1960s and shows the rare sight of an exposed shaft straddled by a partly-built tower. The structure on the right is a temporary support for the contractor's derrick crane. In 2015, Kellingley became the last of the UK's deep coal mines to close, exactly half a century after its opening. It is unlikely that Britain and other Western nations would reconsider their climate change policies, but if gas and oil prices continue to soar, who knows? NCB/COURTESY STEVE DAVIES

Glossary of terms

NB. Many terms in the mining industry have more than one meaning, depending on era and/or area. The definitions listed here are those most commonly used and in all cases are based on British practice. It should also be borne in mind that in an industry as ancient and complex as mining, there is at least one exception to virtually every rule! (In order to make this directory as comprehensive as possible, some terms are included that do not appear in the main text of the book.)

Abutments: Sections of coal left in place to support the walls and roof of narrow roadways.

Adit: A horizontal or slightly-inclined entry into a mine, usually driven into the side of a hill for access, ventilation or drainage purposes. Horizontal adits were also known as Levels and those whose slopes enabled water to drain from the workings were sometimes known as Soughs. Some adits were self-contained, others interfaced with a shaft.

Advance Mining: Traditional method of coal-getting in which the direction of progress was made away from the shafts. See Retreat Mining.

Aerial ropeway: A 'cable-car'-style system for conveying colliery waste to a spoil heap.

Afterdamp: A mixture of noxious non-inflammable gases left in a mine after a firedamp explosion.

Air doors: Heavy doors inserted at strategic positions in underground roadways to create airlocks, ensuring correct ventilation flows while allowing men and mine cars to pass through safely. Also known as ventilation doors.

Anthracite: Highest-ranked coal in terms of hardness and quality. Virtually smokeless, it possesses a high carbon content giving off intense heat when burnt.

Anticline: A dome-like upfold of the coal measures as a result of geological pressure. Opposite of syncline.

Arch girders: Curved steel supports lining the walls and roofs of underground roadways. Their semi-circular shape provides strength to resist downward pressure from the strata above.

Armoured Flexible Conveyor: The conveyor component of a heavy-duty longwall shearer or plough system. Usually shortened to AFC and sometimes referred to as Armoured Face Conveyors, these articulated devices are capable of being hydraulically 'snaked' towards the face without dismantling. Also known as 'Panzers'.

Ash: The non-combustible residue left after coal has been burnt.

Ash content: The percentage of incombustible material inherent in coal, which varies from type to type.

Bank: The raised area around a shaft at surface level, also known as the pit brow. (Originally an alternative term for a coalface.)

Banksman: Person in charge of cage operation on the surface. Based at the top of the shaft, he is in contact with the onsetter and winding engineman. In pre-automation days when tubs were taken to the surface, his team would have dealt with loading and unloading as well as man-riding operations. See also Onsetter.

Baring: Removal of overburden in opencast mines.

Bats: Plastic bags containing either stone dust or water hung from the roof of a roadway (hence their name). In the event of a coal dust explosion, they would burst, fill the air and thereby prevent the blast from spreading.

Baum: A washing plant, named after its inventor and designed to separate coal from stone by means of specific gravity.

Beam: A bar or girder supporting a span of roof between two props.

Bellpits: Shallow hand-dug pits pre-dating the establishment of proper collieries. They were wider at the bottom than the top, hence their name, and the coal was either manually carried to the surface via ladders or wound up by horse-powered windlass.

Bevin Boys: Young men conscripted to work in the mines during the Second World War.

Bind: See Shale.

Bing: Scottish term for a spoil heap.

Bituminous: The most common type of coal. Widely used in domestic household fires, for steam-raising and for coking, although higher-carbon varieties are preferred for the latter.

Black coal: A wide-ranging generic term for bituminous coal, to distinguish it from brown coal.

Blackdamp: A toxic mixture of carbon-dioxide, nitrogen and other gases. Also known as chokedamp or stythe.

Blind coal: An archaic alternative name for anthracite.

Bord & Pillar: See Pillar & Stall.

Brattice: A timber or canvas partition for deflecting or separating intake and return air in shafts and airways.

BR: British Railways.

Brown coal: See Lignite.

Bunker: Large storage receptacle. Most were on the

surface but underground versions were positioned between face and shaft bottom in order to even out peaks and troughs in a conveyor-based coal-loading cycle.

Buttyman: In the early years, miners were not employed directly by colliery owners but by self-employed contractors known as buttymen, who supplied their own teams of labourers and paid them accordingly. Following abandonment of this contractor system, the word 'butty' became an informal term for a workmate or colleague.

Cage: The structure in which men and materials were lowered and raised in a shaft. Some were double-decked and those in coal-winding shafts were fitted with rails for tubs or mine cars. Normally, there were two cages in simultaneous operation in a shaft, travelling in opposite directions, but some (known as Shonkeys) had only one chair plus a counterweight. In some mines, a cage was known as a Chair.

Caking: The tendency for coal particles to fuse together or soften to a semi-liquid state on heating. Varieties with the greatest tendency to act like this are known as caking coals and, confusingly in view of the names, are suitable for coking.

Canaries: Birds taken underground in cages to provide miners with early warning of carbon-monoxide.

Cannel: Lowest-ranked bituminous type. It burns with a bright flame and can also be polished and carved into ornaments. Also known as parrot, crackerjack or splinter coal.

Caving: The practice of allowing the unsupported roof of an extracted district to settle or collapse into a waste area, thus avoiding the need to pack.

CEGB: Central Electricity Generating Board.

Chair: An alternative term for a cage.

Checkweigher: In pre-mechanisation days, an impartial representative of colliers who would compare the weights of individual tubs with those recorded by the company to ensure fair payment.

Chokedamp: Another name for Blackdamp.

Chock: A large, sometimes square, assembly erected with timber or steel blocks to support a roof.

Clarifier: A circular tank on the surface of a colliery in which coal slurry is allowed to settle until the solids sink to the bottom and the water becomes clear enough for re-use in the mine. They are similar to thickener tanks, although the primary role of the latter focuses on the production of solids rather than on the quality of water.

Cleats: Naturally-occurring joints within coal seams.

Clinker: A hard but brittle slag created by the fusion of minerals and impurities in certain poorer-grade or high ash-content coals during combustion. Could be exacerbated by poor fire-management technique.

Clod: A variety of clay or shale often found adjacent to a coal seam. Also a term for dirt or waste.

Coalification: The geological process by which, in most cases, vegetable matter becomes converted into peat, then coals of increasingly higher rank up to anthracite.

Coal Measures: A geological term referring to coal basins and other regions containing coal seams. In broad terms, the cycle of strata upwards in most fields is: coal, shale, sandstone then coal again.

Coal Preparation Plant: A large component of modern mines, combining the functions of screens and washeries in a more technically-sophisticated manner. Raw 'run-of-mine' coal was separated from shale and other dirt, washed, sized, graded and loaded into rail wagons or lorries for onward transport.

Coffer: Temporary lining installed by shaft-sinkers.

Coke: A virtually smokeless fuel obtained by heating coal in the absence of air to expel its volatile matter. It continues to perform a vital role in the steelmaking industry.

Coking coal: A high carbon variety of bituminous or semi-bituminous, suitable for carbonisation to coke for use in the steelmaking process. Also known as metallurgical coal.

Collier: Originally, a man paid for producing coal from a stall allocated to him. In later years, the term came to refer to miners generally. It is also a name for a coal-carrying coastal sea vessel.

Concealed coalfield: One in which the measures are overlain by newer rocks. The county of Lincolnshire sits above a massive concealed coalfield, yet has never possessed a single colliery despite numerous trial borings, one of the reasons being fear of upsetting surface dykes and rivers.

Continuous mining: A method of mechanised working in which coal is simultaneously cut, loaded and transported to the surface without any transfer stoppages or delays.

Contraband: Cigarettes, matches or any potentially inflammable item that could cause an underground fire or explosion. Miners were periodically searched for such articles before entering the cage.

Convergence or **Creep:** Gradual coming-together of roof, floor and sides due to geological pressure.

Corf: A primitive coal-carrying basket. Corves fitted with wheels were the precursors of tubs.

CPP: Coal Preparation Plant.

Culm: The slack or smalls of smokeless coal. Also the name of an imperfect form of anthracite.

Damp: A general term for gases found in coal mines, particularly noxious ones deficient in oxygen. See Afterdamp, Blackdamp Chokedamp, Firedamp, Stinkdamp and Whitedamp. Damp is derived from the German word 'dampf', which (in addition to meaning steam) translates as mist or vapour.

Davy lamp: A methane-detecting safety lamp taking its name from deviser Sir Humphry Davy. Its flame was contained behind a metal gauze and there have since been many variants and improvements, including those based on the contemporaneous Clanny and Stephenson safety lamp.

Deputy: Official with responsibility for an underground section of mine. Usually reports to an Overman, depending on individual policy of the colliery.

Dinting: Lowering of the floor to increase the height of a roadway or to compensate for the effects of heave or convergence.

Dintheader: A machine for cutting roadways in thin seams.

Districts: Term for the various underground sections into which coal mines are divided.

Downcast: The shaft, or division of a shaft, through which fresh ventilation air enters the underground network of roadways and passages. At most UK collieries, it was commonly known as the No. 1 shaft and was usually (but not always) used for man-riding. See also Upcast.

Drift: An underground road running at a slant underground, usually linking two seam levels. The term is also used to describe a roadway entering the ground at a sloping angle and which at many pits, particularly small or shallow ones, acted as an entrance or exit.

Drift Mine: A colliery possessing no vertical shafts or headstocks. (Some mines had drifts as well as shafts).

Dry coal: One from which no liquid product of decomposition is exuded upon heating.

Endless rope haulage: A double-track rail, roller or cable system on which tubs are clipped to a rope powered by a motorised pulley.

Engine House: The building containing the stationary steam or electric cage-winding engine(s). Also known as Winding House.

Evasee: A tapered wide-rimmed chimney on the surface through which air is drawn by the ventilation fan.

Exposed coalfield: One in which the edges of the seams outcrop at, or close to, the surface. See also Concealed coalfield.

Face: The wall or seam from which coal is won. Superpits and other large collieries featured numerous faces in simultaneous operation.

Fans: See Ventilation.

Fan drift: The airway connecting a fan to an upcast shaft.

Fault: A geological fracture in rocks causing a coal seam to break and become distorted or displaced.

Filler: In pre-conveyor belt days, a labourer or apprentice faceworker who transferred freshly-hewed coal to tubs.

Fines: Tiny particles of coal that once went to waste but which can be retrieved by modern coal preparation plants. (See froth flotation).

Firedamp: Odourless flammable gas, mainly methane (but can also contain traces of nitrogen and carbon dioxide). Firedamp explosions have been the cause of the worst coalmining disasters in history.

Fireman: In the 1700s and early-1800s, a man employed to rid a mine of firedamp by wrapping himself in thick water-soaked garments and igniting the gas with a naked flame on the end of a pole. In some mines, deputies were known as firemen.

Flameproof: Term describing diesel locomotives, electrical machinery and other equipment insulated against sparking and therefore allowed to work underground in 'gassy' mines.

Footrill (also spelt Footrail): A form of adit or level. The term has also come to refer to an extremely small private mine featuring a drift or adit entrance and usually worked by fewer than ten men.

Free-steered vehicle (FSV): A modern, rubber-tyred diesel shuttle car for underground movement of supplies and coal in mines with no rail tracks. Also used for man-riding in some mines.

Friable: Brittle, disintegrates easily upon impact.

Froth flotation: Process in a coal preparation plant in which fines are retrieved by suspension in the froth of a chemical fluid while slightly heavier particles of dirt sink to the bottom.

Furnace ventilation: A 19th century system in which a furnace at the bottom of the upcast shaft caused the shaft to act as a chimney and create an air flow through the workings.

Gaiters: Strong plastic covers worn to prevent lower leg injuries.

Gale: A type of footrill particular to the Forest of Dean.

Gallows: A frame at the top of certain headstocks used as an over-wind safety device and/or to facilitate the lifting out of pulley sheaves. Also known as a gibbet.

Garage: Mining term for a locomotive depot.

Gate road: An underground roadway, usually positioned

at right angles to each end of a longwall face and linking the face with a trunk roadway. For each face there is a main (air intake) gate, usually used for coal dispatch, and a tail (return) gate normally used for moving in equipment and supplies. Gate roads are extended as the face advances.

Geothermal gradient: The rate at which the temperature of rocks increases with depth. In British mines the rate averaged 1 deg Fahrenheit for every 50 to 100ft the men descended. Temperatures of over 100 deg F explain why many deep pit mineworkers wore only briefs, boots and helmet and why some almost passed out with heat exhaustion!

Gin: In the early years, a horse-powered means of hoisting coal up a shaft. Short for the word 'engine'.

Goaf or Gob: Worked-out waste area vacated by advancement of the coalface. Such voids were either packed with stone or allowed to collapse in a controlled manner, depending on whether the advance or retreat method of mining was being employed. Goaf is believed to have derived from the Welsh word 'ogof', meaning cave.

Graphite: This is 99% fixed carbon and therefore almost impossible to ignite. Although classified by some authorities as a 'coal', it is not mined for the same purposes as the other ranks. (Given enough time and pressure over millions of years, some graphite turns to diamond.)

GWR: Great Western Railway.

Haulage: A term covering locomotive, rope or pony operation of wheeled vehicles underground. (It does not include conveyors as they were not formally classified as a haulage system).

Headgear, Headstock or Headframe: Winding towers on the surface of a colliery. With their great sheave pulleys, they remain the internationally-recognised symbols of coal mines even though more modern mines feature slab-sided towers of friction-winding types, which tend to conceal the pulley wheels from public view. Traditional lattice-work frames were originally made of timber but as requirements grew for safer, stronger and taller towers, steel or reinforced concrete became the norm. Upcast shaft frames were fitted with air-lock chambers to prevent leakage. The terms generally include both the tower and the pulleys.

Heading: A roadway in the course of development, either through a coal seam or in rock strata, and therefore usually with only one entrance.

Heapstead: The buildings and associated facilities on the surface surrounding the tops of the shafts.

Heave: The lifting of the floor of an underground roadway as a result of geological stresses.

Hewing: The cutting of coal with a hand-pick in the pre-mechanisation era. Also known in those days as Getting or Winning.

Hilt's law: The theory that the deeper a seam of coal is found, the higher its rank will be. This generally holds true but there are numerous departures, especially where faulting and rearing has occurred.

Hitcher: Man who attached and detached tubs on an endless steel rope haulage. Also known as a clipper-on.

Hoppit: Large bucket-shaped container used for lowering and raising shaft-sinkers. Also known as a kibble.

Horizon mining: A system whereby horizontal or near-horizontal roadways are driven at different levels to intersect steeply-inclined coal seams. The levels are then joined by vertical 'staple shafts' for the upwards or downwards movement of coal or materials for loading into locomotive-hauled mine cars.

House coal: A generic name for thermal forms of bituminous coals suitable for open fireplaces.

Hurrier: A person who in the early years of mining moved underground sleds or rail tubs by hand. Also known as a drawer, thruster or trammer. In some mines, a hurrier pulled and a thruster pushed. The work, which in the very early years was often undertaken by women or children, was later taken over by ponies..

Igneous rock: An intrusion formed by volcanic action that has replaced a section of coal in a seam, not only vertically but sometimes horizontally. The action of the intrusion sometimes turned coal to coke. Also known as a dyke.

Inbye: When underground, the direction away from the shafts and towards the coalface. Opposite of outbye.

Journey: A mining industry term for a train of tubs or mine cars coupled together.

Kibble: Large bucket-shaped container used for lowering and raising shaft-sinkers. Also known as a hoppit.

Kirving: Another term for undercutting.

Knocker-upper: A person employed to knock on the windows of miners' homes in the middle of the night in order to wake them up in time for their shift.

Koepe winding gear: Friction-based form of cage-winding, named after its inventor and usually deployed in very deep shafts where other systems would require excessively large drums.

Lagging: Wood or steel boards placed behind arches or girders to provide additional security in roadways.

Lamp room: Surface-based stores department in which lamps, batteries, self-rescuers etc were kept. Also contained battery-charging apparatus. Relightable oil lamps were issued to officials only.

Landing: A platform or point in a shaft at which a cage can be halted for the loading or unloading of men or materials.

Landsale: Part of a colliery set aside for direct sale of coal to road vehicle-based merchants and local customers. Also describes the coal sold therefrom.

Level: See Adit and Footrill.

Lignite: The youngest and lowest-ranked coal in terms of quality. Harder than peat but softer than bituminous, it is prone to spontaneous combustion if not handled carefully. Also known as Browncoal.

Loader Gate: See Main Gate.

Locomotive haulage: Subterranean narrow gauge railway system featuring diesel, battery, compressed air or trolley electric locos hauling mine cars and miners' 'paddy train' carriages. From the 1940s onwards, this form of motive power replaced almost all endless-rope and horse-drawn haulage systems.

Longwall: A method of mining in which the length of seam being worked is far greater than is the case with the pillar & stall technique. The earliest type of longwall featured numerous men working simultaneously in stalls along the full length of the face, but they were later replaced in almost all large and medium-sized collieries by the faster and more efficient shearer-loader/conveyor system in which the coal is mechanically sliced off from end to end.

Macerals: Microscopic organic plant components of coal from which precise types and ranks can be determined by laboratory analysis.

Main: A generic term to variously describe the principal colliery in a local area, the main seam in that area or the main (i.e. best) grade of coal marketed by the mining company concerned. Many collieries, particularly in South Yorkshire, incorporated the word in their formal title.

Main gate: The principal gate road leading to a coalface. It usually acts as the intake airway and is normally used for the outbye conveyance of coal. Also known as Loader Gate or Mother Gate. See also Tail Gate.

Manchester gate: A safety barrier across an inclined railway to prevent mine cars from running away.

Man-rider: System of transporting miners to coalfaces (usually by train, monorail or conveyor).

Measures: The strata within which coal seams were usually located. Also a term used by survey staff when plotting advancement of faces, headings etc.

Merry-Go-Round: Normally abbreviated to MGR, this system was introduced in the mid-1960s to streamline the transport of coal from collieries to power stations. Looped track enabled main line trains formed of hopper wagons to discharge their loads at slow speed without stopping and return directly to the colliery for re-loading, thus forming a continuous supply chain.

Metallurgical coal: See coking coal.

Methane: Odourless colourless gas, lighter than air and highly explosive at certain air-mix densities. Non-toxic in its own right but can become lethal when combined with other gases. Main constituent of firedamp.

MFGB: Miners' Federation of Great Britain.

MGR: See Merry-Go-Round.

Mine car: Larger, more modern form of tub.

Mineral: Inorganic matter such as rock and ore. Technically, coal is not a mineral as its composition is primarily of organic origin, although its contents often include varying traces of mineral substances.

Mudstone: One of several types of stone found in mine workings, formed of compacted mud. Others included siltstone, claystone and sandstone.

NACODS: The National Association of Colliery Overmen, Deputies and Shotfirers.

NCB: National Coal Board.

Nick: To make cuttings, usually vertically, in a coalface prior to hewing or shotfiring.

NUM: National Union of Mineworkers.

Onsetter: Person in charge of loading and unloading of cages underground. Based at the shaft bottom, he is in contact with the banksman (his opposite number on the surface) and the winding engineman.

Outburst: A sudden high-pressure emission of methane from a seam. Sometimes known as a blower.

Outbye: When underground, the direction towards the shafts. Opposite of inbye.

Outcrop: Coal that appears naturally at, or near, the surface, due to tectonic upheaval and/or rock erosion.

Opencast: A mine completely open to the surface. Operation of such sites is similar to that of quarries.

Overcast: A ventilation air-crossing in which air travelling in one direction is bridged over that travelling the opposite way.

Overman: An official responsible for one or more underground districts. Reports directly to mine manager or undermanager (depending on individual policy of mine). Sometimes known as an overlooker.

Overwind: Failure of a cage to stop at the end of its journey up or down the shaft. Special safety catches are fitted to prevent loss of life in such an eventuality.

Packing: The filling of a goaf or other worked-out area

with tightly-packed stone and waste material to form a permanent roof support. With retreat mining, this is not necessary.

Paddy, or Paddy Mail: Miners' nickname for an underground man-rider train.

Panel: A large section of virgin coal allocated for extraction. A mining company would normally have to pay royalties to the surface landowners in order to take the coal.

Panzer: Nickname for an armoured face conveyor.

Peat: Soft brown partially-decayed vegetable matter considered by geologists to be the immature stage of coal formation.

Pillar & Stall: A traditional form of mining in which colliers worked individual stalls, leaving square or rectangular columns of coal in situ to support the roof. Several roadways would be driven parallel to each other and cross-cuts made at planned distances, joining the roads and creating a ventilation circuit as well as pillars. Also known as Stoop & Room. (See also Room & Pillar.)

Pillar-robbing: The practice of removing supporting columns of coal during withdrawal from a worked-out mine. This was a perilous operation normally achieved by cable at a safe distance. Also known as pillar-drawing.

Pit: Originally referring to a hole or shaft, this word has for many decades been a widely-used alternative term for a colliery generally.

Pit bank: The raised bank or platforms surrounding a shaft collar. See also pit brow.

Pit bottom: The underground area around the foot of shaft, particularly the main man-riding shaft. Sometimes known as the pit eye.

Pit brow: Old term for a pit bank or heapstead.

Pit brow lasses: Females employed on the surface, usually in the coal screens.

Pithead: The top of a mine shaft, including the buildings, roads and equipment around it.

Pithead gear: See Headgear.

Pitman: One trained to inspect and repair shaft walls and the guides and pipes therein, usually while standing on top of a cage.

Pit pony: Small horse used for tub haulage and other underground duties. At the start of the 20th century, an estimated 200,000 were at work in British mines.

Plough: In the early years of mechanisation, a type of cutter-loader machine using fixed blades to slice off the coal. Most were replaced by rotary shearers.

Prop: A strong timber post or hydraulic steel pillar for supporting a roof.

Pneumoconiosis: Disease of the lungs caused by prolonged dust inhalation.

Putter: See Hurrier.

Regulator: An air-door containing a smaller door through which a limited flow of air can be allowed to pass.

Rearer: A vertical, or near-vertical, coal seam.

Retreat mining: A system in which roads and gates are driven prior to coal production so that longwall shearing can proceed back towards the shafts. Although this requires high financial capital ahead of income, it speeds production by dispensing with the need to pack the goaf. Almost all other forms of subterranean coal retrieval are known as Advance Mining.

Rings: Steel roadway arches.

Ripping: Increasing the height of an underground roadway or heading to provide room for vehicles or equipment.

Roadheader: A machine for cutting and ripping new roadways. Statistically, a roadhead is the most dangerous part of a mine due to the high frequency of roof falls prior to the fitting of bolts, props or arches.

Roadways: Underground tunnels leading from shaft bottom to coalfaces.

Rock-bolting (also known as roof-bolting): A relatively modern form of roof support in which bolts up to 10ft long are drilled upwards into stronger rock, clamping strata together and thereby dispensing with the need for roadway supports such as arches, legs or girders. Large steel mesh panels held in place by the bolts provide additional protection.

Roll: An undulation in a seam, or an irregularity in a roadway caused by a washout.

Room & Pillar: A traditional form of mining in which square or rectangular columns of coal were left in situ to support the roof. Strictly speaking, it differed from the Pillar & Stall system in that it was usually deployed in small drift mines with a single entry, whereas pillar & stall was more commonly a feature of larger collieries that had not yet adopted the longwall system. Also known as Bord & Pillar

Run-of-mine (ROM): Raw coal as it comes to the surface, unscreened, unwashed and complete with dirt and rock if the coalface has been mechanised.

Safety lamp: Insulated oil lamp used for illumination and detection of gas.

Scouring: A roadway driven through a goaf or other non-virgin ground.

Scraper-chain conveyor: One fitted with metal cross-beams, which move the coal better than conventional conveyor belts on steep inclines.

Screens: Large surface structures, usually combined with a washery, in which run-of-mine coal was sieved, sorted and delivered into railway wagons. Predecessors of coal preparation plants.

Sea coal: In early days, coal washed up on a beach. Also coal shipped from the North-East to London

Seam: A stratum of coal measuring (in Britain) anything between a few inches and 15ft. Seams are usually sandwiched in long strips between layers of shale or other non-combustible rocks and there were often numerous seams of different depths, ages and qualities lying beneath each colliery.

Self-advancing supports: Powerful hydraulic roof chocks that move forward electronically after each pass of a longwall face shearer. They work in concert with armoured flexible conveyors that 'snake' forward simultaneously. The cantilevered top sections of the chocks perform the dual role of supporting the freshly-exposed roof and shielding men working beneath them.

Self-rescuer: A type of respirator issued to miners and others before they are allowed underground. It is worn on the belt and in the event of escaping gas or excessive dust, is designed to give the wearer sufficient time to exit the mine or reach a safe fresh air area. They were designed to last an hour but many became uncomfortably hot.

Semi-bituminous: Higher in rank and less smoky than bituminous coals, this grade includes steam coal, whose high calorific value and low levels of volatile matter make it ideal for boiler use.

Settling ponds: Open pools on the surface, normally arranged in descending order, in which slurry water was allowed to settle and clarify.

Shaft: Means of vertical entry and exit to a deep mine for men, materials, machinery and (in one direction) coal. See Downcast and Upcast.

Shaft collar: The normally raised area surrounding the mouth of a shaft.

Shaft pillar: A large area of coal left unworked around pit-bottom area to maintain rigidity in the shaft and protect it – and the surface buildings – from damage caused by subsidence or geological earth movements.

Shale: A variant of mudstone commonly found adjacent to coal seams. Sometimes known as Bind.

Shearer-loader: Longwall face machine that moves in association with an armoured conveyor and simultaneously cuts and loads coal.

Sheave: A winding wheel. Those up to 8ft diameter were usually built whole, but above that size they were made in halves and bolted together. Large British collieries featured sheaves of up to 24ft diameter but those installed in modern Koepe headstocks were normally hidden from public view within a concrete tower.

Shot-firing: The practice of bringing down coal from a seam by detonating explosive charges inserted in pre-drilled boreholes. This method largely replaced the time-consuming manual extraction of coal using hand-held picks but was itself superseded in large collieries by longwall plough and shearer systems.

Shuttering: Air-tight enclosure around an upcast shaft tower ensuring that ventilation air (drawn by an extractor fan mounted near the upcast shaft) is encouraged to enter the mine's workings via the downcast shaft and not get drawn down the upcast shaft to short-circuit straight back to the atmosphere.

Silicosis: Disease of the lungs caused by prolonged inhalation of stone dust.

Sinker: A skilled worker involved in the excavation and construction of new shafts.

Skip: A large steel container, capable of holding up to 30 tonnes, in which coal (and in many cases dirt too) is hoisted to the surface in a specially-adapted vertical shaft. In such cases, the mine's other shaft would normally be used for men and materials, although most skips could be utilised for man-riding in emergencies.

Slack: Small residual pieces of coal, larger than fines but too small for sale as individual lumps.

Slant mine: Another term for drift mine.

Slinging: The lowering of large bulky items down a shaft by hanging them underneath the cage.

Slurry: Usually a mixture of fine coal and water.

Snap: Miners' term for sandwiches or a snack, normally kept in a snap tin. Also known as 'bait'.

Snicket: A small road made between two parts of a mine for ventilation or short-cut purposes.

Sough: Adit primarily used for draining water, usually from a drift mine.

Spoil heap: A large hill (originally cone-shaped, later rounded) at or near a colliery, formed mainly of shale and other waste material extracted in the mining process but not used for goaf-packing. Also known as spoil tip, waste heap, stack or (in Scotland) bing. Laymen and members of the media often refer inaccurately to such tips as 'slag heaps'.

Sprag (1): A short timber post used as support in thin seams and other low-height areas. In more modern times, the term sprag plate is used to describe a hinged section of roof shield on a self-advancing hydraulic support.

Sprag (2): A rudimentary brake preventing a tub from running away.

Stables: Spaces at each end of a longwall coalface enabling a cutting machine to be turned for a return run. (The place where horses were kept was more commonly known as a Stall).

Stall: In a pillar-and-stall mine (or a longwall mine in the pre-shearer era), the working area allocated to a collier and his mate. (Also a place where pit ponies were kept.)

Staple shaft: One that connects two or more underground levels but does not reach the surface. See Horizon mining.

Steam coal: See Semi-bituminous coal.

Stilt: A sliding or extension at the foot of a prop or arch to allow convergence without bending or buckling the support. Some roof arches were telescopic and adjusted automatically to the earth's movement.

Stinkdamp: Hydrogen-sulphide or similar pungent-smelling poisonous gas. Also known as 'Gob Stink'.

Stint (or Stent): A section of coal worked by an individual collier and his mate in the pre-mechanisation era.

Stone-dusting: The liberal depositing of crushed limestone along underground roadways as a defence against coal dust explosions.

Stoop & Room: See Pillar & Stall.

Stopping: An airtight wall erected in a roadway to seal off a disused part of a mine.

Stowing: Another term for packing.

Stripping: Clearance of coal from a non-mechanised face after shot-firing.

Stythe: Another word for blackdamp or chokedamp.

Subsidence: Settling of strata following removal of coal. The rate of subsidence depended on many factors, including the strength and depth of the stone layers above. Many efforts were made to minimise the impact and in some sensitive areas, coal was left in situ, but numerous dramatic effects were nevertheless seen on the surface in the form of damaged buildings, dipped railway tracks, sunken fields and so on.

Sump: A water- and sludge-catchment reservoir at the bottom of a shaft.

Superpit: In the 1950s, '60s and '70s, the National Coal Board built a range of huge all-new collieries and enlarged and modernised several others in order to take over the workings of older and smaller pits in the neighbourhood. These 'superpits' almost invariably featured full mechanisation, underground locomotive haulage and concrete-clad Koepe winding towers and, from the mid-60s onwards, coal preparation plants and rapid-loaders based on the Merry-Go-Round system.

Supply Gate: See Tail Gate.

Surveyor: Person responsible for the direction and depth to which underground workings can safely be made; also for locating the likely presence of water and old workings etc. As a result of the 1911 Coal Mines Act, surveyors entering the profession had to be qualified by examination.

Sweetener: Coal from another pit or pits mixed with that of the home colliery to make its product more acceptable to a particular customer, such as a power station.

Sylvester: A hand-operated ratchet device for withdrawing props from old workings. A long chain enabled the user to stand at a safe distance!

Syncline: A trough-like downfold of the coal measures as a result of geological pressure. Opposite of anticline.

Tail Gate: The subsidiary gate road connected to a coalface. It usually (but not always) acts as the return airway and is normally used for the movement of supplies and equipment to the face. Also known as the Supply Gate or Return Gate.

Tailings: Extremely small particles of waste left after the processing of fines in coal preparation plants.

Take: An area of coal owned by, or allocated to, a particular colliery or mining company.

Tectonics: The science that deals with the causes and effects of structural movement in the earth's crust.

Thermal coal: General term for bituminous coal suitable for heating and electricity generation (as opposed to metallurgical purposes).

Thickener: A circular tank on the surface of a colliery in which chemical reagents are added to effluent to encourage solids to separate from water. See also Clarifier.

Thirl: The joining-up of subterranean roadways, including ones driven from each end that met accurately in the middle. Thirling was also the means by which neighbouring collieries were connected underground.

Thruster: See Hurrier.

Tower winder: A modern form of headstock in which the pulley wheels and other equipment are enclosed inside a tall concrete or steel block.

Tram, or Dram: A mining industry term for a tub or small mine car. Also known as a 'hutch'.

Trapper: In Victorian times, a lad responsible for opening and closing airway doors.

Tree, or Timber: Another word for a roof support prop.

Trepanner: A face-cutting machine featuring a vertical or side boring wheel; so called because it resembled a surgical instrument used for drilling small holes in human skulls!

Trolley: An underground railway powered by a catenary wire electric supply. In Britain, the gas levels in about half a dozen collieries were considered sufficiently low-risk for the Mines Inspectorate to approve the use of such railways. Other pits used either battery-electric or flame-proof diesel locomotives.

Tub: A small wheeled wagon running on narrow gauge lines known as tub tracks. In the early days of mining, they were pulled or pushed by hand, later being hauled by ponies and eventually by locomotives.

Tubbing: Cast iron or steel segments used by sinkers for lining a shaft and protecting it from water ingress.

Tunnel: Curiously, the word 'tunnel' is not used as extensively in the mining industry as might be expected. It is normally reserved to describe a drivage – often through rock – to connect the underground workings of one colliery to another (also known as thirling). Some bores were open to the surface at one or both ends and used for drainage, ventilation or as service tunnels for the movement of men or supplies.

UDM: Union of Democratic Mineworkers, set up in 1985 by moderates who wished to break from the NUM.

Undercast: A ventilation air-crossing in which air travelling in one direction is bridged under that travelling the opposite way.

Undercut: A slot cut into a seam at floor level prior to hewing or shot-firing. The incision encouraged the coal to fall more easily when hewed or blasted. Also known as kirving.

Undermanager: Man in overall charge of underground operations. Reports directly to mine manager or deputy mine manager.

Upcast: The shaft, or division of a shaft, up which stale ventilation air (return air) flows after circulating through the underground network of roadways and passages. It was normally known as No. 2 shaft and usually (but not always) used for coal-winding. See also Downcast, and Shuttering.

Ventilation: The use of powerful electric fans to draw an adequate flow of fresh air through the underground network, not only to enable miners to breathe but to reduce temperatures, counteract dust and remove noxious and flammable gases. An extracting fan would be connected to the upcast shaft and if a forcing fan was also installed, it would be linked to downcast shafts. (See also next entry).

Ventilation furnace: In the years before electric fans, a large fire would be lit at the foot of the shaft of (non-gassy) mines and the updraught so created would produce a flow of air through the underground workings. Such methods ceased to be effective once subterranean networks began to extend too far beyond pit-bottom.

Viewer: An old term meaning a senior manager, agent or surveyor employed by a coal owner to oversee or control a mine, or more usually several mines in a group.

Volatile matter: Hydrocarbon, sulphur and myriad other gases driven off when coal is heated. (Technically, it has to be heated in the absence of air at around 900°C under laboratory conditions to determine its exact volatile matter content.)

Washery: Large surface structure, usually combined with a screens building, in which run-of-mine coal was cleaned. Sometimes known as a Wet Separation Plant. See also Screens and Coal Preparation Plant.

Washout: Geological term for a gap in a seam caused by an ancient subterranean water flow.

Waste: Another word for Goaf. Also a general term for spoil or dirt.

Web: The amount of coal sliced, sheared or ploughed off a coalface in a single pass. Thickness can vary from a few inches to 6ft but averages about 3ft.

Weighting: Roof movement, especially when it can be seen or heard. Normally a creaking sound.

Whitedamp: Air mixed with a high percentage of carbon-monoxide: So called because lamps tended to burn with white fumes in its presence.

White finger: Ailment caused after prolonged use of high-powered vibrating machinery.

'Windcutter': Nickname given to high-speed coal trains on the former Great Central main line before its closure in the 1960s. Such trains used 16-ton coal wagons, the last few of which have been preserved by the Great Central and can be seen there and at other heritage lines, including the Pontypool & Blaenavon Railway.

Winding house: See Engine House.

Winding gear/winding tower/winding wheel: See Headgear.

Winning: The process of extracting coal from a seam and moving it to the surface.

Yardstick: A stick carried by overmen and deputies, primarily for checking measures between props etc, but also acting as a ready means of identifying a person of authority when underground.

INDEX

(See also Glossary, page 244)

(A bold page number indicates a major entry)